What's Next?

What's Next?

How Professionals are Refusing Retirement

Dona Roche-Tarry
and
Dale Roche-Lebrec

palgrave
macmillan

First published 2011 by
PALGRAVE MACMILLAN

Palgrave Macmillan in the UK is an imprint of Macmillan Publishers Limited, registered in England, company number 785998, of Houndmills, Basingstoke, Hampshire RG21 6XS.

Palgrave Macmillan in the US is a division of St Martin's Press LLC, 175 Fifth Avenue, New York, NY 10010.

Palgrave Macmillan is the global academic imprint of the above companies and has companies and representatives throughout the world.

Palgrave® and Macmillan® are registered trademarks in the United States, the United Kingdom, Europe and other countries.

ISBN 978–0–230–29125–6

This book is printed on paper suitable for recycling and made from fully managed and sustained forest sources. Logging, pulping and manufacturing processes are expected to conform to the environmental regulations of the country of origin.

A catalogue record for this book is available from the British Library.

A catalog record for this book is available from the Library of Congress.

10 9 8 7 6 5 4 3 2 1
20 19 18 17 16 15 14 13 12 11

Printed and bound in Great Britain by
CPI Antony Rowe, Chippenham and Eastbourne

*This book is dedicated to FPR and Nancy
who redefined this road a long time ago.*

Contents

List of Illustrations

Figures

Tables

Boxes

Introduction

The idea for the book *What's Next: How Professionals are Refusing Retirement* came from Dona Roche-Tarry's work as an advisor to very senior executives for over a decade. Today Dona is an executive recruiter leading the Board Practice in EMEA for CTPartners, and over the course of her career (with Heidrick and Strugles and BT) she has had the privilege of working with a large number of highly successful executives in many industries and countries. During the dot-com period and then again over the last few years she noticed an increase in the number of "younger" (between 48–60) professionals who were looking to leave their top-level corporate careers and "do something different." She helped place them as Non-Executive Directors and Chairmen as well as advising them on how to restructure life after a full time corporate career. In her discussions with them, Dona noticed that while they were excited about the change, they were also seeking direction. Many were unsure of how to move forward into this new chapter or even how to define exactly what it was they were looking for. In fact as most of these folks were CEOs of large corporate divisions, and they had not had to reach out to others for help in a very long time. They had become used to continuous support in a world with advisors, assistants, and a strong team. The idea of transitioning into a nebulous space without a title or a business card was daunting and difficult. In these encounters Dona met with men and women throughout the world who had followed the linear path of a corporate career moving from one role to another and one promotion to another. They had gained visibility and a reputation in their industry, accompanied by institutional support and recognition. Opportunities had fallen into their laps, allowing them to rub elbows with economic and political power. Despite all of this, they were motivated to move on, were looking to organize themselves differently, all the while wondering what they could possibly do for an encore.

On a broader scale, all of them are members of the Baby Boomer, or B2-generation, as we like to call it. After decades of a successful career they were nearing the glass ceiling of age and facing traditional retirement. The problem was that nothing about this traditional "next step" corresponded to their aspirations or potential. All of them still felt in the prime of life, had no intention of getting in the back seat and playing a passive role, but no longer wished to pursue the linear corporate, academic, or industrial career path to its bitter end.

Intrigued by this tendency, we began gathering their stories – for in their search to reconcile both professional and personal needs at an age that was no longer young and certainly not old, a certain number of these executives had taken risks, and sculpted made-to-order solutions through trial and error, sometimes with a little help from Dona. To see whether this process was pertinent outside of the scope of the corporate environment we opened up our interviews to other successful boomers: and we found politicians, scientists, and entrepreneurs who have also felt the need to transition "out" of their singular career and begin defining a new paradigm. Read together, we saw a pattern in these separate stories, the woof and the warp of a process of change that could be pertinent for many others who are contemplating this professional and personal crossroads.

To place this pattern within the greater context of the Baby Boomer Generation, we delved into the research on Aging and Baby Boomers: in particular Ken Dychwald's work at *Age Wave*, Tamara Erickson's "*Retire Retirement*," Helena Ibarra's excellent book for mid-career changes *Working Identity*, as well as Hazel Markus' fertile theory of potential selves. We would like to thank all of them, and the others in this field for the theoretical foundation this has provided for the book.

Although we do not pretend to present a theoretical model on how the Baby Boomer generation is going to change the developmental stage of old age and redefine retirement, these interviews do give a voice to some responses to the question, and have been placed within the context of a process of transition.

These first-hand accounts follow one of the first groups of the Boomer generation – a group of top-level professionals – through their steps out of a linear career path into an uncharted stage somewhere in-between middle age and old age and somewhere in-between a professional life that is lived 24/7 and retirement in the traditional sense of the word.

We discovered certain similarities in the preparation for the transition out, as well as in the final structure of the lifestyle chosen by our interviewees. Although their needs and expectations were very different from people making career transitions in their 30s or 40s, they had nothing to do with traditional retirement.

Most important, unlike in earlier stages of career change, where one choice must often be made among the many possibilities, for people at this stage, plurality and flexibility seem to be keys to the final choice. As we shall see, this desire for plurality and to extend the prime of life by a decade or more, means maintaining a business connection through Non-Executive Board work for some, living out a passion, working with family, mentoring or academic work for others; and for most in this book, some of each. All of the choices reveal a deeper and urgent desire to take control and fulfill some of the dreams that were set aside when the B2-generation began their careers: resolving the work-life balance with a new paradigm, making a difference and refusing outmoded definitions by doing it their way. Thanks to the hindsight of these interviews, as well as Dona's continuing work in coaching senior executives, we have also sketched out a roadmap with a framework to help other professionals contemplating this type of change. Based on the overall contents of the interviews, we discuss steps to be taken to prepare for and live through this process. Some of them can and should be taken while still working in a full-time career, while others provide directions and subjects of reflection for planning and for the early days out and beyond.

In the first few chapters we look at the reasons motivating the move out of a high-powered career: the losses and the gains, the surprises and the "oh-shit" moments, then trace the process from the early days of planning to leave, through the first steps out to the choices made when rebuilding. Each step is accompanied by first-hand accounts to illustrate the process. The interviews themselves lasted approximately one hour and were loosely structured. We asked each person to describe the end of their career (in industry, politics, or research), the difficulties encountered, how they were organized today, what advice they would give to someone else in the same situation, and how they would define retirement. The one consistent message which we received is that none of them consider themselves retired. We then asked them to give a title if they were to write a book about their life.

Everyone we interviewed was very generous with his/her time and as you shall see the stories are fascinating. We were particularly struck by the amount of focus and discipline they applied to the challenge and also the generosity in giving their time to not-for-profits, family members and the community. Most wanted to give back at some level and have done so by using the skills they acquired during their career and applying them to this next chapter. We appreciate their honesty, as this transition is an emotional and intellectual journey and many faced a loss of confidence at some stage. They all worked through these challenges and their insight and suggestions should provide guidance for the others who face this exciting transition in the future.

Part I

Age is only a number, a cipher for the records. A man can't retire his experience. He must use it.

Bernard Baruch

Retirement at sixty-five is ridiculous. When I was sixty-five I still had pimples.

George Burns

1 The disappearing point on the horizon

This chapter defines the boomers statistically and demographically, for Europe, the United States, and East Asia, discussing the influence they have had on society as they have passed through each stage of life, because of the sheer numbers. Presenting interviews with Patricia Hewitt, former Minister under Tony Blair, Loh Meng See, a former Minister in Singapore, and Stephen Davidson an investment banker.

In this book we have interviewed several dozen highly successful individuals who are all members of the Baby Boomer generation and who found themselves at professional crossroads for one reason or another, generally between the ages of 48 and 63.

As you will see, these are not just the "stars" at the top of the news, but the movers and the shakers behind the scenes, corporate leaders (CEOs, CFOs, HR Directors) in telecommunications, banking and finance as well as doctors, lawyers, politicians, entrepreneurs, a media specialist, and the former managing partner of an executive search firm. We interviewed boomers from the United States (US), the United Kingdom (UK), France, and East Asia (Singapore, Hong Kong, and China) to try to identify any obvious cultural exceptions, differences according to career industry or culture or specificity on the question of gender.

Who are the boomers?

Born between 1946 and 1964, there were more than 78 million members of the postwar B2-generation born in the US – compared to the 46 million in the next "generation X" – and they represent one-third of all Americans living today. A similar demographic pattern can be found in Europe, Canada, Australia, New Zealand, and Iceland during that period.[1] In Asia, Christopher Woods, global emerging-markets equity strategist for Credit Lyonnais Securities Asia (CLSA), states that including China and India there are an astounding 1 billion boomers across this continent[2] with over 7 million in Japan and two million in Hong Kong while in Singapore they make up 74 percent of the population. Unlike in Europe and the US, the increase in population in the Asian countries is a direct consequence of the increased life expectancy during this period. While in the US, the life expectancy was around 70 in 1952, it was 42 in Asia. In 1980 that average

Asian life expectancy was 61.7, just over the official retirement age for Asia. Today it is approaching 70.[3]

But the Baby Boomers, more then just numbers, are a group which has had an enormous cultural impact and the first signs of their coming of age were also worldwide, with Beatlemania in Britain, Woodstock and the Vietnam War in the US, the Mai '68 student protests in France, and antiestablishment movements in India, Japan, and Australia.

The Baby Boomers were teens in the '60's and '70's, and if, as Tamara Erickson states in her book *Retire, Retirement,* one's life perspective and most powerful impressions are formed during the teen years, the teens for the B2-generation were years of causes, revolutions, and unrest. For this impatient generation, "the world needed change", so they set about changing it.[4]

As a result, the boomers have a mistrust of tradition, and in a US study 84 percent of them felt that they "would have been better off without their parents," a sign of the generation gap, the development of youth-oriented cultures around the world, but also of a group that was on its own and would make it on its own, which they have.[5] During the period of social and political upheaval in the 1960s and 1970s, the B2-generation made its first indelible marks: bringing women into the workforce and fighting for racial and social equality as well as seeking change in education, politics, and life choices.

Once they hit the workforce the boomers were fiercely competitive (because they were born in a crowded world), but not revolutionary, and driven, becoming a generation of work-intensives and corporate warriors in traditionally structured environments during a period of substantial economic, technological, and scientific progress. The Dankai generation in Japan is emblematic of other boomers worldwide, fueling the country's economic growth, and tirelessly toiling for their companies.

Boomer careers have included the dot-com boom, the real-estate boom, and the financial boom. They have participated in the development of quantum-leap new industries: biotech, the Internet, telecommunications, and financial services and have been the motor for the globalization of markets and the industrial processes. This was a period of incredible economic development in the US, Europe, Asia, and India. The highly developed newly industrialized economies of Hong Kong, Singapore, South Korea, and Taiwan maintained incredible growth and rapid industrialization from the 1960s onward, while Japan's postwar economic miracle was an example for many.

With all this growth, even with the most recent economic crisis, the most successful of the generation have lived in continuous wealth. To date, the boomers have the highest median household incomes in the US, dominate the top five highest-paying jobs in Japan, and hold 80 percent of the UK's wealth. They are also more educated than past generations, so it is not surprising that for many years now, and still today, they have truly "ruled the world," controlling the political, cultural, industrial, and academic leadership roles worldwide. Bill Clinton was the first US president from the B2-generation, like Tony Blair in the UK and Nicolas Sarkozy in France.

But this is on the verge of shifting. While the large majority of the boomers are still fully active, between 2007–8 (depending on the country and age of retirement), the first wave of boomers to officially retire – now dubbed the Golden Boomers – left their work spaces empty: 7 million in Japan, 93,000 in Hong Kong, 4 million in the US with comparable situations worldwide. And this process will continue, but how?

What's all this about retirement?

Because of the sheer numbers, B2-demographics have profoundly influenced every stage of life they have gone through – childhood, teen years, and adulthood. In a well-known quote Ken Dychtwald said, "watching the Baby Boomers evolve is like watching a python swallow a pig."[6]

Thus, this massive shift of people into the traditional age of retirement and out of the workforce has sociologists and economists holding their breaths. There are theories and studies and papers and articles about how the boomers were going to retire but now it is beginning to happen.

Retirement: East vs West

In Western countries, in particular the US, France, and the UK where our interviews were done, the institutionalization of retirement dates from the twentieth century. In Asia, until very recently, there was no institutionalized gold watch with a life of vacations, and because of the low life expectancy, many Asians who did not work within official corporate structures expected to work until they died. Those who did retire relied upon the support of families in their old age.

Everyone (or nearly) agrees that retirement will not happen the way it has in the past, but the "how" remains theoretical. There are some who see a major crisis (with a workforce retiring in droves causing a wave of spending for retirement and health costs, and a market meltdown) while others have a less catastrophic vision (suggesting a more gradual effect and impact).

However, these theories must also reckon with the personalities of the Baby Boomers themselves, for even before the recent economic crisis, numerous studies have shown that most of them have no intention of stopping working at all. "Almost 32% of boomers said they never intend to stop working for pay. An . . . AARP study in 2004 said that many boomers expect to go back to work after they normally retire – approximately 79% said they intend to work for pay in retirement."[7]

Thus at the outset, an important trend has been identified in the working patterns of this generation. Though work driven, they retire from jobs at an earlier age, then continue to work long after retirement. The reasons for continuing work include continued activity and daily structure and a better sense of self-worth including the ability to provide valuable information and guidance to the next generation.[8] This intention "not to stop" stems from both economic and personal reasons and brings up as many questions as it answers. But it suggests that this group is motivated to change the paradigm of work itself during a new life stage.

From a sociological perspective it is clear that thanks to advances in science, medicine, and lifestyles, this generation, already greater in numbers than others, will have an extended life span. Beyond the traditional age of retirement, the boomers can count on living a period of high energy and good health, many for nearly 25 years, without the responsibility of raising children. They will be extending the prime of life into what was once defined as retirement, requiring new definitions of middle age, old age, and retirement itself.

Our group of successful boomers jumped the gun on traditional retirement and is a few years ahead of the rest of the rest of the B2-generation. The stories in this book are a glimpse at the unique choices that can be made to reach a professional/personal balance that satisfies the specific needs of this uncharted life stage as well as the underlying desire of the boomers to have it all. They provide a look at what's next as this first group of Golden Boomers redefines the patterns of work and retirement.

Patricia Hewitt: The list of the great hereafter

Before transitioning into her new role, Patricia Hewitt was a Labour Member of Parliament for thirteen years, serving for most of that time under Tony Blair's government – initially as Economic Secretary to the Treasury and Minister for e-Commerce (during the dot.com boom), then in the Cabinet as Secretary of State for Trade and Industry, Cabinet Minister for Women, and then Health Secretary. Patricia Hewitt is a good example of a Baby Boomer who sought to integrate the values of her youth into her career early on by working in not-for-profits as an equality activist and a feminist, and then by moving into politics.

But Patricia Hewitt didn't write up a career plan in her twenties that said, "*I will become a member of Parliament.*" She says "*I was much vaguer and more idealistic than that*" and like so many Baby Boomers she "*just wanted to change the world.*"

Patricia began by doing not-for-profit work. She became the first women's rights officer for the UK's National Council for Civil Liberties (now Liberty) in the early 1970s, then became General Secretary for nearly ten years. Politics came afterwards:

> *The transition to change to politics came from not wanting to move from one voluntary organization to another, or become a professional campaigner, switching*

from one issue to another. I'd spent ten years in Civil Liberties and helped make big changes in the law already.

I was very active in the Labour Party, but I'd also come to know several members of Parliament, in particular one woman, Josephine Richardson, and that made me think that I would like to become a member of Parliament and be able to make changes from there.

I stood for Parliament in 1983 as a Labour candidate in Leicester. That was the year that the Labour Party was losing seats all over the country, including the one I was standing in! The Labour Party was near death then, but I then went to work for Neil Kinnock who had just become the Labour leader and learned so much from him. Neil was a superb leader, he could get out there and make difficult decisions. This was an incredible turn around where I learned a great deal from him about leadership and played a part in bringing the Labour Party back to electability.

Later, Patricia helped found the think tank, the Institute for Public Policy Research (IPPR), and became deputy chair for the Social Justice Commission. Finally when Tony Blair became Labour leader, she stood again in Leicester West and got elected.

That was how I came into Parliament and some years later found myself with the NHS (National Health Service). By then the NHS was hitting the targets to cut waiting times, so when Tony Blair appointed me, I thought the hospitals were fine and I could concentrate on public health. But when I got into the department I found a team that was brilliant at hitting targets but that was not equipped to move the NHS forward, to take it from a nationalized monopoly to a patient-focused service, with new private and not-for-profit providers as well as the public sector. The second problem was the financial crisis that became apparent a few months after I arrived. Despite huge budget increases, the NHS had overspent; although the amount was small, we could see that it was doubling every year. I found myself with an organization with a big financial problem and without the right people or tools to deal with it.

So I settled down for a two-year turn around. Granted this did not make me popular, but we ended up with a financial system that was far fairer, as well as more efficient. And we extended patients' choice and banned smoking in enclosed public places – a huge step forward for people's health.

The catalyst for Patricia's decision to transition out involved a reappraisal of the cost of her career to her family as well as a creeping unwillingness to accept a situation where there was no time for herself.

She says:

I was a dedicated Labour Party member, but the Labour Party had eighteen years in opposition. There was quite a long period when I thought that my generation would completely miss out on government, that even if we rebuilt the Labour Party, none of us would ever become Cabinet Ministers. Which was not true, but it happened later than it would have if Labour hadn't spent so long in the wilderness. So I became a Member of Parliament when my children were 10 and 11. It is very difficult to have children and be in full-time politics when they are little and even worse when they are adolescent. It's very, very hard for them. If I had been a minister earlier, I could have said "I've done that" and given up when my children were becoming teenagers. But I decided to become a member of parliament and then became a cabinet member, which means when Commons is sitting, you're working 70–80 hours a week, and even without that you are juggling the constituency and Parliament as well as your family.

Today my children are 23 and 24. My mother, who lived in Australia, died this year at the age of 95, after several years of becoming increasingly frail, and my father is 94 – though still active and traveling between Australia and Britain. Recently my husband, who is four years older than me, became a full-time judge, which is less demanding than when he was a barrister, often working late into the night. I was desperate to have more time with my husband, my children and my parents, which also meant spending more time in Australia. As a Minister, I'd introduced the flexible working law which gave parents of young children – and now older workers and carers – the right to request different working hours. I've been campaigning on flexible working since I wrote a book at IPPR, About Time, which argued that people are increasingly choosing to combine paid work, family and other activities in different ways at different stages of their lives. I never managed flexible working when our children were young, but I thought it was time for me to have some time for my family and myself before it was too late.

Patricia spoke to various people about her plans:

They said do it now and not later. It took me some months to decide. And I knew that the right time to do it would be a moment of big governmental change.

Patricia considers her life since she transitioned out: *"wonderful because I prepared for it."* Her preparation was "mental" including

a list which I had been making for many years which my mother called the list of the great hereafter. My mother used to say 'We'll get round to this one day – in the great hereafter' so it's a list of things you would do if you had the time. Like seeing all the friends I've neglected for the last decade, taking up yoga, walking, getting the piano re-tuned. Not retirement because I was not retiring. Things that make you well rounded and balanced which you simply cannot make time for in a full-time career. Things to get your life back in balance.

But also very practical:

I thought very carefully about it, and I had a mentor, who I have worked with a long time since I left the think tank. That was incredibly helpful. The advice was: "don't wait – do it now" and that's what I've done. I thought about how I would tell people, but except for family, I didn't tell most people until I actually did it. I told Tony Blair and Gordon Brown (who was about to take over as Prime Minister) a few weeks before. I could not tell my department, so I said I would be having a "transition party" on the day of the political transition (from Tony Blair to Gordon Brown) so we had a wonderful, and very moving occasion in my office looking out over Whitehall and the entrance to Downing Street. It was a way of reaching completion. Then I went to see Gordon at the end of the day and agreed on the press release ready. I wanted my constituency to know why I was doing this, so I hit the phone and emails telling them before it hit the press.

Yet, despite this, Patricia remembers the final days as a jolt.

For all of us who'd worked with Tony Blair, his departure was a big, emotional wrench. And then, the next day, watching other people get their government jobs was very difficult as well. But I thought "this is the next generation." And besides, it was my decision, I stepped down when I knew it was the right time. It is much more difficult when people are told they are not staying, or they lose their Parliamentary seat, when the decision is not theirs.

To readjust to her new status Patricia says:

To start, I sorted out my study so that I could enjoy working from home. For about 10 years my office had been the dumping ground, so you can imagine. I put on my sweats and dug in – it took a great deal of work. One of the kids had been sharing it too. I threw away an enormous amount of stuff. This was part of the cleaning out process, part of moving on.

Patricia's long experience in politics has given her a unique understanding of strategic issues that she can now use to serve different industries. Her choices have also given her the new challenge of developing the skill set necessary to be a non-executive director.

After I left government, someone I knew recommended me to BT and I joined the Board some months later. It's a wonderful company and a very good board. I am also now on the Board of Eurotunnel Group, a French company and a member of the Asia Pacific Advisory Committee of Barclays. In a voluntary capacity, I also chair the UK India Business Council and work with an inspirational Indian charity, Katha.

I very much like being on a board. I like the sense of collective responsibility, having a strategic overview but being able to dig deeper into specific areas. Some people find the governance responsibility of a public board too onerous, but I rather enjoy it. And although the substantive nature of the decisions is different, the challenge of making decisions in a very fast-changing and uncertain environment is remarkably similar to what I was doing in government.

Patricia has also taken on significant pro-bono activity, notably for the UK India Business Council, which works closely with the UK government to promote UK-India economic relations. "I had the good fortune to represent part of Leicester, one of Britain's most multiracial cities, and my love of India partly stems from that."

And I wanted more time to travel, particularly to spend time with my mother and sister in Australia. When the children were younger we went to Australia every eighteen months or so; now I go several times a year.

In her new life, Patricia must make a special effort to keep up to date on matters and obtain information that would in the past have been placed on her desk by someone else.

In my case, when you are no longer in government (but this goes for business as well) you no longer have a private office and an entire team who brief you; you no longer have access to huge resources to keep you up to date. When you are full time, there is a huge amount of information available and you can just phone up and get your hands on it.

When you transit out, six months later, things have moved on. So I find that I need to spend a lot of time reading, Googling and keeping up my network. And I am working on building my skills as a non-executive director. I exchange information, I plan lunches and go to a lot of seminars. You need to keep in the swim.

Her advice:

Take time with yourself and your family and then with a person who is a little outside of it, a coach, mentor or friend. Test your idea out and make sure that this is really what you want to do. Think about what you are going to be giving up in your current role. There is a certain amount of satisfaction in the full-time role, making a difference, ego satisfaction, the money. Think about what you are giving up as well as what you are going to gain. Especially if you are giving it up before you turn 60.

Then imagine your new life, when you're walking. Make lists of what you'll be doing. Visualize it. Because of Parliament I had a very structured life. I had to think about what would happen when all that went away which meant projecting myself into a completely different life.

Finally make practical preparations: are you going to use your home office, a remote office, have a paid secretary? How much do you need to earn to pay for the support system? Do you want to be self-employed, start a company?

Definition of retirement:

Retirement is a disappearing point on the horizon. Retirement is a life where you have no responsibilities left except for yourself and your family.

When asked if her work today feels like work she says:

Yes and no, but a lot of time my work has not felt like work – it's always been my passion. Yes, I am paid for it, I have responsibility. It's not just something I do because it's interesting. But I don't want a full-on, full-time job. I no longer want to get up at the crack of dawn feeling as if the whole responsibility is on my shoulders.

Book Title: *On Reflection.*

The paradox of a generation

In her book, *Retire, Retirement,* Tamara Erickson remarks about the boomers: "The paradox is that you are the generation most committed as teens to change – but in the corporate world, at least, you have not done it."[9]

For although they are skeptical of authority, the B2-generation has, on the whole, like Patricia Hewitt, played by the rules. Everyone we interviewed has invested enormously in their careers, and whether they are scientists, CFOs, politicians, or lawyers, they made their way to the top of their mountain. They used the impatience, competitiveness, and drive of those teen years to succeed by "traditional" rules in Medicine, the Corporation, Industry, Law, and Politics.

They all had what one interviewee calls "a fire in the belly" and they used it to reach the top. Even if there was a deep but nebulous motivation to help, they became investment bankers or mainstream politicians to do so, and accepted to pay the price. The women of this generation are the second-wave feminists who sacrificed or transformed the traditional family role to become the first PhDs in engineering or like Patricia to make decisions that were "very very hard" for the children, or not have children at all.

Each of the boomers interviewed reached a position where they played a role in imagining and implementing their company's or laboratory's identity, strategy and future and spent 99 percent of the hours of the waking day doing this. So in the end, it is easy to imagine that most, if not all, of their psychological space – despite discussions about work-life balance – became filled with their job, and that the merger of that job and their personal identity was probably one of the most important joint ventures they managed during that time.

But the payoff for all this work and pressure was title, power, recognition, intellectual satisfaction, and lifestyle. Fortune lunches for some, Davos seminars for others, world-class travel in five star hotels for the scientist reporting on his invention, private jets for company directors. These individuals received in return, in one way or another, for what they had put in.

In many countries in Asia the drive of these successful professionals during the postwar period was directly dedicated to the construction of their nation following independence from the colonial powers, or reconstruction in Japan. They have also participated in the metamorphosis of traditional culture (family, work, women) which is continuing and accelerating, resulting in some differences in the transition out of the primary career which will be explored throughout the book. Moreover, unlike in the US and Europe, this generation will be the first to retire massively within the structure of institutionalized pension schemes.

Loh Meng See our next interviewee was a politician in Singapore, and one of the first generations to live through independence, so it is interesting to place his story back-to-back with Patricia's.

Loh Meng See

Like Patricia, Loh Meng See describes himself as being *idealistic*. He says,

> *with so much wrong with the world I made a decision from the outset not to go for the banks. The banks were the place to go. My generation was the first generation after independence from the British, so we could have benefited. But somehow, I wasn't interested in just making money.*

After going to university, then completing national service Loh Meng See entered the workforce during the first oil crisis in 1974. He trained as a manager in the personnel department of a shipyard in the Port of Singapore, beginning a long career in the *area of people* and becoming part of what he calls *an interesting Singapore story* in a period when Singapore had embarked upon an incredible modernization program to become one of the world's most prosperous nations.

> *The shipyard was a repair arm of the port. And the government decided to privatize it, to make it commercial. Then it was incorporated and listed on the stock market. So I went in and we took over management from the British.*
>
> *We went through a difficult recession in 1985, and I had the unpleasant task of having to deal with the retrenchment and we had to directly lay off more than 800 people. It was an important experience. I believe that no executive that has not seen the full cycle of growth and recession can manage correctly. They keep making the same mistakes over and over.*
>
> *After that I was chosen to succeed my boss. He was in his forties then and the retirement age was 50. The chairman said he wanted me to stay in HR to contribute and serve, and that was enough for me.*

His entry into politics was also uniquely Singaporian, reflecting the multi-cultural dynamics of this new country.

> *In Singapore the political system is a system of induction. I worked in a company that was related to the government (Keppel Corporation Ltd) and one of the people who was involved in politics was a union leader. He was a Malay Muslim and he became a Member of Parliament but he was not English speaking. Since I spoke Malay and English, he asked me to help him with his English-speaking constituency. So I began helping and serving in the community. Then in 1987 I was invited to tea by the ministers and asked whether I would be willing to be a candidate.*

Loh Meng See did not jump right into politics blindfolded, indeed, at first he hesitated.

I thought politics would be too demanding, and would require too much commitment. Because politicians hold two jobs in Singapore so I would have to continue working at Keppel and be in politics. This is good because the people in the parliament are tuned in. It's very dynamic but I thought my career in HR would have been wonderful. Besides my kids were young, and my career was just taking off. But finally I was persuaded that few are chosen, and that you are given the privilege to serve. That was in 1987 and I was fortunate to be posted in the Kampong Glam constituency where the incumbent was the Deputy Prime Minister. That was a big pair of shoes. It was a very poor constituency and I learned to understand human nature better from that experience. I got the vantage point of the poorest fellow right to the top. Human beings are the same, dressed in different clothes and with different roles so we shouldn't have pretensions. I served 4 terms in Parliament and retired in 2006. So politics was another people area where I grew and learned.

Toward the end of his career with typical Baby Boomer drive, Loh Meng See decided to take on a new challenge and became Senior Vice President of Human Resources at Singapore Airlines, and one of the first executives to be recruited from outside the company reflecting a change in approach to corporate governance.

In 1999 I was in my third term in politics, and I was still working at Keppel. Singapore Airlines has always had industrial relations issues and I think that they realized that the board was too removed, that they needed to either shake things up or get another perspective. I didn't need that job, I could have retired from Keppel, but I thought "If I want to test myself, this would be an amazing challenge" because you can't find a more challenging job in Singapore. And I took the job on that basis.

And the challenge proved to be even greater than expected.

When I considered the job in 1999, Singapore International Airlines was unscathed by the Asian Financial Crisis because travelers from the US and Europe were still coming back and forth. So I figured it wouldn't be so bad, but you know what happened? The day after I joined I had to terminate an employee who committed fraud for 35 million Singapore dollars, and 10 months later the first air crash occurred in Taipei. That was in 2001, then after that you had the bombing and SARS, and I had to handle a major retrenchment in 2003.

Like Patricia Hewitt, Loh Meng See decided to transition out to have time for himself and his family several years before official retirement. In 2006 with an election coming up, he wrote to the Prime Minister.

I stepped down at 57. The official age of retirement is 62, but I didn't want to leave after 60 and reach a point where no one wanted my job. I wanted someone to take over, so when one of my Deputies who was already 54, came on board with 20 years experience, I worked out an arrangement so I could leave earlier in the year and he could take over. He was interested, the company was interested, so it was fine.

Loh Meng See felt very ready for the transition out but he was clear that he wanted to continue in the area of people:

> *I have always wanted to share my experience, so I started an HR consultancy. Because life is about relationships and not things. And the area I was in was all about relationships. People remember you because of how you relate to them.*

He began by consulting exclusively for a large family-owned group with companies worldwide led by an entrepreneur who realized the importance of integrating corporate management if he was to be effective globally. This allowed Loh Meng See to scale down gradually and apply his management skills to another environment:

> *He was the second generation of a family-owned business and he was thinking of the family legacy and how to have your company persist for many years to come. He realized that the skill sets are different for an entrepreneur and a corporation so that even if it was a family-owned business, he had better set up independent corporate governance to help him. I worked 4 days a week for him for the first year, which was a good transition.*

He also helped another client set up an office in Singapore and understand local culture and environment. He says: "*So that was the transition.*"

Besides these activities Loh Meng See spends time with his children and grandchildren which is a high priority and a chance to make up for what he missed.

> *I spend time with my grandchildren. The first grandchild was born May 14, 2008, 6 months before I left. The second was born this year. My wife helped because my daughter works. Both grandmothers look after the grandchildren. Now I share that – we have two grandsons, so I am there as a role model.*
>
> *I also make up for what I missed with my children. When I began in politics, my children were around seven, so I hardly saw them during their school years. For example, it was so bad that if one night I found myself at home, my kids would say "how come you are home?"*
>
> *Today I have more family time, and time with my wife.*

Finally Loh Meng See has dipped into his list of his great hereafter, and created space for himself for giving back and working in church.

> *One of the things I was always uneasy about in the corporate existence was how to serve in Church. When I was preparing for retirement in 2006, I decided to embark on an eight-year program of Bible study, with BSF Intl. This entails 52 weeks per year, it's every week. Then in my own church, I started hosting and formed a cell group which meets in my house. That's two evenings a week. The BSF study group is all men. The group in my house is for couples. Also, last year the church appointed me Chairman of the personnel and finance committee. I manage the full-time workers, staff and missionaries. We send out a lot of missionaries. I suppose in some ways this has helped me to let go.*

But the priority, he says, *is still the family.*

> *What I desire is to look at the challenges of the young today, the exposure and risk.*
> *I want to help our grandchildren to be better prepared to confront the world. The*
> *youth face a lot of challenges. Dual careers are the rule in couples, so we can help*
> *this. Then my daughter can be at peace. During our time, there was a lot of stability*
> *but today is very different.*

Loh Meng See's advice is about becoming an "ordinary citizen" again and appreciating the simplicity of life:

> *Even when I was a member of Parliament I always understood that one day I would*
> *be an ordinary citizen. People will look at you differently, so you must move on. If*
> *you think in terms of special treatment, it can get to you because you go to castles and*
> *palaces, places others wouldn't have the opportunity to see. This is not easy to give up,*
> *especially in politics. People want to hang on, but they have to overcome this. Because*
> *in politics the important thing is relevance. I could have stayed, but the environ-*
> *ment is changing and society needs the turnover.*
>
> *I've learned not to let all that "stuff" rub off on me. There is a richness to other*
> *experiences, the simplicity of life. I walk from here to there now, I don't use the car*
> *except on weekends. And time is more flexible. I see things I never got the oppor-*
> *tunity to see and I'm able to interact with people I would not have been able to*
> *interact with.*

He defines retirement as

> *[a] technical term in relation to the full-time executive role. But it is something*
> *you do at your own pace. The first stage of life is success, now it's significance. That*
> *is what we are moving towards. Our time is over for success, we must move on to*
> *something else.*

Book Title: *It all Comes Back.*

So why change, anyway?

The decision to leave this powerful corporate, scientific, or political "family" is never an easy one. To become a senior executive you spend more than 20 years in the corporate environment – whatever the industry: banking, pharmaceuticals, consumer goods, telecoms, and publishing, or country. The work environment is home and you are used to living in its comfort zone.

At the same time, if the trip up the mountain was grueling, the top may be even more grueling. Besides the 70 to 80-hour work weeks mentioned by Patricia Hewitt, today's top-level jobs are considered by some to be in a class by themselves. A recent article concluded that today's most difficult jobs really are more difficult than in the past:

> *because the world economy is going through a genuine epochal transformation on the scale of the industrial revolution 200 years ago. As we move toward an information-based economy in which computing power, data storage, and telecommunications are virtually free, the challenges are fundamentally different and deeply unfamiliar. The toughest jobs are the ones you don't know how to do, and in this new economy those are mostly the jobs we face.*
>
> *Time was when a company could turn the crank on a good business model for decades. No more. Former Xerox CEO Paul Allaire spoke for millions of managers in 2000 when he famously said at conference call of Wall Street analysts: "We have an unsustainable business model."*[10]

And Patricia Russo, former CEO of Alcatel Lucent, says in her interview with us:

> *In the industries of communications and equipment, there's been a huge transformation. It's been the industrial revolution. It means dealing with troubled industries and troubled companies as opposed to consumer products, like making shampoo, which means the more people who are living the more shampoo you use. It's all about the product. You don't see a lot of consumer product companies going out of business.*

And the top of a mountain, if we are to believe statistics, is not the kind of place you should plan to stay for very long – the average CEO, for example, stays in place for an average of six years and in certain industries even less.

Still the reasons for leaving varied:

▷ For some, the awareness of age in an increasingly young environment was a motivating factor.
▷ Others did not get the post they expected – so they "took the opportunity" to agree to disagree and left.
▷ Others left for the challenge, to prove that after being a CEO of a big corporate division, they could prove they could do something else.
▷ Some left because of a plan that was more or less clearly (but mentally) defined, which they called "retiring early," or "retiring after 50" or just "the plan."

For all, there was an increasing feeling that the existing role in the corporation no longer corresponded to what they could give or thought they should be giving considering their level of expertise, experience, and age. Even those who found themselves in the middle of the dot.com bubble burst and were forced out, who might have made a linear choice to look for another similar position, were faced with a sense, forced or intuitive, of nearing what one called his "sell-by date" or feeling that their potential was no longer fully exploited in the corporate environment.

Certain interviewees received more or less subtle messages suggesting that they were nearing the limits of their usefulness. To a certain extent because of their success, their choices within the organization were becoming limited too. They had reached the invisible ceiling at the top. Although linear moves were possible, this could mean a series of serial CEO positions (same 'ol, same 'ol). Beyond that was the prospect of traditional retirement – "retiring from professional life according to age" – with all its psychological and economic implications, while on the contrary all of them felt a need to remain creatively engaged and active that was as powerful as someone in their 30s looking for a career change: but with a difference. This difference had to do with their maturity and experience, resulting in different expectations for the next steps.

Steve Davidson: the young fart in the board room

For Stephen Davidson, who left a career in finance to become Chairman of SPG Media Group plc, Enteraction TV Ltd, Deputy Chairman of Datatec Ltd and Non-Executive Director of Inmarsat plc as well as various other public companies, the decision to leave the corporate environment came when he looked himself in the mirror one morning and asked: *"since when did you become the old fart in the room?"*

Steven continues:

> In the City there is only room for one emissary and I was not it. I realized that if I moved into non-executive roles, I was not the old fart but the young fart. Besides the market had crashed and I felt that it was the right time. I had made enough money and was heading towards 50. I think that everyone wants to be their own boss at some stage and it is usually in the age group of 40–50. It was time for me to be my own boss. To be free and independent.

Before reaching this point, Stephen held various positions in investment banking, starting at Rothschild's in London, then worked as CEO at Chemical Bank. He had a first operational role as Treasurer of US Entertainment Group, Lorimar Telepictures Inc. When Steven moved back to the UK, he joined Bankers Trust and a Technology group, staying for four years. He was the Finance Director and then CEO of Telewest Communications from 1993–8. After the successful build-up of Telewest and its flotation, he participated in one of the largest and visible media mergers of its time (Telewest-NTL). Steve remembers: *"We went from an unknown brand to a FTSE 100, and I went from CFO to CEO and took the company public. When I left Telewest there were over 1 million customers."*

He decided to step down in 2001.

Steve spent the first few months with his family and quietly started networking because he had decided to take a crack at working on boards. It interested him and it was a new challenge.

He remembers that first period and says,

I think you fit into 2 camps when you leave the corporate environment; very hot property where all of the senior people come after you. It is a rare and elite group. Then there are the rest of us. It's a sort of twilight zone. I did go the search route, because it's important to get your CV circulated, but by and large my assignments did not come through that route. Most came through personal networking, recommendations from other professionals I knew in the City.

Steve spent those early days thinking and in conversations with his personal network to understand what he had to offer a board.

He says, "*You need to be very clear on what set of skills you bring to a board or a non-executive position.*" He figured out his strengths and today with his experience in deals, finance, Wall Street, and US/UK governance he has specialized in remuneration, but this did not happen overnight.

It took me two years to have a full complement that I was happy with. These discussions take a long time because both sides are doing the due diligence. It's really important to do things thoroughly and properly the first year, really research the company and the management team and say NO, if you are not sure.

Remember, it's easy to fill a dance card.

Steve learned this when he accepted a board assignment because he trusted the person who recommended him. He found himself with a catastrophe on his hands that he had to solve before he could depart because: "*Once you are committed you cannot just pull out. So lesson learned, do your research.*"

Today Steve works 50–60 hours a week but "*on my own time.*" He is Chairman of four companies and Non Executive Director for two, with assignments in Asia and the US.

When asked what he misses he says:

I miss the wonderful level of support I had in the corporate environment. When you first leave, it's odd not to have a place to go everyday or a single place to operate from. Not to have a team and interaction with the same people every day.

But you become very self-sufficient, learn to operate out of a shoebox and do your work wherever you happen to be. I know where all the good Starbucks are, as well as quiet places to work.

While you miss the support, you gain independence and self-reliance.

His advice:

Anyone moving into this phase needs to be realistic about what they can do. If they set a goal of being a FTSE Chairman in 2 years, that's not realistic.

Most executives have the right to have a least one Board position in their contract. Many do not take advantage of it because of time pressures in their day job. They need to take advantage of being a Non-Executive Director prior to leaving full time. Get on a board, learn, listen, pay attention, recognize what a good Chairman is, what good board practices are. Participate fully, don't just show up.

Make an effort to keep a good rolodex. As an executive, you are privileged to meet a number of very influential people because of your position. Maintain those relationships beyond just your executive purpose. Be diligent about relationships and connections.

Definition of retirement:

Point in time where you and others think you have reached your sell-by date. Also when you want to stop and create another opportunity for yourself.

Steven concludes:

I must have something to stimulate my mind so I am sure I will keep things going at various levels. I can see today in my 50s I am full-time, I may ease off a bit in my 60s but I will play it by ear. I am not retired, I'm self-employed.

2 Reigniting passion

Retirement:
From the French term meaning to withdraw from. (retirer)
To withdraw from office, business or active life, usually because of age.
(Webster's Unabridged Dictionary)

Today I am absolutely engaged, I am not a spectator.
(Chai Patel, former CEO of The Priory)

The definition and negative image of retirement by the different interviewees are discussed and how they define themselves today. The search for an appropriate self-image that corresponds to their expectations and resists ageism, Baby Boomer "subversive thinking" around this topic, as well as the initial "oh-shit" moments in the early days to be dealt with, especially structure and time, are illustrated by interviews with Kathleen Flaherty, former CEO of Winstar, and Patrick T. Gallagher, former CEO of Flagg Telecommunications.

No one we interviewed felt that they had retired and none were sure that they would ever retire in the traditional sense of the word. They, like others of their generation, seem to want to change retirement by not retiring at all.

When asked to define retirement, they answered:

▷ *the point at which others think you have reached your sell-by date.*

▷ *The moment you become a passive observer – you read about life and you discuss it, but you are not an active participant.*

Or more facetiously:

▷ *When a trip to the post office is the height of your day,*

Or prosaically

▷ *You become a book on a shelf that someone might take out now and again to flip through if you're lucky.*

The image is definitely not a positive one and corresponds to what we now imagine for very old age, such as someone in the mid-80s – which was called "absolute retirement" by one and which is associated with being withdrawn from daily life and becoming inactive: "*One of things about absolute retirement – you can read the newspaper and talk about everything, while doing nothing or little.*"

Instead our interviewees were looking to leave the linear career path and seeking to create a definition for themselves that would correspond to an evolving self-image and a professional role that could carry them through the next 20 years of life. Steve Davidson speaks for those several who consider themselves "*self employed*," while many like Patricia Hewitt no longer "*wish to wake up in the morning with the weight of the world on their shoulders.*"

Everyone interviewed was motivated by a profound need for change in his/her working identity that would not be satisfied by another next step up the ladder. Like the mid-career changes in Hermina Ibarra's *Working Identity*, they were imagining doing something completely different that would involve a qualitative break in their structure and behavior that was "much more than transferring to a similar job in a new company ... or moving laterally ... a true change in direction ... (which) is always terrifying."[1]

However, in addition to their working identity, our interviewees were simultaneously looking to define or redefine their personal identity and the role that society once assigned to them as potential "retirees" – perhaps moving into a developmental stage that the social psychologist Levinson called but did not specifically describe as a late adulthood transition (50–65) – a period when "the life structure comes into question, with its crisis in meaning, direction and value, and it is marked by a desire to express the neglected parts of the self."[2]

This desire is clear in all the interviews: each expresses a feeling of "been there, done that, got the t-shirt" and a desire to take control of a life that has been largely determined by the rigors of the professional corporate – political or academic path and rules.

Boomer subversive thinking

But one also senses a renewal of the boomer commitment to change: expressed by Stephen Davidson as wanting to be his own boss and be "*free and independent*" and by Patricia Hewitt as "*to have some time for herself.*" In our next interview Kathleen Flaherty says "*I wanted to get involved in something completely different and something I was passionate about.*" A desire to be free, not of work itself, but of the traditional rules accepted thus far, and on a deeper level of the traditional next step into retirement and old age.

All of the interviewees also have a healthy skepticism and a lack of naivety about the world they have been playing in (Kathleen kids about her last CMO position, "*It's funny, I read somewhere the average life span for a CMO was 23 months, I lasted 18*"). As if they have given it all, and accepted to play the game by those traditional rules without ever completely buying in. Each has been waiting for the right moment to actualize the needs of that other idealistic boomer self on his/her own terms, and like Steve Davidson on his own time. For Patricia, this was a major political change, for Steve Davidson a market crash, and for Kathleen a turning point in the business plan.

And as luck would have, they will have that time. Beyond this late adulthood transition, each has potentially 20 years or more in good health. Indeed, the life expectancy has increased from 48 in 1945 (in the United Kingdom (UK)) to more than 80 today – and people are simply healthier than they were. Today, there are 180,000 centenarians in the world and this is expected to increase to 3.2 million by 2050. Thus this generation, unique in its numbers, will also be the first to map out an uncharted life stage.

In her book *New Passages*, Gail Sheehy calls this period a "second adulthood"[3] and Ken Dychtwald and Tamara Erickson have coined the term "middlescence."[4] These authors have each in their own way contributed to a new way of thinking about age. They have chosen to extend what was once midlife to ten to 20 years later because, like the business models of yore, the psychological life models have also become unsustainable and obsolete.

Beyond this desire to be free of tradition, with this extra time, there is a desire to build what we will see is a complex, rather than simple/singular, life structure by first exploring hitherto unexplored avenues for the all-engrossing career, then dipping into those lists of the great hereafter to get life back into balance.

Kathleen Flaherty. There is a way

As one of the first women to obtain a PhD in engineering at Northwestern, University, Kathleen had a well-planned 18-year career at the telecommunications company MCI of increasing responsibility. She spent three years as President and COO of Winstar International and has lived in Geneva, London, and the United States. She began transitioning out in 2001 and finally transitioned out in 2005. Her transition highlights the will to rediscover and actualize certain passions, while pursuing a new professional activity where she could exploit her past experience.

Kathleen's motivation to transition out came after her three years as President and COO of Winstar International.

> *Winstar was a very intense role for me. I built a company in 15 countries, hired over 400 people and then had to shut it down over the course of three years. When I left in 2001, I was planning on retiring. I basically took the year off to build a dream beach house. I literally left my apartment in New York on Sept 7th and then Sept 11 happened. With all of the destruction caused by that catastrophe in New York, it was unsettling to be demolishing a house, even if it was to replace it with another. The nine months it took to build this house was quite healing and so intense that I perhaps did not feel some of the usual emotions that others might upon leaving such an all-consuming global corporate role.*

When the house was completed, I felt an amazing sense of accomplishment. I had never done anything like that before, been a general contractor, and I realized I might want to do it again!!

Before I left Winstar I also had two board positions which I continued.

After the house was complete, my plan was to get involved in something completely different and something I was passionate about, but I was not sure what that would be. I met a woman who had written a book and was offering active wellness programs in the corporate environment as well as a candy company that produced low calorie, low carbohydrate candy which she had begun to market in New York. I have always been interested in health and wellness, so I invested in her project and joined her as CEO. She was also writing a cook book and I love to cook so I tested, critiqued, and edited her recipes.

I was business advisor and CEO, and I applied all my know-how to writing a business plan and raising funds. But there was no funding out there. And when I dug into the company and the different agreements they had signed, I discovered a flaw in the business model due to the distribution agreement that the original owner had signed. I worked on this venture for 12 months.

I am still involved as an investor and still truly believe in the concept, but we did not raise money and the business was not going to scale up. So after that I went back to ATT as CMO for 18 months before completely transitioning out.

Once the euphoria of not working wore off, when asked what she missed, Kathleen jokes: "*Nothing!!*"

Well, maybe I did miss having a driver . . . and corporate jets were quite nice ... No, kidding aside, I still had my board work and in some ways the 2001–4 period prepared me for the final transition.

At the same time, there were silly things that were incredibly important. You have to imagine that senior executives don't write their own letters and although I had been in technology all my life, the PC came into the corporate environment after I was quite senior. All of this might not seem like much, but that meant I didn't know how to do a spreadsheet, or Power Point! So I had to become computer literate, and get back to doing everything myself again, like travel arrangements.

For example, I remember one incident where I agreed to do a presentation for some very senior science advisors on wireless technology. While I knew quite a bit about the wireless industry, I did my own research, and spent a great deal of time preparing what I wanted to say. After I had the presentation ready, I realized I did not know how to create a power point presentation!!! This was a real "oh-shit" moment for me, and for the first time I had no choice but to ask for help. I have always managed to solve my own problems but this was not something I could do on my own. Quite funny, really.

Kathleen, like others does not consider herself retired:

I consider myself a professional corporate advisor and plan on working on at least two boards until I am 70. Today I am working for Inmarsat and Yell Group, plc., with businesses in the UK, US, and Spain. Board work is definitely work. If age legislation changes, I would work longer than that. I do it both for the intellectual stimulation and to keep abreast of what is going on. I am passionate about corporate governance and the people side of the equations. Succession is a particular hot button of mine.

But I am relieved to be finished working full time. My 25 years in corporate life took a toll on me and my family. Your time is completely monopolized and while you do your best to organize the family and work, the family is usually what loses out. I can remember being on conference calls at home while I was babysitting my grandchild. It never felt right. So I am delighted to have the time to garden, and I can say with pride that the garden is mine, not some landscaper's. I spend about 70% of my time today with my children and grandchildren, and am totally dedicated to this, although this might lessen over time.

In Kathleen's case, plans involve board work but also her family and exploring "non-linear" activities that have been left by the wayside.

I always wanted to work on at least two boards which I have managed to do. But there are many more things I want to do. Get more involved in my gardening, and go back to school for "fun" stuff, the "ologies." For example, I completed a "Mini medical school" at Georgetown Medical School and learned about cardiology, pathology, immunology etc. It was great! I have a PhD in engineering, so I have had a very linear education. I love learning, so I expect to immerse myself in additional formal education. And I will take up music again; I was quite a gifted musician in my early years and plan to pick it up again. My plan is less structured or time-oriented and more about reigniting passions because I have time to do it.

Her advice:

Keep your network active. All four boards I have were from four different search firms. The phone does stop ringing and it's up to you to keep in touch and visible. Also think about how you want to be viewed and positioned after you leave your full time work and what you need to do to keep this position alive.

You will go through confidence crises at times because you have less feedback, you need to ride these through and go back to your roots of planning and making things happen.

Book Title: *There is a Way.*

Dealing with the twilight zone and oh-shit moments

Despite the resounding "*Nothing!*" when asked if she missed anything, Kathleen Flaherty also speaks of "*crises of confidence*," while the very early period after transitioning out left one interviewee "*weepy*" and Steve Donaldson in a "*twilight zone.*"

For even with all their deep determination to finally satisfy the urge to do something different on their own terms and time, each is moving into uncharted territory, and getting out the door can be difficult. First, the corporation does not necessarily make it easy. Although for a certain number of interviewees the transition was gradual and timely: during a major change in government or after a market crash, two interviewees stated that when they announced they were going to resign after 15 years or more with the same company, "*The CEO did everything in his power to discourage me, and made me doubt my decision.*" While the other states "*It felt like getting a divorce and disowning my family at the same time.*" So the decision may be immediately put to the test.

In these cases, the pressure probably comes from two sources: a decision to move off the beaten track is a threat to the others who stay on, and a desire to convince you to stay, because you are good at what you do.

Hermina Ibarra states in *Working Identity*, "When it comes to reinventing ourselves, the people who know us best are the ones most likely to hinder rather than help. They may wish to be supportive, by they tend to reinforce – or even desperately try to preserve – the old identity we are seeking to shed."[5]

Indeed, as we will see in a later interview, this resistance can also be found after one leaves: close family members may be skeptical about your new choices – tending to place you in a box.

For others, who do not directly choose to leave and control the timing, or who find themselves in a dot-com bubble burst or another burst, there is first the shock of unprepared loss. This additional shock must first be overcome with its associated frustration, feelings of betrayal, and sense of powerlessness. Within the wake of this, the decision may be made not to pursue the linear career path to its traditional end and to redefine the next 20 years or so of life and work on other terms.

So whatever the exit scenario, for many, like getting a divorce or leaving your family, the split is often a very emotional affair, even if they are convinced it is the right thing to do. Our next interviewee, Patrick Gallagher, a global telecommunications executive with 30 years experience says "*I was overwhelmed by the number of calls I received from people I had worked with, for, and had worked for me. Everyone was sad to seem me go and I found these calls to be quite emotional.*"

Patrick had time to prepare before leaving, and his story illustrates this early period in some detail, the difficulties encountered and the rigorous approach that he had to the ups and downs of the process of rebuilding.

Patrick Gallagher. A life of London buses

Patrick Gallagher spent 30 years in Global Telecommunications. Between 1995 and 2000 he was President of BT Europe, Group Director Strategy & Development, and a member of the BT Executive Committee. Patrick then served as Co-Chairman and CEO of Flag Telecom, a UK headquartered, NASDAQ-listed, global company with offices in over 20 countries. While there, he restructured the post-Chapter 11 [bankruptcy] balance sheet, and defined, developed, and successfully executed Flag's three-year business plan leading to the sale of the company to Reliance Industries. As Vice Chairman of the Moscow headquartered company Golden Telecom, Patrick led the sale of this company to Vimplecom in February 2008, making it the largest acquisition by a publicly listed Russian company of a NASDAQ listed-company. Patrick was also Chairman of Macro4 Plc, a global software company, when he led the sale to a private American buyer in March 2009. Today Patrick is on the Boards of the Harmonics Inc. and Ciena Corporation; is Chairman of the Ubiquisys Ltd; and on the board of the Russian-listed automotive company, Sollers.

Patrick began discussing an exit from BT in 2000 because he felt he had accomplished what he could there.

> *There were no opportunities that I felt would continue to challenge me. We agreed to the exit and I was asked to stay on for six–seven months to complete the strategy, which I did. So even though I knew I was leaving, I kept working and it was 24/7 to the very end. The exit package included a very tight non compete so I was almost forced to take ten months off.*
>
> *It was very emotional split for me as I had been there for 17 years, and when the announcement went out, I was overwhelmed by the number of calls I received from people who I had worked with, for, and had worked for me. Everyone was sad to see me go and I found those calls to be quite emotional. In some ways you do not know how much impact you have on people's lives until you leave and they tell you!!*
>
> *So I had ten months to decide what I wanted to do. During the early days of my notice period, a number of Venture Capitalists (VC) contacted me and asked me to help with due diligence on a number of the deals they were sourcing. I found this very interesting and also got to understand the VC community. In working with them I realized it was not a route I wanted to go down. An operating partner was something I toyed with, and in working with them I disqualified it as a role I would enjoy having been so full on as an operating senior executive.*
>
> *I was also contacted by a small electronic pharmaceutical distribution company and I accepted a short-term role as Chairman which was a good experience as well.*

The early days for Patrick was a period of "shifting his thinking" and reshaping his time, personal and organizational structure.

> *As an executive, the 24/7 working and constant pressure is stimulating and I was used to it. It was important for me to structure my time and to realize that if the day was not full on 24/7, I was not going to fall off a cliff.*
>
> *I had to learn to look after myself again. I could have employed a secretary but I decided not to, and to do it myself. I did not even have an email address because*

everything always came through BT, so the first thing I did was to get a Blackberry and a Yahoo address so I could keep in touch.

I spent the first few months getting back in touch with people I had not had time to see when I was working full time – business colleagues, family, and friends. One comment I will always remember was from my brother-in-law. My wife and I started spending more time with them and he said to me one night "you know it's nice to know you are human after all." Up until that time even if we were together, I was always multitasking and not really engaging the way I should have. I made it a priority to be sure to be in touch with my family and friends from that point forward.

To fill my time I got back into sports, which I have always loved but had no time for, and read lots of books both for business and pleasure. I love to read and learn so this was and continues to be a delight.

To reach his goal, Patrick then decided to take a risk:

I was not someone who was drawing down a lucrative pension, so I needed to work and I took a personal risk at this point. I decided that in order to find the right role and to begin networking properly, I needed to be in central London. So with my wife's support we sold our out-of-town flat and bought one in London, complete with a fairly hefty mortgage! The whole transaction meant that I had exactly eight months of cash available for us to live on and after that life would get more than a little difficult. It worked out, but it was a very high-risk decision at the time.

I felt that in order to network effectively I had to be available and I had the confidence that something would come through. I networked with everyone I could think of, search firms, business contacts, friends of friends etc. It was my job to be in the market talking to as many people as possible to assess the opportunities and I was very disciplined about it.

I had a number of approaches and said no to almost all of them, because they were not quite right. It's very much like London buses … there are no opportunities at all and then suddenly they all come at once.

During that time I learned to play the piano and spent more time with my family. And there was a family crisis at this time that I would not have been involved in if I had not been home. In fact, I even said "no" to one board opportunity to help take care of it. It was very satisfying to be able to contribute to a family issue and see it through to completion – something I had rarely been able to do.

As we saw with Kathleen, the transition out is not necessarily a straight line, but a process of exploring avenues of interest, and gradually realigning them. For Kathleen and Patrick, who were interested in having a portfolio of boards, this also included a decision to return to the corporate structure one last time to fill in certain gaps before finally settling in.

Patrick says:

Then I had to make a decision: "Do I go plural and take on a lot of boards on or take on one more operating role?" I decided to take on another operating role.

It was important for me to become the CEO of a stand-alone company where all of the responsibility stopped with me. I knew I would learn a great deal, and in the end it would make me a better board member. It was also a bit of a catch-22 situation, because search firms say you don't have the experience to be a CEO of the stand-alone publicly traded company, so once again you need to be focused on finding the right role and the right company. It may not be a big or high-profile company but it's important to find it. So when I was approached for the FLAG role, it seemed the perfect fit. It was quite complex (NASDAQ-listed coming out of bankruptcy with a board of bond holders, financial executives and others) but it was a worthy challenge. It was absolutely the right thing to do. I thoroughly loved the position and the team I worked with right up until we sold the company to Reliance. The board was looking at me to turn the situation around, and with a great new team, we did.

After Flag, in 2006 I was ready to have a portfolio of boards and chairman roles.

Planning for Patrick also involved reappraising one's experience to identify one's added value in potential new roles, which in these first few interviews involved board work, but as we shall see later on can be transferred into very different activities or industries.

Patrick says:

I was very clear about thinking through exactly where I could add value and what would interest me intellectually so I said no to a number of roles.

For example, I decided to work in emerging markets. My added value was in the telecommunications industry with my experience in mergers, acquisitions, high growth, and transformation. So I applied those skills to emerging market companies. I was involved in cultures and markets that were unfamiliar to me and this forced me to stay sharp and learn new things.

Once on a Board I also asked to get involved in all sorts of things and immersed myself in understanding IFRS [International Financial Reporting Standards] (I enjoy understanding the numbers and was always on the Audit Committee) and all of the governance issues associated with European and US boards. I also did a lot of reading about this to keep current and to learn what was expected of me.

Patrick has a clear idea of how to create opportunities:

1.   *The old boys' network is not enough.*
2.   *Luck ... you need to be available.*
3.   *Networking – I met every recruiter who would see me and then decided who I liked working with which cut the list by half. Business Contacts: customers, partners, informal lunches. You need to meet a lot of people who understand the range of opportunities that are out there.*
4.   *Be clear on what you have to offer, of what your value is.*

Patrick advises learning by observing; not filling up your agenda too quickly; and taking initiatives so that you keep the adrenalin flowing and not lose the sparkle in your eyes:

> If you want to become a board member, you should find time to commit to a non-executive position before leaving full-time corporate role. Don't just show up. Take it seriously because you will only learn by doing. I was very lucky to have the opportunity to sit on the boards of various European companies at BT so I was able to observe excellent Chairmen and also not-so-good ones. I learned by observing and reading everything I could find.
>
> More generally, it is important for anyone who is transitioning to realize they don't need to fill the diary on day one, but take time to choose the right things. If after six–nine months you only have two board assignments, the world will not fall apart.
>
> I would also suggest that you challenge your own conservative conventions, push yourself out of your comfort zone. Part of what keeps us motivated and engaged in the corporate world is that we are constantly pushed and challenged. This is what creates the edge and the adrenaline. When you no longer have the structure to push you, you need to push yourself to remain simulated and challenged.
>
> And you need to question yourself every day: am I doing the right thing? Life is full of choices and if you need to change the path, then change it, not necessarily a U-turn but at this time of life you have an opportunity to veer to the right or left.
>
> I have seen people who leave work and expect these things to come to them on a plate. After a time they lose the sparkle in their eyes and the energy that allows them to do what they do. They loose touch but do not understand why they don't have "calls" coming in.

Patrick does not consider himself retired. He says:

> It's like a ful-time job but with more flexibility of time and variety. I am available to my board members and chair 24/7 if they need me. I tell the people I work with that I will be back to them within an hour if they send an email, text, or phone. We have the great privilege of having technologies that allow us to stay in touch and run our own diaries. As a Chairman I do the same thing I did as a CEO. I create a team and make sure that everyone contributes and feels a part of the success of the company. I am also not afraid to admit when I do not know the answer. I actually work four days a week but if you allow for emergency situations, travel, and conversations with people, it ends up being five–seven days sometimes.

When speaking of the difference between his work today and his corporate career, we discover a lifestyle in which personal and professional activities are integrated and interwoven:

> Managing your working time and creating and weaving personal time into your life is a huge difference. It has more balance. I love what I do and I am enjoying this era. I am always challenging myself and continue to have an open mind to the future.

Book Title: *The End of the Beginning*.

Structure and time

As we have seen, getting out the door itself, and in the first few months after the transition, there is a whole list of prosaic "oh-shit" moments that must be confronted – the absence of secretaries, email addresses, and BlackBerries, full access to information and resources, and on a deeper level confidence issues when the phone stops ringing and the question comes up of the title on the business card without the prestigious company name.

For no matter what the final choices are, the loss of structure remains formidable. As Patrick Gallagher mentions, the structure *"constantly pushes you and keeps you challenged, creating the edge and ... keeping you motivated and engaged."*

This structure must now be arranged by you. It is the price of making an independent choice and stepping outside the box. First, by deciding whether you wish to maintain the more classic organization with an outside office or to organize this yourself at home and work out of a shoebox, discovering the best Starbuck's. Elisabeth Brenner-Salz says:

> *"There is a difference in being executive and non executive, and if you have to ask how to become an entrepreneur, you may not be meant to. Some people jump out because they are really meant to be entrepreneurs and then there are others who may not be. You have to think about 'Can I cope with being truly independent?' 'Can I cope with truly hiring and paying for a secretary, employing and paying for a driver? About having to think about how to do my own IT and having my own Black Berry?'"*

Mike Critelli, former CEO of Pitney Bowes also speaks of all there is to learn:

> *The first thing was from a technology standpoint that I needed a different and better system. Large companies have technology systems and spending processes that are designed for standardization and control rather than effectiveness and support. For example, I had a meeting to go to in Cambridge and I was still with a company assistant. She went through the company's travel department and the best rate they could find was 239 USD for a night in Boston. I had someone fixing my computer system at the time who traveled a lot and I said "how do you travel?" He said he used Hotel.com. We did that and we found a very good higher caliber hotel for 179 USD per night. I found a lot of examples like that, for air flights, rental cars. I now use the metro in Washington, the T in Boston, and the public transit systems.*

And about becoming resourceful:

> *The surprise was that I could function far more inexpensively than I had in the corporation. The other thing was with the iPhone and the iMac I could be much better connected and have much better technology capabilities than in the company. Also the support at the Apple store really guides you to where you want to go. I discovered*

that there are many ways to create meeting spaces and function virtually compared to the corporate structure. I was traveling with an entrepreneur and where I usually would have gotten a hotel, taken a shower, then rented a limousine to get to the meeting, I learned from him. He said "first you can go to the American Airlines lounge and take a shower, you can have a full hot breakfast there. Then you can take a high-speed train to Oxford which costs about 75 dollars, compared to 200 for a limousine." And we held the meeting at one of the American Airlines lounge at no extra cost because he had membership in the lounge.

So I've become resourceful. In the start-up businesses I work with, I've taught the executives and employees how to get more out of less, which was fun.

The corporate structure also managed your time. Patricia Russo former CEO of Alcatel Lucent says *"your calendar, how you spent your time, the panels you are on, the speaking engagements, the conferences, industry trade shows, customer visits, and operational meetings are all shaped for you. It is totally structured. And how you spend your time is defined."*

Although Patrick Gallagher is now available 24/7 to his board members if they need him, today he feels that his time has become more flexible which might allow him to make a few phone calls after a game of tennis. He has gained the freedom to live by literally mixing business with pleasure, taking advantage of the liberty of deciding how and when to engage in these different activities.

Managing this requires significant discipline, for without the corporate structure, time is suddenly a malleable dimension. Taking, making, and filling time while not losing it is now in your own hands. One interviewee said *"If you aren't careful, you can take more and more time to do things. Something that took you ten minutes before is going to take you an hour now, and on an on until you end up feeling too busy!"*

Dealing with this relationship is an important underlying element when redefining one's self image and place in society. It is restructuring in the deepest sense, a way to give basic definition to the new priorities as they come up and are woven into this more complex and independent role.

Finally, the continuum between having too much and not having enough is a challenge to all our interviewees who wish to remain active in a professional arena of 24-hour global communication.

When speaking of her book *About Time*, Patricia Hewitt states:

Global sourcing creates a world with no boundaries. So if you can do your email at any time of the day or night, you have to create your boundaries for yourself. If you are completely responsible for life except for the fixed points of meetings and airports and you have a portfolio of things, but everything else is a great formless space, you have to create the forms and fixed points and decide the limits of how long you are going to work and all that kind of thing. No definition. Just the rest of your life.

3 Preparing for an encore and plurality

The question "what am I going to do for an encore" is explored through two interviews, one with Patricia Russo, former CEO of Alcatel, and Henri Balbaud, former Director of HR and Communications at Indosuez and Credit Agricole Group. The process of deciding what's next is begun, and the period of searching, the importance of not locking in too quickly, and the ultimate choice of a flexible and "multiple" or plural lifestyle is discussed.

As we have seen, during the initial months after transitioning out and in response to the early twilight zone period many, like Patrick Gallagher, spent more time with their families and picked up old hobbies. This sometimes meant getting back in touch with people they had not seen when they were working full time, people "who discover that you are human after all" (and help you discover it too); seeing more of their children and being present to manage a crisis; or babysitting for grandchildren without having to teleconference at the same time. This is all about what Patrick calls "shifting your thinking" away from constant multitasking both on a human and professional scale, and learning that if the day is not full 24/7, you are not going to fall off a cliff.

Steps may also be taken to physically rebuild and create structure. Like Patricia Hewitt, one's private space must be set up to include a professional domain, a study, or office, or on a larger scale, Kathleen Flaherty tore down the old to build a new dream house. All of these are early incremental actions to symbolically reconstruct/separate personal and professional identity by giving oneself time to reflect before reorganizing, and to find the echoes of the familiar in personal relationships.

Key questions, key words

But finding the answer to the key question *what am I going to do for an encore* involves a period of searching that may (and often does) begin before the final departure and continue through a year or more after leaving. Although some come out with a fairly clear, but general, idea of the next steps like Patrick Gallagher, for many this transition involves a long process including visualizing and speaking with others like Patricia Hewitt, learning-by-doing and participating in boards like Steve, or trying out a new business the way Kathleen did when she left in 2001. During this period of search all agree that it is important to remain flexible even if you make mistakes. Patrick says: *"you must be willing to change a path if you need to, not necessarily a U-turn but varying to the right or the left."*

Patricia Russo – What a ride

Patricia Russo joined Lucent's predecessor in 1982. In 1992 she became the president of its Business Communications Systems division, then executive VP of corporate operations in 1997 and executive VP and CEO of the Service Provider Networks Group in 1999. After a reorganization she left in 2000, returning in January 2002 to become its CEO. After cutting costs and focusing on sales of wireless equipment, Russo was credited with returning Lucent to profitability in 2004, after three years of red ink.[1]

Russo took on the CEO role of a new combined company resulting from the merger of the French communications company Alcatel and Lucent in 2006, while Serge Tchuruk, the former CEO of Alcatel, remained as Chairman.

On July 29, 2008 Russo, along with Alcatel-Lucent chairman Serge Tchuruk, announced that they would step down by the end of 2008 in a broad-reaching restructuring to pave the way for a fully aligned governance and management model going forward.

In the following interview, Patricia Russo provides remarkable insight into the many issues that come into play when deciding "what's next" after the roller coaster ride of working in an industry that has undergone "dramatic transformations" leaving Patricia feeling as if she's *"had a CEO career of 30 years in 10."*

Compared to Patrick Gallagher, Patricia Russo had no real time to prepare or search before leaving, she *exited from a very difficult situation* in a high-pressure, high-profile CEO position. When she talks about the exit strategy itself she says

I think timing is everything and when you choose to leave something it often helps to shape what your opportunity set may be. In my case I had a couple of opportunities. There were time periods where breaking away from what I was doing – stepping back and looking to do something else – would have been logical. For example, when I came back to Lucent in 2002. I had left Lucent in July of 2000 because I had a falling out with the CEO who four months later was asked to resign. I was at Kodak. The company had had merger talks with Alcatel in 2001 which failed to conclude late in the process. Lucent concluded that they were going to have to go it on their own and they needed someone to run the company who knew the industry and was not going to come in and suddenly do a completely different strategy. I was asked to go back as CEO which I did in January 2002. At that time the industry and Lucent had just started to feel the pain of the Internet and telecom downturn like all the equipment manufacturers. Lucent felt it a bit more than others as they had benefited from the "boom" more than their competitors. By January of 2002, the industry was projected to be down that year by roughly 5%. So the revenue plan was for 19 billion and the costs were set up accordingly. We did 12. The market literally crashed. We were bleeding cash. I was there for six or seven months and our stock dropped to 57 cents. All hell broke loose. As you can imagine, we were dealing with a number of issues. We had an ongoing SEC investigation, pension issues due to the market downturn, shareholder lawsuits due to the stock drop, etc. So I had an overflowing plate of issues to manage. On top of that, of course, when our stock dropped to 57 cents, it was clear the investment community was betting we were going bankrupt. In fact, I had three firms in who said the only thing you can do is file for Chapter 11 [bankruptcy]. And I said "over my dead body." We had 125,000 retirees, 95,000 additional dependents, not to mention employees, customers and I said "I'll die trying." Well, we made it; we got back to profitability by the third quarter of 2003, and had a good growth year in 2004 and 2005. That would have been the time for me to leave, to say I'd gotten the company through the worst of it and I would have been a hero, or a heroine.

But Pat, in a reaction which is typical of this work driven generation says:

I didn't spend a lot of time thinking about it because I felt like I had recruited the board and there was a dimension of loyalty that caused me just to keep going. There was a lot of change in our industry. It was clear that the industry structure was not sustainable. Our customers were consolidating and there were too many players. As we discussed with the board ... we either needed to become more global or become irrelevant. I really believed that, so we talked with a number of players, and ended up negotiating a deal with Alcatel.

(Alcatel SA, a global company, headquartered in France, that sold equipment for mobile and fixed voice communication networks, data networks, and television and video delivery merged with Lucent to begin operations as the world's leading communication solutions provider on December 1, 2006.)

The merger made sense. They had the European coverage, Lucent had great North American coverage and we had complementary products. It made strategic and industrial sense although I have to say that I underestimated the complexities and challenges of cross-border governance. I agreed to run the company from Paris. The former CEO became the Non-Executive chairman and we merged the Boards. It was roughly half French/European and half American. But during my time there, the board never fully came together. My personal intention going into the merger was that I would run the company for up to three years. My husband did not move to Paris: we had an apartment, I traveled all over the world, we were separated quite a bit so it was personally difficult. And the first year of the merger, 2007, was a very tough year for the industry. The pricing aggression by the Chinese suppliers destroyed margins and we had to make some tough price decisions. What became particularly difficult was the governance model. As things got tough, the Chairman and I had increasing difficulty working together. I think, while perhaps well intended, in his heart he did not believe that anyone could run the company as well as he could. He had a history of failing to find successors but I thought it would be different in this case. It wasn't. In addition I found there were different views regarding the role of a board vs management. After reaching the conclusion that the situation needed to change and after difficult discussions at the board level, we announced that we would change the composition of the board and that Serge and I would both leave to create the opportunity for a better aligned governance model and a fresh independent perspective. From my perspective, in a tough industry, executing a complex merger, I needed to spend my time and energy on running the company with the full support of all of the board members. Without that, it wouldn't work. The whole exit was difficult, the media which so likes "palace intrigue" was painful ... In the end, we took these steps: I agreed to run the company until we found a replacement, which I helped with. After we made the announcement, things moved quickly.

Patricia Russo's interview is a perfect example of the "grueling" aspect of being at the top. Moreover she was someone who *"was still working 24/7 right to the last day."*

This meant I didn't have time to think about what I was going to do for an encore. Not only until after I left but until after I left and disconnected myself completely.

As a result Patricia Russo says:

I didn't know what I wanted to do next. I didn't know whether I wanted to work full time next. I didn't know if there were CEO opportunities whether I would even be interested.

Because when you leave and you are 24/7 and you are a high-energy person which I am, even if you know there's something more to life besides working 20 hours a day, and thinking about work 20 hours a day you think "but I have to work," because it's just who you are, because you've done it for so many years.

Patricia goes further than most in her reasoning, going so far as to say "What if there is no other chapter?"

Because you see, the presumption is "there needs to be a defined next chapter." Because that's the way I've lived my life. So in my case, people will ask ... So what are you doing? I say, "mmm ... nothing!" There are these paradigms that someone like me has to be able to articulate what my next chapter is. But maybe it's ok not to. That's a question. What if there isn't a next chapter? What if it's just that I'm enjoying life? I'm traveling, I'm spending time with my family. That's acceptable if you are ok with it. But I must admit ... a year into it, I am still figuring out what's "OK" for me. I'm still feeling my way and it's a process.

From there, Patricia says the challenge became: *but "what is it for me? What is IT for me?"* And then, she began the transitions.

She speaks of

> *the macrolevel transition of what do I want to do, what do I like doing? I've been a*
> *CEO, I've been a Chairman & CEO. I've run companies. I've run United States*
> *(US) companies, I've run a French company on a global level. I ran what is now*
> *Avaya, Lucent, and Alcatel-Lucent. But at this stage in my life, I don't know.*
>
> *When recruiters say, "Do you want to work full time? I say 'I don't know unless*
> *I see it.'" It depends. I know this: I would not go to work full time unless it was in*
> *a business that I was really interested in and with people that I really liked and*
> *respected. Because life is too short.*
>
> *The second transition when you are a CEO of a company is that what you do and*
> *where you go and how you spend your time is shaped by the problems and opportuni-*
> *ties you are trying to pursue on behalf of the company. When you transition out of*
> *that kind of a role, you need to get some discipline around how you spend your time,*
> *what you spend it on, what you want to spend it doing.*
>
> *So the first is the macrotransition about who you have been. You've been defined*
> *by your job title, your position, and then all of a sudden you're gone, and all of that*
> *disappears and you're on your own.*

At the same time she had a Baby Boomer's lucidity about this role:

> *I was always a believer, notwithstanding the congratulations on being on the*
> *Fortune list of most powerful women, one of Time's most important people, and*
> *the like, that once I was not in the job anymore, I wouldn't be on any of those. They*
> *would go on to the next crew. Nobody should get confused that the reason you're*
> *asked to be on those things is because of the role you're in. It's not because you are Pat*
> *Russo. It's because you are Pat Russo who happens to be CEO of ... whatever.*

During this macrotransition, in order to figure out what the next step is, about
whether to dive in to another full-time CEO position, or something else,
Patricia had to back away from being Time's most important person to look at
herself in relation to the rest of her environment, herself, her family, and the
society, and she begins to see what she calls the "complicating factors."

> *The paradigm for age and runway has changed. It has really changed. I'm a mid-*
> *fifties person who believes I am 20 years younger than I am, who acts and behaves like*
> *I'm 20 years younger than I am, who has an incredible amount of energy. So on the*
> *one hand, I look back and say. I've been 24/7, I've been this, I've been that. But, so*
> *what? What am I going to do for the next 20 years, because I like working, I like doing*
> *things, I'm not a go-out-and-play-golf-everyday person, I'm not a hang-around-the-*
> *house-and-read everyday person. That's a complicating factor.*
>
> *Another complicating factor is that my husband happens to be nine years older*
> *that I am. So he's been retired from ATT since 2001 and he's young and he's healthy.*
> *So how can we take advantage of the benefits of all the work we've done? When are*
> *we going to do the things we didn't when we were working so much, like take a golf-*
> *ing cruise, like going to Europe for three weeks, like going to visit the seven wonders*

of the world. I've been to a lot of places but seen less than one would think. I'm in
and out. And that's another complicating factor.

So say a CEO job came along, that would mean putting in five years, which
would mean that we would be five years older. Is that an issue or not? It's a decision.
It would surely need to be something really interesting in a desirable place. So part
of the message is that there are a lot complicating factors in a person's life. And get-
ting to a place of clarity when you haven't done a lot of preplanning for a transition
is difficult. Not because you can't decide but because it's complicated!

In this way, Patricia gets distance from her situation, beginning to balance
the "trade-offs" and seeing that her options have changed. Rather than just
evolving into the next step, she is making decisions, because the way of
approaching it has changed.

And yet again it is a set of trade-offs. But now instead of evolving into the trade-offs
the way I did during my entire career, I'm taking those trade-offs and making deci-
sions. I evolved into a trade-off when I first became a CEO. But now, I can sit and
think about it should that kind of opportunity arise again. I would consider another
CEO job. I would because I like the business of business. I love motivating people.
I'm young, I've got a lot of energy. I like inspiring people, I like turning businesses
around. I like dealing with customers, I like seeing results. What's the likelihood of
that happening? Who the hell knows?

Suddenly you have a lens on decision-making that you didn't have before when
you have been in the roles I have and when you are no longer compelled to be the boss.
For me, it has to be something where I can make a difference, with people I like and
respect in a positive environment.

With this new lens, Pat, because she is no longer willing just to evolve into the
next step, considers other possibilities, different models of working. She says:

Then a second possibility, which is what I'm doing now, is a patchwork or portfolio of
interesting activities. I am on three large company Boards, and I'm thinking about
taking the chair position of the board of a not-for-profit called The Partnership for
Drug Free America. I could get passionate about helping the team take this charity
to the next level. I would like to do more to give back. I have been very fortunate.

The current Chairman of the Partnership is a terrific person who has made a big
difference there. I liked him and would enjoy working with him. I liked the staff;
they are passionate. It's New York-based which is helpful. I admire their mission.
In exploring this with the current chairman, we concluded that this would be an
interesting opportunity and a platform to reach out toward other non-profit inter-
ests. And it's like a little business. For example, one of the issues that is growing is
prescription drug abuse among teens. And I'm on a Board of a pharma company
and I think ... this is an issue the pharma industry should be interested in attacking
more aggressively ... let's talk to them.

I'm also running for the Board at the golf community in which we live. Not some-
thing I have ever done. We own property, my family does also. Things are happening

there. The club is being turned over to the members. I have been asked to run for the board in this community. (Some have said: "You're overqualified to work on this board" and I say "based on what?"). This affects my life here.

I'm also teaching a couple of Exec Ed sessions at Wharton on leadership. And lastly, I am having exploratory discussions with some private equity firms but I'm not sure about that. There are very different models and I don't know if they'll work for me.

Patricia also imagines a third path, "doing something radically different"

which I haven't yet gone down at all. On one hand I think I might like to do something in the public service arena, but I'm not a Democrat so there is no real role within this administration. And I haven't laid a foundation to position myself in politics. I find at times I would like to have a platform to speak out on things I believe are important ... but I would not like to go through the public scrutiny that you must go through to run for office. I don't have the stomach for that. I've experienced the spectrum of media support ... been the one who led Lucent successfully through a crisis with all kinds of positive press ... and the "embattled" CEO of a French company. So, I know what it feels like to be supported and clobbered.

Or pursuing a passion like Kathleen Flaherty:

One of the things I'm really passionate about – if you've read The Omnivore's Dilemma by Michael Pollon for example, is the issue of obesity in America. I have strong feelings about it as I think it is a far-reaching issue for this country. While I am empathetic to the issue, I think we overdo "political correctness" in talking about the issue and the role personal responsibility plays. There's a problem, a real problem, a drain on our health system. We eat too much, restaurants serve too much, it is fixable if we had the will. So I do have a passion about that. That's a cause I could get behind.

But Patricia uses her new lens to qualify her choices, even when imagining working for something she is passionate about, she is seeking to transfer her skill set into the "radically different," and imagines a transversal change.

If there were a group of people who had already formulated a not-for-profit cause that was all about obesity, I would do it in a heartbeat. But the notion of starting from nothing is not what I am good at. I am not a creator. I take the seeds and with a little bit of work I shape it into something. Grow it. Expand it. So I need creators and I take it over. And I think that is part of the process of transitioning, about getting in contact with who I am really. I love working with people, solving business problems, engaging. I like complex business problems. I'm hoping that as I get involved in this not-for-profit, for example, I will be running a charity more like a business. In this charity all the people involved are in business, so I'll see.

From these various choices Patricia sees her "psyche shift":

Because today if I had to go back to the 8 to 6 grind, full time, I know what I'm getting into. So maybe the plural life, this patchwork, some boards, and perhaps a chairman role. In the UK model the Chairman and CEO positions are usually separate. When you are a chairman of a company you are engaged but you don't have to run it day to day. That would be interesting for me even in smaller companies in the US. That's one of the attractions about the private equity area. Those kinds of opportunities come up more often.

That might be a perfect balance, because I would be engaged and have a platform to engage from because you are entitled to engage in that position. It's more than a director role, but not running something day to day, so it's a little different model. Except for a full-time job that I am not at all sure I want to do, that might round out the other things I am doing.

Patricia concludes by saying,

In five years I would love to have established something that attaches to me, that makes a difference, something that could make a difference in this country, that's big. But I am still evolving my thinking here and therefore a plan. I don't mind being visible on issues or opportunities that are important to me, that I feel comfortable with, can articulate and can defend. I like it as long as it's in a positive context. But I don't have to have it. But that also is an adjustment.

It's about finding the right equilibrium. A patchwork. And about coming to terms with it. But that takes longer. Then defining what it is, defining who you are without the title and leveraging what you have established.

And she advises:

Part of it has to do with what your vision is. If you think "when I leave, I want to be on two Boards and that's it," that's easy. It's when you think you want to move into something different, a new chapter, another run at something different. In that case don't say "yes" to anything in the first six months. When people call, say "call me in six months." Don't sign on too early because once you make Board commitments you've got schedules. You are locked in. So that I would strongly encourage someone who is entering transition stage to take some time to get some perspective on your life without the consuming nature of a full-time job and a title.

For Patricia and others even after a year, the many complicating factors may remain intertwined, pulling and pushing during the transitional period: family obligations, community and the work identity whirl around, claiming their right to expression, demanding a voice. Establishing priorities among them is central. Confirming that you really are not a play-golf-everyday kind of person is part of this process which as Patricia Russo mentions can be surprisingly long, especially when one is used to working to deadlines and controlling when things happen yourself.

I guess the only expectation I had which was probably unrealistic is I thought it would all happen faster quickly. The definition part ... That's because your life is lived at such a pace. As a CEO you work to quarterly earnings. You work at a pace.

At warp speed. But life's not warp speed. And I figured I would have had more definition and clarity than I currently have after a year.

One way of approaching all the possibilities, and which was discussed with Patricia is to prioritize one's commitments (and time) into groups: personal (family, friends), professional, community, and even the world. Once this has been clarified, it is a question of understanding "what is enough?," "what is too much?" and even "What if there is no other chapter?"

Patricia Russo says,

Before my life was a lot of work a little bit of pleasure and of course, family. But everything was in the context of my work which could be all-consuming. Now if I say work, community, family and friends, the world, it's a very different picture. And what everyone has to do is dig deep inside and say, is that picture satisfying for you? I'm still figuring that out. Some of it is defining the circles and figuring out how much time you want to spend in each circle.

Although Patricia has had the courage and the wherewithal not to lock in too quickly, one senses the depth of this transition, as important as that from childhood to adolescence, then from adolescence to adulthood.

Still, her advice is

Just "pause." Sit down and think about what have I not done? When you're working you are always saying I wish I had more time to do these things. In my case it was exercise and reading. And say okay that's what I am going to start to do. And do it. Then see. Ok, I'm shifting priorities, I'm making things important that I didn't have time to get to now I'm going to make that a priority and then see how much time do I have left? And say, do you like it? Was that a fantasy, or do I like it?

Book Title: *What a Ride.*

But when you take the pause button off and move onto the next chapter, what will it look like? (See figure 3.1)

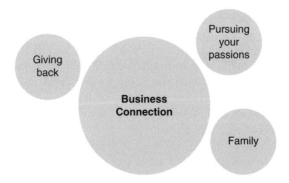

Figure 3.1 **What's next? Primary career**

Why refuse to lock in?

As Patricia Russo has clearly understood, the danger of saying yes too quickly is finding yourself back on the same path in a lateral move and dissatisfied, defeating the purpose of the entire maneuver. By refusing to immediately lock in after you have removed the corporate (or academic, or entrepreneurial) suit, you can take the time to try on other outfits.

Obviously as we have seen, not locking in during those early months does not mean doing nothing. Indeed Hank McKinnel, former CEO of Pfizer, feels that there may be a window after leaving; six months to a year of opportunities. *"And if you wait, the bad ones will be left, and the good ones will be gone."* Thus, it is more about being thoughtful and selective and using these opportunities to help you redefine the new role that truly fits.

So whether you start trying on new outfits before or after leaving, it is all part of an essential try-and-learn process suggested by Hermina Ibarra in *Working Identity*, a process which may include saying "I don't know," then sifting through existing opportunities, and creating new ones until the answer to the question "What is IT for me" gradually becomes clear.

Underlying this refusal to lock in may also be the desire to identify what the social psychologist Hazel Markus calls one's "possible selves" before making choices. For Markus, one's identity is not a fixed entity, but multiple possible selves including both what the person is now and also what s/he imagines s/he could be in the future. 'These future possible selves include who a person hopes to become, who the person expects to become, and who the person is afraid of becoming. Possible selves act as incentives that guide future behavior. Negatively-evaluated selves engage avoidance to prevent the realization of "feared possible selves," whereas positively-evaluated selves engage an approach motivational system to promote the realization of "hoped for possible selves."'[2]

For Patricia Russo, these hoped-for selves include being a CEO, working on a patchwork of community, non-profit and for-profit Boards, traveling and just living life, playing golf, and doing something "radically different" like politics or a program against obesity. Pat's negative selves include becoming a go-out-and-play-golf-everyday person, or a hang-around-the-house-and-read everyday person.

Understandably, in the younger stages of life, priorities must be established and choices made so that some of these hoped-for selves are placed on the back burner, or perhaps abandoned completely. Kathryn G. Jackson, another interviewee, puts it this way:

> *When I graduated from college, I majored in human biology. A lot of grounding in the sciences and social sciences. People come out and go to medical schools but others come out and can work in areas such as climate change which includes science and public policy. That was where my head was at when I got out of*

Stanford. I worked for two years at a women's clinic then I went to business school. And when I went to business school, I pretty much flushed all of that out, forgot it. And did not revisit that until I started exploring and looking back and got interested and engaged and looking at microfinancing – it woke up that altruistic aspect.

If we are to believe Tamara Erickson, these selves are lost but not forgotten for the boomers. She says "Most of ... [the boomers] have ... not ... had the discretionary time [they'd] like to make a change in the broader world. Many Boomers today are finding themselves hit hard with a sense of midlife malaise ... with a desire to make a positive difference with their remaining time."[3]

Whereas in their younger years, they (certainly) felt they had all the time in the world, once again time, and its limits have now stepped in creating a sense of urgency and pushing these more mature boomers to actualize the idealistic potential self that was going to "change the world and make a difference." This urgency is further reinforced by society's (not so) subliminal message: "ok, you can get in the back seat now, it's time to retire soon," and the negative potential selves associated with the traditional retiree.

Henri Balbaud, former Director of HR and Communication for Indosuez and Credit Agricole Group, provides a thoughtful analysis of how his relationship with three essential elements changed when he left corporate life, and an account of how these positive and negative potential selves played a role as he recreated another work-life balance which effectively responded to his needs.

Henri Balbaud. Change is a reality with a future

Henri Balbaud spent 35 years working at the Indosuez then Credit Agricole group, in particular as Director of Communications and Human Resources and where he was on the Board of Directors. Henri feels that his case was slightly unique because the end of his career made it both easier and harder to leave.

Easy because I was Head of Communications and HR and member of the Board of Directors of a commercial bank which was Indosuez but hard because this bank was not doing well at all.

When Indosuez was sold to Credit Agricole, I was 57 and in the process of negotiating out. After the merger with CA they didn't want me to go, and the President of Credit Agricole asked me to manage the HR aspects of all the senior executives of the group. That kind of position did not exist before that. It meant managing the President of Indosuez (on an HR level) and all the senior executives of his group, as well as all the senior executives at CA. It also meant I moved from a team of 150 people at Suez, to Credit Agricole with no one, knowing no one. I was in charge of this for four years, gradually hiring a team, and it was very successful. Thanks to this, the President of Credit Agricole took me on as a Senior Executive at Credit Agricole, giving me a pension system which allowed them to retire at 57. I was already 59. As of April 1, 2002, I was free to say what I wanted. Then when Credit Agricole bought Credit Lyonnais, I worked with the President to set up the new top-level management organization for this new structure. I stayed for another year, worked with the HR Director they hired, and when I left, I turned the entire package over to him.

So I chose my departure date, and it was a complete departure. I wasn't torn by negotiations, or placed on a shelf. It wasn't like other situations I know where the person may feel bitter. They're 59 and they feel like there's nothing left for them. The essential element is that I decided. There was no shock. The corporation didn't say "you're too old." I decided down to the last detail. I didn't leave in the winter, I left on June 30, because you go away on vacation on that date anyway, then I came back in September and began to build a new life. I also left without losing any buying power, which is not true for everyone who retires. This is very important. I have seen people who have had a hard time and this adds to the frustration that you can have during this transitional period.

He also feels that his position as HR Director gave him an understanding of the process of transitioning out that helped him prepare to leave:

I was head of HR so I had seen and accompanied many people during lay-offs or retirement. So the mechanism of "retiring" or "separating" yourself from professional life was not a mystery because of my job. Perhaps I was more aware of the pitfalls because I had accompanied many people through the process during my career. I'd seen how traumatized people could be by this.

There is a triple relationship that changes when you leave the corporate world:

(1) Your relationship with society. That is you can have the impression that you no longer matter. And its true, in society if you don't do anything, you are considered a passive participant, who consumes what you can with limited means. But you don't count. You vote, but you are not someone who counts in society. You are not asked for advice. So that is the first type of relationship which you must learn to manage and adapt to.

(2) Your relationship with your friends and your family (intimate relationships). This means you are always at home. I didn't want to find myself with two empty shopping bags on my arm. There is a relationship which changes when you leave your corporate structure: with your spouse because you live in a limited space (the apartment) and if you find yourself face to face with each other at lunch everyday, this changes, and with your friends, too. There are the friends who are retired, and the friends who are not retired.

(3) Your relationship with time. Once the corporate structure is gone, time suddenly counts differently. Something that took you ten minutes before is going to take you an hour now, and on an on until you end up feeling too busy! This is silly, but true. I have seen that happen to people once they retire. It's noon, and they haven't done anything. They get up later, take hours to have breakfast. When you work, breakfast is a ten-minute thing. When you no longer have those obligations, it's easy to get up after eight, have a long breakfast, read the paper, and find

yourself at noon. A retired friend of mine has a joke; "Thursday? I can't. I have to
go to the Post office." That's the relationship with time. Your agenda is empty so you
take the afternoon to go to the PO.

Based on this, Henri thought about what he could do to manage his relationship with these three elements when he left.

I worked on managing this triple relationship so that "society" would not abandon
me. For example, I never have lunch with my wife during the week, or very rarely.
I try and save Wednesdays now and then to have lunch with my grandchildren and
my wife (no school on Wednesdays in France). Otherwise I take the initiative and
organize lunches every day from a list I've made of everyone, retired or still working
that I want to stay in contact with.

Doing this is about being "faithful" to the people you know, and about being
motivated to keep your network alive.

In fact the network that you built during your career can be the thing that moves
you forward after you leave. This network made it possible for me to become a con-
sultant in HR. For example, one day I got a call to help rebuild the HR dept in a
bank in Morocco. That project lasted a year. In another recent assignment, I was
asked to organize a seminar on "managing change" – it went well and we came
up with a brochure "change is a reality with a future." I didn't go looking for these
missions specifically, but I am not passive. If you are active, things come back to you.
It's indirect. There is a snowball effect. You get other offers.

As we shall see, these other offers include teaching, volunteer work, as well
as sports and music. Henri explains the importance of each in the bigger
picture of his life choices, and how they help him manage the changes in
relationship that come with leaving a single career:

He says:

I teach, and as long as I have experience to transfer, I would like to continue. I teach
adults in Masters or Post Docs in management. In fact I started this before I tran-
sitioned out; I did one year at the University of Paris Dauphine, and through my
network I was invited to work with Hospital MD's to teach management skills. With
teaching you find yourself face to face with people who are amazingly stimulating
mentally. They are not easy on you. If you are not good, if you don't satisfy them,
you won't teach more than one semester. It is an activity which forces you to keep up.
I read Les Echoes (Business Newspaper) every day, cut out articles on HR, trade
union negotiations, and such. It is an intensive activity, one semester, an afternoon,
three hours at a time.

And then I do non-profit because it seems to me that if you reach a certain level
professionally and you can share your experience or your values with others who need
it, you should. I had no desire to be on the management level of a large association
because I didn't want to find myself face to face with people problems. I had been
managing people problems for years, and I didn't want to do that. So I chose Suicide
Ecoute (SOS suicide). I was trained and now I am on the phone once a week.

I am also Financial Director of an association of psychiatrists on a volunteer basis and Administrator of a very small publishing house. All this took time to decide to do, and to set up at least six months, after I left.

There are no medals to win in these jobs. It's just you and your telephone, or you helping people establish basic financial rules so the association won't lose money. And it's about taking little risks. Certain people suddenly become afraid of taking risks once they leave.

Finally I also manage a hotel and golf course owned by the Credit Agricole for professional seminars – the staff, the budget etc. That takes half a day a week and many emails at home. I go every week.

Henri has completed his patchwork with sports and music activities:

I did sports before I left but I seriously started running and biking after I retired, and I now have a personal trainer to develop a program to keep my body toned. I did my first semi-marathon at 60 on a dare from my son-in-law. We ran it together. I took up the challenge and have continued.

Finally, I play the clarinet.

Henri concludes:

Having different activities solves the problem of your relationship with society, your family, and time. I feel like I am totally part of society. Through the non-profit work, the consulting, and the hotel, I have a social role. In relation to my family, my wife, and my friends I am still as active as before, and my relationship with time has not changed. I eat my breakfast in 10 minutes! I had an appointment at 8.30 this morning, I have a lunch date, the afternoon is free.

Still, I am in a period where I choose the time, I manage my time. An hour is an hour not a day, but at the same time I spent eight days in Lebanon and this week I'm working from Monday–Thursday and on Friday I'll be in Corsica where we have a summer home. But I won't spend six months in Corsica. This year we will be coming home from summer vacation on September 7, we won't be coming home on October 15. I want to be centered in Paris. Paris is the home base.

Henri sees this evolving over time, and slowing down little by little:

I think that the hotel activity may be this year I could give more time to my family, and traveling. Today I don't have a lot of time, and if I get more time I have plans to visit France. I have done some traveling overseas – (Madagascar, Morroco, and Lebanon this year) and want to continue that.

I think that little by little, you must accept to slow down, but for the moment I haven't accepted that. It is very easy to give up, and sometimes tempting. You hear people say about someone "Boy, he's gotten old." So I'm careful, even about how I dress. Day to day, I don't get up and put on an old sweater and jeans. I put on my dress shirt, with a tie and am off to my lunch. For the students in my Master's class, too. I notice that some of the teachers come in jeans, but I represent "business" for the students, so I wear a suit and tie.

His advice:

> *Keep your network alive of friends and professionals. Take the initiative. People don't call you. You call them. If you keep moving, people look at you. See you. If you don't, you are invisible.*

Like everyone else, Henri doesn't consider himself retired, he says *"I've forgotten what that term means. I put 'consultant' on the airline immigration form."*

Book Title: *Vieillir est un combat difficile qu'il faut savoir mener joyeusement* [Aging is a Difficult Battle That Must be Fought with Joy].

Changing the reality of the future

In his process of transition, Henri has directly confronted the "negative future selves" which he associates with retirement. He has done this in his analysis of others in the same situation: fear of risk taking, change in the conception of time (an hour is not a day), inactivity (having two grocery store bags as a role), and finding yourself face to face with your wife at lunch every day. Other interviewees have this same approach; for example, one says "I don't want to be the guy who says 'when I worked at so and so....'" These negative demons motivate Henri and others to make his final positive choices, allowing him to take actions to directly overcome these feared future selves by being willing to continue to take risks, by managing time carefully, and most importantly by remaining active. In so doing, he arrives at a conclusion which will be central to his choices: if you are moving, people see you and look, if you stop, you are invisible.

Henri also says: *"having different activities solves the problem of your relationship with society, your family and time,"* and his final choices: HR Consultant, managing an events chateau, Masters seminar professor, and volunteer worker (besides jogging/biking and singing), are indeed remarkable for their multiplicity and variety. Thus, Henri has settled upon multiple choices to solve the problem of what's next, living out many possible selves at once rather than one.

And yet in her book on mid-career changers, Ibarra states, "As our possible selves list grows beyond an intellectual exercise, we must establish some means of selection ... most people simply cannot tolerate such a high level of fragmentation for an extended period of time. The time comes to reduce variety ... and to select a new favourite."[4]

So, is Henri's merely the story of an overactive individual refusing the inevitable?

Plurality as a possibility

It would seem not. Henri, and most of these boomers, seem to resist this imperative to reduce variety to merely one favorite, as if the urgency of time were pushing them to actualize as many of their potential selves as possible in the time remaining; we find them seeking to live out several possible selves at once, called by Patricia Russo a patchwork, by another a smorgasbord – so their final choice includes keeping the control and flexibility to allow them to do so. In marked contrast to earlier stages and to younger career changers, *plurality is a possibility, and even a need.*

The term "going plural" was originally coined by Allan Leighton, former chief executive of Asda, a leading chain of UK supermarkets, in September 2000 when he resigned from a full-time position at Wal-Mart to take over a number of boardroom roles.[5] In the case of our interviewees however, this plurality is not limited to boardroom roles (although some have made this choice) or even to professional choices alone, but involves integrating personal and professional choices into a life package – work, family, friends, community, and the world. As Patrick Gallagher says "*You can manage and create personal time and you can weave it into your life. It has more balance.*" These professionals have moved out of the singular organizing principle of their professional careers to pursue "many ends at once," building a multiple, flexible working, and living structure that might represent a work-life paradigm for this new developmental stage.

The new paradigm

> *One thing that I find fascinating, and I don't understand the cultural background of this, is before I "retired" I'd meet people and we'd talk about 25 different things; it was a very active intense period. Now I see the same people, and the first words out of their mouths are: "you look great." And nobody ever told me I looked great before! Well, there are two explanations, one is I didn't look great before, that's possible. But the other is that people have this expectation of deterioration, once you leave, I don't know. It's a strange thing for people to say, but they all say it, all of them. Nobody ever said that to me in my life before ... maybe I am defying expectations of how you look after retirement.*
>
> Hank McKinnel

Our interviewees are also more or less consciously resisting the glass ceiling and barriers of age with this new paradigm. Inherent in their choices is a refusal to live in what Margaret White Riley, one of the world's leading scholars on aging called an "age differentiated" model of life in which "one finds oneself limited to age-activity homogenous environments. Extreme examples of age-differentiated structures are schools, where children in same age grades have little opportunity for interaction with children even a few years older or younger than they; or nursing homes, where old people have little chance for interaction with younger people."[6]

Instead the flexibility sought in this lifestyle also includes remaining in contact with different ages through different activities. Teaching, running a marathon with a son-in-law, going back to school for the "ologies," and refusing to live in Florida are all ways of refusing the negative self associated with age. They are all participating in creating a life-work pattern imagined by Riley and called an "age-integrated model" (from school when you are young, work in middle age, and leisure when old, to education, work, and leisure occurring simultaneously in close proximity or in repeated cycles of work, education, leisure) in which structures are open to people of every age (within the limits of biology) and people of all ages are brought together."[7] Ideally, in age-integrated structures, older people can interact with the middle aged and the young; and individuals can intersperse over their long lives, periods of education, or work with periods of leisure or time with family.

Thus, by seeking to remain in contact with all ages rather than within a box of (old) age and (single) career choice, by managing to pursue many ends at once during this new stage, these members of the B2-generation may be participating in a quiet revolution, and fulfilling their earlier commitment to change. In order to do this, certain barriers are being confronted: age discrimination, the "oh-shit" moments of learning to deal with constantly changing technologies, the need to learn, to define a new role, and then to live it.

Part II

When you retire, think and act as if you were still working; when you're still working, think and act a bit as if you were already retired.
Author unknown

Don't simply retire from something; have something to retire to.
Harry Emerson Fosdick
American clergyman
1878–1969

4 Multiple questions, multiple choices

When you do multiple activities, it's a single machine with multiple jobs. So you have to plan, and it gives you the variety.

Siaou Sze Lien

The shift in the road to retirement and the working paradigm which will be quiet but significant, and the negative image of the Baby Boomers as the greediest generation are discussed. Are they really greedy? A blueprint for this multiple lifestyle is presented illustrated by the interview with Hank McKinnel, former CEO of Pfizer, and his "smorgasbord of activities," including a business connection, giving back, family, and his passions to show how he has organized this.

So, this revolution will be a quiet one: a shift in paradigm rather than an explosion, away from the all encompassing career, with a commitment to continue working on new flexible terms; a shift toward using time differently, refusing the age-differentiated box, and maintaining or gaining new access to personal pursuits, family, community, and the world.

As we have seen, "what's next" involves the desire to live out not one, but multiple, unfulfilled choices. In Part I we sketched out the early difficulties and the process involved with leaving the single career and sifting through the choices. In the following chapters we will take a look at the choices themselves. Some of them, such as board work, are specific to this group of professionals, available as a direct result of their single career choices. Others such as running a horse farm, creating a science foundation, or becoming a judge, provide a glimpse at what is actually motivating the choices of these boomers at this stage, and a chance to discuss some gender and culturally specific issues as well as to revisit and evaluate the paradox of a generation which has been blamed for all the world's present ills from destroying the economy and the environment to the breakdown of social structures.

The greediest generation

Although there is a general consensus that they are hard-working, opinions about the B2-generation are not all rosy, unanimous, or complimentary. Behind the idea of hard work during a period with sustained economic growth is the idea of accumulating personal wealth; behind "wanting it all" lies conspicuous consumption, and waste of the world's resources; and behind the youthful idea of "wanting change" is the breakdown of social values, the rise in sexually transmitted diseases, divorce, and a loss of moral values. The B2-generation have been accused of it all, called by L. W. Diuguid "the greediest generation"[1] and more cynically by Joe Queenan "the most obnoxious people in the history of the human race."[2] Besides the desire to make headlines or sell books, these accusations are an interesting point of departure when looking at what has motivated the "multiple" choices of our interviewees.

A blueprint for failing retirement

Our next interview with Hank McKinnel former CEO of Pfizer and his "smorgasbord of choices" provides an illustration of the pattern of choices made once the initial period of reconstruction has passed, and a first response to the accusations and stereotypes that are often wielded about this group (see Figure 4.1). As we shall see, McKinnel's pattern of choices proves to be prototypical of many in this book.

Hank McKinnel: Failing retirement

Hank McKinnel spent 36 years at Pfizer which he says is a little unique in today's world. He says *"I kind of had an accidental career and spent 36 years in one company and ended up being CEO."* He also says he didn't give a lot of thought to retirement until about the last year when several things became evident.

One is when you leave an organization after that period of time, it is unproductive and unseemly to try to maintain some kind of a role. Your plan should be on the day

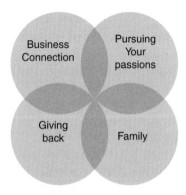

Figure 4.1   **What's next? The blueprint**

you leave, you leave. You can be available but you shouldn't try to stay on the board or in some other role. This meant that I did not want to have an ongoing relationship with Pfizer. I was also very conscious of any eventual conflicts of interest, so when I left I agreed not to take on any competitive role for three years.

Hank didn't want to go from a 150 percent career to zero, because he says "*you can't go from 100 mph to zero overnight.*" Thus like others, he planned on ongoing involvement in the for-profit segment which he achieved by beginning a number of directorships and consulting relationships as well as a number of non-profit enterprises.

Where?

One of Hank's first steps was to "ground" himself for this transition out which meant deciding where to live.

> *All my life I've enjoyed living in the outdoors, and I wanted to be somewhere other than in the big city where I lived most of my life. I decided to go to Wyoming and I found a house in Jackson, Wyoming, which is now our full-time home. I gave a lot of thought to that. We'd lived in New York for 20 years and I'd lived around the world. My home was in Greenwich Ct. which is stuck in the middle – not city, not country. I thought, I can always travel, I want to live in an outdoor environment where I can hike and fish and ski and do the things I love and at the same time be close to an airport to do the other things.*
>
> *I know a number of people who have retired. And the saddest were often people who retired to Florida. This is a euphemism but you can't go from CEO in a major corporation and go and play golf everyday. I saw people who tried that and frankly it didn't work. They weren't happy, their health deteriorated. In Wyoming you are in contact with young people, you are part of the community, you're outdoors. It's a healthy situation.*
>
> *So that was the Where.*

Besides being a place to live, choosing Wyoming resolved the negative age-differentiated self he associates with Florida, laying the groundwork to allow McKinnel to live "in a community with young people," as well as to cultivate his passion for the outdoors. He could then begin defining the *What?* in this new structure which he describes as "*one third for-profit, one third not-for-profit and one third for me.*"

What?

A business connection

> *The plan that I developed in the last year was a third for profit, a third not for profit and a third for me. What I found very quickly was that the part that kept getting squeezed out was the one-third for me. So I had to be somewhat disciplined in saying no to things. But I agreed to stay as Director of the Moody's corporation, where I am*

now the lead director. I was on that board for five–six years before I left. And I began working on a board in a Biotech Company in Western Canada. I got Pfizer's approval for that. It's a small company that's doing very interesting things in infectious disease related-areas. I serve as a senior advisor of private equity company and I serve on the advisory board of Toyota that meets in Japan, those are all paid.

Hank did not "plan" his departure, because he says *"The traditional advice is start early. But I don't find that very helpful. Nobody can. If you're in a high-pressure career, you can't, so good advice, but thank you."* Nevertheless as Steve Davidson and several others have recommended, he had already begun certain for-profit Board activities (Moody's) before leaving, and found others when he left. At the core of all of McKinnel's choices are his intellectual and personal passions – science and the great outdoors. These become a central vector and serve as a magnet for a cluster of activities. By breaking down his choices into for-profit, not-for-profit, and personal he is able to satisfy the desire to continue to achieve professionally, live out his passions, exploit his business expertise in another setting, but also to give back to the community and the world – which emerges as a central motivating factor.

Personal passions and giving back

For Hank McKinnel,

There is a season to these things. Like there is a season to a career. You move on and are evaluated. As a young employee, you're evaluated based on your own personal contribution then in the next stage you are evaluated based on the division you're running, then you're running the whole thing. Each of these chapters is different, and retirement, which is not the right word, is another chapter. Just as you progress through a career, you progress through life. And there comes a time where you are more interested in developing others and giving back to the community than in your own career progression.

In the early days he continued to share the work at the Connecticut Science Center, an effort which he began seven years before leaving.

We created a science center in Connecticut to get kids interested in math and science. We raised 180 million dollars, we built the building, we opened in March and I recently had my last day as board member. I've been the chairman since the beginning, for seven years. It's built, it's successful, it's up and running so this is a good time to hand it over and move on to something else. That is not-for-profit.

To fulfil his passion for passing on the heritage of the great outdoors he joined the board of the Grand Titon National Park Foundation. He says, *"its a great foundation, our national heritage. Something I'd like my children, grandchildren and great grandchildren to profit from."*

Finally McKinnel participated in endeavors with a worldwide focus:

I've continued as founder and sponsor of the science and technology and society forum in Japan which meets once a year with 800 people. And I chaired what was originally called The Academic Alliance, a group of companies and academic medical leaders devoted to strengthening academic medical centers in Africa. Six or seven years ago we brought together a number of the top experts in infectious diseases in America, Canada, and Europe, and the Infectious Disease Society of America and we started an initiative based in Campala, Uganda. We built the clinic, its up and running, its very well funded and we've trained more than 5000 healthcare professionals who in turn have trained about 40 000 healthcare professionals to help fight infectious diseases. We're funded by a number of private corporations, by the Gates foundation, by the US Government. It's doing exceptionally well and I am still very involved in that.

Mentoring

We also find McKinnel engaging in another type of community activity, which we call "mentoring" and which he calls *"Bringing your business skills and applying them to some of those organizations. Helping them develop their knowledge."*

I now live in Jackson, and I'm doing two things there, I'm on the board for the Center of the Arts, which is a great organisation in Jackson that needed help. Both there and in the local hospital I've done some work on improving corporate governance. I have become known as someone who can educate boards on how do be effective as a board, how to be effective in that role, what is the role. This turns out to be a big need. I have also been on the business round table and we have done white papers on governance so it is an area that I have interest in. This is mainly helping the organization think through and clarify what their expectations are for the board and board members.

Actually it's quite astonishing what some people in smaller business structures don't know and have not experienced. I've found I can help out in these cases and it's very much appreciated. The not-for-profit sector is all about giving back and being involved in something bigger than yourself. So that's my one third not for profit. And it's very community-oriented.

Hank McKinnel had a lot of offers – a smorgasbord of choices and he was very selective about what he chose. Today he says:

My calendar is pretty full. The one thing that has helped a lot is living in Wyoming. Eight in the morning in Wyoming is ten in New York so I can participate in conference calls as long as they are over by 11 o'clock New York time, which means that I do them from 8 to 9 then I have the rest of the day. Then this week I've been in New York all week. Moody's two days, the Science Center tomorrow, then a couple of other meetings. But this would not work if I went to New York for one thing and then had to go back again for another, instead of doing 5 things this week. I group them together. This week is 100% work, most weeks are not and there are very few weeks that are 100% me.

Hank's new activities on four or five profit and not-for-profit boards expose him to more people and allow him to develop another kind of knowledge. He says *"as a CEO you're prepared in a deep narrow area of your business. It's a mile deep but not very wide."* Although he does not actively network, and *"the Facebook thing has left him behind"* he says *"it's the people you know and talk to,"* which he does. *"I continue to maintain my relationship with people in Asia through the Science Forum. And I do stay in touch. If I stayed in Wyoming and didn't answer my emails it wouldn't be the same."*

He also uses technology to keep in touch and to keep his own calendar. *"I have a really good travel agent which helps. I found I could do it on my own. I have an iPhone now which does a lot of what an assistant did for me."*

McKinnel's time for himself, which was the hardest to control includes *traveling and quite a bit of hiking and fishing. I try to be in Wyoming as much as possible in February and March. I have a season ski pass. But even with skiing, I can have a conference call from 8 to 9 and then I'm on the ski slopes. I'm 20 minutes away. But I have to fight a bit to maintain the one third for fishing and hiking and traveling, which was harder at the beginning and is a little easier now, a little more balanced.*

And family

Today McKinnel also clearly spends more time than before with his four children (and two grandchildren), spending more time with his son who lives closer by and likes to ski, and his three daughters who he sees when he goes to New York.

Besides all this, Hank always keeps has an eye on the bigger picture:

The other thing I'm giving more time to is a vision for philanthropy. Because when you have made a lot of money, you want to take care of your kids, I've done that, created trust funds to take care of my kids and grandchildren. Everyone has that obligation. And you need to have enough reserve for yourself of course. But unless you have five homes, and boats and planes, you only need a relatively modest amount of money to do that. And when you've reached the level I have, a lot of the people I know do not spend a lot compared to their relative worth. So you think, now what am I going to do?

And to some extent, I may have left that a little too late. But I hope I have 20 or 30 years to figure that out. I'm contributing. I started a foundation, the community science center, but you need to think it through. There are a lot of worthy organizations. But money is not all of it. Sending checks to 20 different people is not having an impact. It's about your personal time too, getting involved. Because not only do you support with money, you support with time, too. I've done this kind of by accident, because I thought the Connecticut Health Center was a good thing. But that chapter's now closing. What else do I feel strongly about? Education. Health. Ok how can I have an impact on health and education? Where should I spend my time and money? That's something I am just starting to think about.

When asked if he misses anything, McKinnel says:

I enjoyed doing what I did, when I did it. Now I'm doing something different. Would I go back? No. In fact I was on the top of a mountain in Wyoming, with a pack on my back a few weeks ago. It was daybreak and I realized it was 8.30 am in New York and this was the day Pfizer announced earnings. I knew the drill. The press release would go out at six and you would then be on the phone with analysts, CNBC interviews. I know how it would go. And I was standing there on that mountain top, I thought, "I'd rather be here." I did that for a lot of years, but I don't miss it.

His advice:

They say the future will take care of itself, which it will. But you can guide it. And in my own case it was a third, a third, a third. That didn't work for a while, so I had to push back and readjust.

I think everyone is an individual. It's a great adventure and if your health is good, because health is very important, you can make your choices. It's a great time to develop others and give back to the community and there are a lot of things you can do at this stage in your life which you were too busy to do before.

Hank's definition of retirement is open ended, a Baby Boomer's definition. "*In the dictionary retiring is moving from an employed state to an unemployed state, basically, and from a salary to a pension. Some do, but many don't. The people I know don't live that kind of life. They are doing five different things before they retire, and five different things after. It's just a different mix but they're still very active and healthy.*"

Hank comments that if someone asks if he is retired, he tells them "*I'm failing retirement. I'm doing something different. The word is not right.*"

When asked about a title for his book Hank says *A Thousand Kindnesses* belying the accusations of the self-centeredness of the B2-generation.

Because I've been helped by a lot of people along the way. Everywhere from my parents, to teachers, to colleagues. The one very strong sense I have which I try to communicate but don't quite manage is that we have all benefited from what our parents did. They fought wars to keep us free. Sacrificed their lives. Worked hard. The tradition I came from is that you worked hard and sacrificed for the benefit of your children. We benefited from that. I am very concerned that we are the first generation that might be leaving less for our children than we had. In education, in freedom, in absence of terrorism, in environment. You name the area. Almost any area seems like it's going to be worse for our children than it was for us. And I think that we are the first generation in history to have u passed on a worse legacy than what we received. And I feel a great debt to parents and teachers and people who helped me. I can't pay that debt back, because they aren't here anymore. I hope I said thanks when they are around. I can't pay it back but I can pay it forward. The inheritance is that you invest for the future. And we are not doing a very good job of that. Not collectively. We are a selfish generation. The debt we are running up. Education is not what it was. How do you face your children and grandchildren. Which is why I did the Connecticut Science Center, to get kids interested in Math and Science. To compensate for the lousy education system. That's working. And I'm doing some in Africa. That gives meaning to life.

If looked at from above, Hank McKinnel's interview provides a bird's eye view of the landscape of this multiple lifestyle, a blueprint of the new paradigm that emerges from these stories. We find his smorgasbord of activities clustered around his passion for science and the great outdoors, and an attempt to manage time "equally" so that he can pursue his personal passions, continue working in a professional context, and spend more time with his family, but also "pay forward" to the community and the world. Far from the stereotype of the greedy, overconsuming yuppie, McKinnel's choices are motivated by an acute and socially conscious awareness of his responsibility to past and future generations. As we shall see, this pattern can be found in many other interviews. Clustered around a central focus – a passion, the family or a professional activity, the interviewees develop their activities while often keeping an eye on the bigger picture to leave space to pay forward to family, the community, and the world. Thus at some point during the transition process, the interviewees make decisions on whether and how much they want to fill their "activity circles" of work, family, their personal passions, and giving back so that they become facets of this new life package in different proportions, interacting in certain cases, and with one or two primary motivating forces serving as a vector. Time remains the flexible element, controlled by the person, making it possible, like McKinnel, to group things together, and go to New York to see family and have several meetings while still having time to be at the top of the mountain on skis at dawn. We will now look at the facets in more detail, digging a little deeper into each with pertinent interviews, to see what lies beneath.

5   The business connection

So some things I've continued and some things are new, but what I did keep in the back of my mind is I wanted an ongoing business connection and I have found that very satisfying.
Hank McKinnel

The importance of the business connection is discussed for this new lifestyle and the different alternatives. The concept of bridge work and the structure, intellectual stimulation, and connection it provides is presented as well as the importance of the network in creating choices.

Although the level of involvement varies, all of our interviewees maintain some sort of business connection. As Hank McKinnel and others state you can't go from 150 mph to zero and for our interviewees, this connection represents the dividing line between being retired and not retired. Indeed, the initial goal is not to stop working at all but to "do something different" transitioning out of the full-time singular career to a more flexible working structure. Called "bridge employment" by Kim & Feldman (1998, 2000)[1] (Employment after leaving a long-term job but before permanent withdrawal from the workforce) and successfully applied in certain countries such as Sweden and Japan as a transition period between full-time employment and complete exit from work through flexible employment options, it has been shown as a way to ease into and facilitate adjustment to retirement and increase overall life satisfaction.[2] It may also result in people moving more gradually toward complete retirement by zigzagging in and out of the labor force along the way.

Not surprisingly this need to build a bridge is especially true of the professionals we interviewed, whose career embeddedness – social, personal, and professional interdependence with the career[3] – is extremely high, making it essential for them to pave the road that defines this intermediate stage with a basic foundation of work. For although an AARP (American Association of Retired People) study shows that the intention to engage in some kind of employment after retirement applies to more than 2/3 of those over 45, the motivation for this activity varies, with those on the lower end of the socio-economic spectrum working to make ends meet, while our interviewees, so many of whom state "I can't imagine not working" fall into the category of those at "the upper end of the socioeconomic spectrum, who work even when they could afford to retire ... presumably because they derive satisfaction from their work."[4]

Even Carole St Mark, former senior executive at Pitney Bowes, who has chosen to live out her passion and has built and runs a horse farm, continues to run the business itself *"for the structure."* She says: *"I'm very disciplined. When papers come in they get organized; I still do things because I am driven, I still have a time – organization structure. I won't ever relax completely."*

This business connection provides our interviewees with a wealth of things: intellectual stimulation, a connectedness with life in general – which for them is so closely associated with work – but also contact with a more age-integrated environment, and the challenge of learning, to keep abreast of new technologies, to transfer skills as well as for a continued income.

As we will note, the particular type of "business connection" varies including consulting within the field of the single-career activity (Henri Balbaud, J. J. Strauss), board work (for profit, or not for profit) (Patrick Gallagher, Patricia Hewitt, Kathleen Flaherty, Steven Davidson, Hank Mckinnel, Jeff Yusi, Elisabeth Brenner-Salz), transfer of skills (founding/running another type of company, working in a different field) (Kathleen Flaherty, Carole St Mark, Marv Berenblum, Eric Christin), private equity (Chai Patel, Eric Christin), advisory work (Patricia Hewitt, Hank Mckinnel) and part-time salaried work (Henri Balbaud). (Figure 5.1)

But more interesting to us, the motivation for doing this activity has also shifted. In more than a few, the intensity of work is similar, nearly full time, but the underlying motivation to work now has less to do with the career and more to do with one's relationship with oneself, the community, the family, and the world or sometimes with just work itself. Thus the business connection usually overlaps with these facets. As Hank's blueprint story shows, the goal has now become to live out unfulfilled desired selves with more control or to give meaning to life.

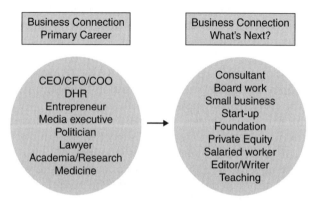

Figure 5.1   **What's next? The business connection**

The network, a poison apple?

A central element to making this possible is choice.

Henri Balbaud's final choices, consulting, teaching, managing an events chateau-golf club and doing volunteer work, involved imagining new roles, but actually having the opportunity to gain access to these wished-for selves was only possible by his proactive approach. After visualizing himself outside of the age-differentiated box, Henri had to actively seek boxes allowing him to live along an age continuum and fulfil his desired roles. In order to make these multiple choices, it was necessary to have multiple opportunities.

Henri, Patrick Gallagher, and others had only one word of advice for this: keep your network of friends and professionals alive. Take the initiative. People don't call you. You call them. If you keep moving, people look at you, see you. If you don't, you become invisible.

While this may seem self-evident and is given as advice by many of the interviewees, somewhat surprisingly, others seem somewhat uncomfortable with the idea, or like Pat Russo says "*I haven't really thought about it.*" Hank McKinnel says he "*is not a fan*" and another interviewee even states in relation to setting up a portfolio of board work that "*raising your hand and saying you want to do something may be the best way not to get it. You're poison then.*"

What is this hesitation all about? Pat Russo's comment provides a hint saying "*I never really worked my time when I worked. I was focused on the business. But now you are focusing on you, and you are defining your future. Which you have never had to do before, so it's a shift.*" And Hank McKinnel states frankly that during your primary career you put yourself and your own personal future in second place and you think about the business.

We are reminded here of how much so many of our interviewees – called by Larry Sonnefield "work intensives" – actually gave to their careers, resulting in a nearly fusional relationship between self-work-life. These work intensives are highly motivated individuals engaged in personally involving work who reach for bold goals for life accomplishment. Because they have a need to create (rather than the workaholic who has a need to keep up), they are fully immersed in work as a way of life.[5]

Thus during the single-career stage, our interviewees were completely focused on "the business" and their "commitments" to the people involved, the goals set, the Board and the shareholders. All of them have a wealth of contacts that have been earned through their hard work. However, for many this network grew organically during the career, it came with the territory, and was less a question of taking specific initiatives than a natural development of their central, decision-making role in the organization.

Thus, the idea of having a network of professional/personal contacts which must be kept alive may seem incongruous to some, and represents another important shift in approach and thinking during this transition.

Once out in the very early period, depending upon whether they are what Steve Davidson called a hot commodity or the others, for some the calls do come, giving the impression that this organic relationship has a life of its own. But as Patrick Gallagher and others note, these opportunities are like London buses, sometimes there are none....

In order to get it moving again, Gallagher called *"everyone he knew,"* taking direct initiative which might not have been necessary in the past. And in fact, even those who say they are not actively networking, like Hank McKinnel, go on to speak of talking to the people they are on boards with and arranging breakfasts, lunches, or meetings.

Depending on the approach taken, these breakfasts, lunches, and meetings can become a playground for rethinking one's identity and stepping outside the career-limiting box. This is part of the process described by Hermina Ibarra in which "identities change in practice as we start doing new things (crafting experiments), interacting with different people (shifting connections) and reinterpreting our life stories.[6]

It will obviously be of use when seeking lateral moves in similar fields but can also be a way of sending out messages that one is interested in exploring new avenues and obtaining personal and professional feedback or ideas about the next steps to be taken. In the early stages, it is a process of "knowing thyself" and as ideas are developed, it can become a forum to define transferable skills, or to gain support for a personal project like Kathleen Flaherty. Through these exchanges the old network will gradually evolve as one sheds the singular self, overcomes the negative retired self-image, and fashions a life structure along the age continuum.

And our interviewees are in a unique position in this respect. For although the majority of B2-generation have been shown to wish to continue working after retirement, and many might seek to actualize several unrealized avenues during this new stage, escaping the "old leisure" box, access to these multiple choices, are not necessarily available.

However "in the case of top executives the possession of a top management seat gives them access to a political and cultural elite also."[7] "By virtue of their senior executive status they are often given seats as board of directors of interlocking businesses, major not-for-profit agencies and even local and national policy-making decisions."[8]

But time once again enters into play. Those who actively "work" their networks all speak of a window of opportunity the consensus being the first six months to a year. Hank McKinnel says: *"I think the 'do nothing' for six months conventional wisdom is wrong. There are opportunities in six months. If you dither for six months the bad ones may still be around and the good ones may be gone so you have to be thoughtful about that period. If you are a person who has reached a certain level, you are serious and you want to be successful. Trying to achieve is important and you've got to screen those opportunities with that in mind."* Keeping the network "alive" means connecting with people, communicating one's ideas and wishes, and getting feedback to readjust.

Thus, whether these contacts remain formally informal, or become a forum to broaden the scope of possibilities, separating from the single-career path also involves taking stock of this essential resource, a key element in making the desired changes accessible and of optimizing one's freedom of choice. During this transition, the network becomes an untapped mine, a dynamic raw material of relationships that can evolve as the person does, to become the connective tissue, then the faces of this new chapter.

6 Giving back. Foundations, volunteering, and mentoring

The main problem is not the haves and the have-nots – it's the give-nots

Arnold Glasow

This chapter explores the many ways of giving back: foundations, mentoring, and volunteering with two interviews, Chai Patel, an MD and former CEO of the Priory, and Marv Berenblum, an executive search partner who have used this as the focus of their business connection. This suggests that the greediest generation may not be as self-absorbed as certain may claim, and shows how, in this area as in others, society may have to adapt to these professionals by giving them the flexibility they are looking for.

Thus, our interviewees continue to work because they enjoy it, but now dedicate some or all of their working energy to fulfill other causes, tapping into the wellspring of desired selves and exploring new avenues. One of these avenues is giving back.

In a report entitled "The 75% Factor: Uncovering Hidden Boomer Values," James Gambone and Erica Whittlinger note that 75 percent of boomers came from poor, working-class, family-run farms or small businesses, and feel indebted and thankful to those persons and institutions that helped them along the way. This attitude combined with the focus on self-fulfillment has resulted in one of the defining characteristics of boomers – the desire to give something back to society.[1]

Although this may be true, bets are still out as to whether the greediest generation is going to give something back to society, and in what form. Of those who have the capacity, it has been shown that more than half intend to engage in some sort of community service as they get older, and today Boomers volunteer at a rate of 33 percent, in contrast with 24 percent for those 65 and older. We did indeed find that giving back motivated the choices of a great many of our interviewees. It is part of the smorgasboard in nearly all of those we talked to, ranging from participating in an association to helping women in business, to one third of Hank Mckinnel's activities.

But the B2-generation is not a homogenous entity. There are cultural differences in the commitment to volunteer work with a study in the United States, Canada, Britain, Germany, France, Italy, Spain, Belgium, Japan, Hong Kong, and Australia showing that Australians are leaders in volunteer work

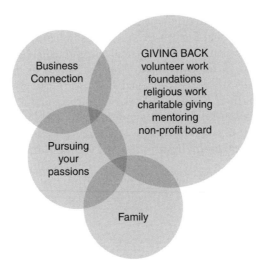

Figure 6.1   **What's next? Giving back**

after Hong Kong with Canada in third place, for example[2] while Americans are the leaders in charitable giving compensating, perhaps, for the limited government healthcare and social support compared to Europe.

There are also differences according to education and earnings. Our interviewees clearly make up the highly educated upper-earning bracket of this generation. Called the self-reliants in a Harvard-Metlife study, these individuals have significant retirement savings and imagine remaining connected to the community through employment or community service. They also have a higher than average anticipation of doing more volunteering during retirement.[3] Thus, most of our interviewees have enough disposable income to make choices above and beyond meeting their personal and family needs. As Hank McKinnel says: *"My kids are well taken care of. I'm well taken care of, so how can I have an impact in society."* Where and how they will choose to have an impact will vary depending on their culture, education, earnings, and career path.

In the following interviews, giving back is the driving force of this new stage, the motor to use the business connection to forge one's own personal avenue to pay forward to society and the next generation. These interviews explore ways of giving back in the form of foundations, private equity, non-profit mentoring, and philanthropy, both hands-on and through charitable giving (see Figure 6.1).

Foundations and philanthropy

Philanthropist: n. A rich (and usually bald) old gentleman who has trained himself to grin while his conscience is picking his pocket.

(Ambrose Pierce, *Devil's dictionary*)

Chai Patel is the first entrepreneur interviewed in this book, and his path from an NHS (National Health Services) researcher and MD in the UK, to international investment banker then entrepreneur CEO of the Priory Group, and today, in his own words "retired" gives us a look at another career path. Chai's story is exceptional because the large majority of this population of boomers has pursued salaried careers and a small proportion (less than 10%) has pursued an independent route. Patel is also the first MD to be interviewed, a career which he saw more as a vocation and did not pursue but which still looms large in this story. Like Hank McKinnel, Chai's choices are driven by a keen sense of social responsibility which has meant that he has kept his eye on the bigger picture from day one. Today his focus is on giving back in a way that is decidedly entrepreneurial.

Chai Patel: The journey

Chai Patel qualified as a Doctor from Southampton University in 1979 and was a Research Fellow at Pembroke College, Oxford. Even before finishing his medical studies when he was working as an MD and doing research in the NHS, Chai Patel says "*I knew that the NHS as a structure was not going to work for me. I felt that the system was abusing people in it. I saw a lot of my friends around me who were frustrated and burnt out. There I was 30 doing my research and I thought, 'I've got one more hoop to go through and then I will become a Consultant.' And I thought if I don't get out now I'll end up on a different course.*"

Chai says he had always been entrepreneurial and one of the thoughts he was toying with at the time was, "*Could I become a businessman and set up my own healthcare company? Can I stop complaining and do something?*"

He says,

> *I had no money. I was a research fellow and obviously my family was from a very modest background. So I thought that if I went into investment banking I could learn something about money, make money in the process, then go back and set up my own business. If I look through my papers I probably still have a little blue piece of paper headed Zantac where I've scribbled out the 12 pros and cons of why I was leaving and what I would do and what "the journey," would be about.*

For Chai the idea of a journey and that little blue piece of paper was critical.

> *Because I had this Christian ethos that I had to deal with at the time. The whole leaving medicine and going to make money was a struggle for me. I had to deal with this with the priest who supported me back then, with myself and my family. My father couldn't understand why I was giving up medicine to make money. So the idea of "a journey" and the integrity of what I was doing was very critical and*

important. The idea that I was not just going to make money and have a great time and that I didn't care how I did it was very important. There had to be a purpose.

Inherent in Chai's idea of the journey was meaning or purpose, and an underlying plan to move from a purely capitalistic business entrepreneur into social entrepreneurial work.

This was always on the agenda. I had always planned to work in the community, to invest some of the money I had made in the not-for-profit activities. The wealth creation was always with the idea of giving back or making a difference. I have always been on boards of charities and worked with the government even before I left the Priory.

Because the other strand that links everything for me is a passionate belief that the root of all evil is not money but poverty. So social justice only takes place if there is an economic system that gives people the chance to make a living of some kind. Thus all my endeavors about work, social policies and the government, with the charities and with private equity are about enabling people to be independent in some way or to be self-supported. This gives one dignity, pride, and rights, then compassion for other people. Investing is about creating jobs, not investing to kill a company. It can preserve jobs and in return the people who work there support people.

Fire in the belly

Chai got his first break on the journey when *to his amazement* a friend of his arranged a lunch with a senior investment banker at JP Morgan. He invested in a pinstripe suit,

because I like pinstripe suits and I felt it helped me look the part! Then I went and had a very long and what was then a boozy lunch. During that lunch I convinced him that the framework of medicine, what you learned in medicine, and what it teaches you was the same as what was expected in investment banking. They were both about listening to people, creating a set of options, excluding some of the options and coming up with choices. They're analytical and people based. I convinced him that I was committed to doing this and I would love to do it. So he put my name forward for the JP Morgan trainee position.

Chai got shortlisted for JP Morgan *"but the HR person had a really hard time understanding how a 30-year old guy who was an MD would want to do this. He was an American, so he couldn't understand how badly paid doctors were here in the UK, and he was looking for the "fire in the belly."*
Finally, Chai ended up at Merill Lynch where he met up with

some very impressive, brilliant aggressive young men, Americans, and that's how it started. I was naïve, the cleaning ladies knew more than I did. I started from scratch and the spent the whole summer reading everything I could find on finance, basic economics, what was a stock, what was a bond, then doing the Merrill program in New York and coming back and teaming with these guys.

Chai spent four years at Merrill and then Lehmans, and in 1987 when he had made a bit of money, he began looking to see if he could set up the healthcare business he had thought about.

It seemed like a good place to start because of my background with the NHS and as a doctor. I saw an opportunity in services for the elderly which were pretty appalling at the time. There had been some changes in public policy which allowed businesses to participate in this sector so I started investigating it from a commercial perspective and seeing if I could add value.

When things started to look possible in 1987–8 he put a business plan together and the first company, Court Cavendish was founded in 1987–8. They bought their first care homes *"in a big leverage buy out in 1989."* Chai was not spared difficulties when *"like all good stories it went wrong in 1990."* Interest rates went up to 15 percent and Chai had to restructure.

So I had a very fast learning curve on how to keep an organization together, how to stay true to your values, and manage cash and keep people, shareholders and banks confident, which I managed to do. I always say that if you don't have to look down into the abyss at least once in your career then you haven't really lived. And we came through. Then we built it up to a series of acquisitions and mergers to become the largest nursing home group at the time.

For Chai, there was a whole Baby Boomer vision behind Court Cavendish.

There was this vision of wanting to make a difference, a commitment to care. "If it's not good enough for your mother, it's not good enough for us." I got involved in the training programs, in the whole culture, in the vision.

I'd speak at meetings and you could see that certain people were attracted to this ideal, and they would call me and become part of the team. There was this amazing situation where people were attracted to the idea, so there was inevitably going to be a certain amount of success because of the talented people who were attracted to it.

Court Cavendish started with three people and ended with 18,000, a completely varied team, from management, to nurses, to therapists. *"Each point in time, we were trying to keep people together, keeping the core values and purpose of the organization together."* He left during the last merger in 1996 with Takecare. *"The company ended up in BUPA (An international healthcare company) which was the right place for it to be, they had a longer-term view, were private and meanwhile I built up new relationships in private equity because that deal had a lot of profile at the time."*

After that Chai worked with Goldman Sachs, led a deal and became CEO for Westminster Healthcare in 1999, putting money in it himself. This private healthcare company had a small division of mental healthcare at the time, which they kept, and Chai began working on an idea which had been the next step in the journey. He says:

> *I had The Priory written down on my little piece of paper as a target if I ever got involved in mental health. That would be the company to buy, which we did. So we expanded this very small business into something that became more profitable than the senior living business – and the senior living and mental health were separated in 2002. We built up The Priory further into new areas of service delivery, such as children's specialist education and did extremely well. The brand got stronger and stronger.*

Chai decided to leave in 2005 during the buyout of The Priory by ABN.

> *The background of this new journey, the leaving part, was that once I'd reached a certain point in my career, one of my transition plans was that I wanted to stop working for money and go into public life or do public service work.*
>
> *The idea was to say that at 50 I was economically independent enough to sustain myself. I had already begun moving toward that with the ABN deal. I was already doing things with the government, and if the time came to do something in public life, I could. I was doing it on my own time, pro bono, and even before ABN I had taken two days a week to do my own thing (so I was working seven).*

Chai's idea was based on a background plan of "reshaping his time," and finding a way to combine his skills and his desire to help.

> *I wanted to combine the investment skills that I had learned in banking, my private equity skills and the investments in my own company businesses and pro bono activity. So I started looking at how I could rearrange my life to transition from being a hands-on CEO to a person who brought in some of these other skills to help out other executives CEOs. Then I could move over across into the operational role if necessary, although it was not what I wanted particularly.*

The changing face of philanthropy

Chai's approach to the idea of giving back will remain quintessentially Baby Boomer, involving a transfer of skills and a hands-on approach throughout. For Chai and others of the B2-generaration this "new philanthropy" is no longer something the extremely wealthy do when they die and is not limited to making charitable donations to a good cause. One finds those with enough wealth to give back investigating ways to be more directly involved in the organization, and as one interviewee put it, there is a desire to be "more than just a wallet."

And philanthropists engaged in charitable giving are also looking for direct results. They "not only want to see their money in action during their lifetime, they want to measure their philanthropic success. Philanthropy becomes a way of giving that articulates one's values and allows you to be engaged in finding a long-term solution. It's about developing relationships with organizations and the cause. It's not the dollar size that matters."[4]

Finally, besides the extremely wealthy new philanthropists such as Buffet and Gates who have brought philanthropy back into the news (at the 2010 Millennium Replenishment Meeting, the Gates foundation gave the equivalent of Australia's contribution), there is a growing trend to develop giving circles – a grassroots approach to giving in which individual donors – often a group of friends – pool their charitable donations and decide how to use the money to benefit the causes they care about most.

And Boomers are obviously not waiting until they die:

> We're seeing gifts made during lifetimes that were unimaginable during the previous period. It's tax changes but also societal changes. Families are smaller. There're fewer people to distribute your wealth among. More and more people are thinking "we have enough money, we'd like to share it".[5]

Chai's choices for giving back reflect his entrepreneurial approach and he has restructured his time to the image of this passion by creating a foundation, a structure to help healthcare companies and a private equity fund, while at the same time coming up with a new idea for funding non-profits.

Family foundation: Bright Future

> *This is my own family foundation, which is a grant-giving foundation so we don't actually run anything, we invest or back other organizations. But we apply the same techniques as in business. We chose a theme, for the first five years it's children; the educational, health, and transitional years from childhood to adulthood. We seek out the projects that appeal to us for start ups or grants then we look at the details: what difference they make, why them, what's their management like. Often these are start-ups where the founders have invested their own money and time and they need a business angel.*
>
> *It is diversified portfolio, some UK, some Africa, some Asia. But the strand that connects it is enabling kids to have an option for a better future.*

Chai says their focus may change after five years to support organizations involved in environmental- or poverty-related areas or something else. But he uses similar skills to private equity. They look at the goals of the project, and what percentage has been achieved. They analyze whether the start-up organization has reached the ability to be self-sustaining and has strong enough position to raise its own funds.

Chai says

> *It's a new framework. I've learned an enormous amount; the people are amazing and incredibly inspirational. And most of the choices are made on an emotional basis, so I always say the right brain is sold on the idea and the left brain finds its reasons, tries to catch up.*

Although creating a private foundation is not available to all, this choice is typical of entrepreneurs and business owners. In fact these individuals often opt to create foundations such as Bright Futures when they reach this stage. This allows them to take concepts from venture capital, technology, or business management and apply them to achieve their personal philanthropic goals. It also allows them to satisfy a desire which has been identified as important to this group of "keeping the business in the family." Finally as impatient Baby Boomers in need of instant gratification, it allows them to have full control over how and where their money is spent – and see the results of their giving.

Private foundations

Private foundations are generally founded by an individual, a family or a group of individuals, and may be organized as a non-profit organization or a trust. There are different types of private foundations, and the structures, purposes, distribution of sums and amounts to be invested vary from country to country. In Canada, for example the minimum capital is $10 000. It is also possible to contribute to existing foundations as "donor advised funding" or seek foundation service organizations to manage your funds.

One type of private foundation is a family foundation, such as Chai's but which in Siaou Sze's case was a way to create a platform for her and her family to work together, and to preserve the cultural legacy of Chinese literature

After I retired I started a foundation in my father's name. My father was a writer and we set up the foundation among the family members to encourage the love of Chinese literature for the youth. We publish books, we organize meetings, we work with the schools and we republished my father's books. This is the fifth year of the foundation and I am trying to raise more funds so that we can do more. I was very happy to do this because it brought the family members together. Now we have an endowment fund which means we work together. Every Sunday my brothers and sisters and my mother and I get together. We have a meal, we share articles, we prepare for seminars together, we have projects.

Siaou Sze Lien, former Manageing Director, Hewlitt Packard

A new model: merchant banking for the third sector

Chai's experience with the foundation and his other activities has brought up some interesting issues, and he imagines a new model:

> *You realize that just because you are in an environment of doing good, it doesn't always do good. There are duplications. Also it's raising some interesting issues,*

especially in the aftermath of the financial debacle because I think there is a real opportunity to create an investment bank that actually works in the third sector, a bank that raises funds for not-for-profit organizations but that brings in the discipline of having propositions, prospectors and due diligence. It goes back to my original choice of the name Court Cavendish which I created because it sounds like a merchant bank. So the idea is to get back to the idea of an old fashioned merchant bank. Because merchant banks used to invest their own money in businesses. They wrote letters of credit and they were the private equity investors of the day. Their client would come up and say "Would you put some money into our mill?" and they would raise money but also put some of their money into the project. So they were both merchants and bankers and the idea is to bring back this idea.

Chai continues:

These charitable investments could have an income stream because tons of money is wasted in the current methods of raising money. The institution would qualify the investors on one hand, like a bank does, and qualify the people coming with their proposition. There would be accountability: key performance indicators and reports. So the measure of success in this case would be the achievement of the objectives that are set out. These can be just as tangible as making profits in a commercial organization.

Court Cavendish: helping healthcare companies

Today Chai has also returned to the original idea of Court Cavendish and is making it work.

The core idea of Court Cavendish (CC) was to help the healthcare companies that got into difficulties. So we have created a fairly unique specialist consultancy for the healthcare business. CC parachutes management in and helps banks prepare business plans to restructure these companies without having them get into major difficulties. It helps prevent them from going into Chapter 11 (bankruptcy) and helps banks better understand their options.

We did our first restructuring in February. We took over 140 million debt from the bank, then restructured and salvaged a business (CMG) that looks after people with severe learning disabilities. This was a situation where lot of jobs would have been lost and a lot of vulnerable people would have suffered. So it was win-win by going in early enough.

Chai can play the role of mentor in these situations, supporting and inspiring the younger executives.

Today we are getting back to and revisiting the core values, the purpose of the orga-nization, what makes us different, what the vision of the company is. That's when I come in because it's something that younger executives find quite hard. It's not hard to go in and ask the younger executives the simple questions like: why do we exist? what are we exactly? because they are just used to being on a moving train. It's brilliant seeing them suddenly feel passionate about it because they are so used to working on the nuts and bolts. So hopefully, Core Cavendish, will do others like this, it will consolidate around the Health Care sector.

It's great fun, remarkably flexible and it's exciting because you can get in as deeply as you want.

Private equity: Elysian Capital

Finally, Chai has also created a private equity company with a partner, targeting a sector that needs funding. He says:

We put our own money in it and have successfully raised money from the market. Elysian Capital is about "buy and build," about helping people to restructure, and growth. There are no particular sectors, but our investments will be about growth, moving to the next level for these companies, which is a sector that needs funding.

Although Chai admits to being 'retired," he says his kids do not believe it, because they see him doing work in a different format. *"But it doesn't feel like work. Because I am not hide bound by structures. I do what I want during the day, and all the alternative things I want to do."* Like so many others, Chai can never imagine not doing anything. Today he is "absolutely engaged" and "not a spectator." In fact, he differentiates between absolute retirement when *"you become a spectator – you can talk about everything but you are passive,"* and anyone who is involved in a community project or a club or anything else.

If they are involved in making a difference, even if they consider themselves "retired," they are not. They are productive in one form or another, they are part of the community, they are still engaged in the process; it's about what it is to be alive in a community. There is a relevance in what they do. That's the difference.

Resolving the contradictions

In his final comments and throughout his story Chai places his finger on one of the dilemmas of the B2-generation which is reminiscent of their detractors. How, with so much wealth accumulation, can one give back in a significant way? And Chai goes further, showing how, for those who no longer have a "club faith" but for whom spirituality is still important, creating meaning, in his case through the journey, is essential. Despite this, one remains "full of contradictions." Chai speaks of the coat of arms he designed for Court Cavendish and the motto on it: To be happy and to do good.

The essence of living is being happy, which we don't talk enough about in the Western culture, anymore – not frivolously happy. And the do-good part of it because I no longer have a "club" faith, I don't believe in a religious institution, but the spiritual aspect is still important. That makes you think of Ecclessiates which starts out "it's meaningless, its all meaningless," which is odd to find in the Bible. It is existential, Sartrian, and every sentence has some application to modern existential questions.

Because we do look for meaning, but I am not sure there is any meaning. Because scientists know that atoms are inorganic with no sense of who they are, it is only the collection which begins to have a sense of self. So if you see things that away, you can say "if I had a journey and I could write what would the narrative be?" For me it's the one that I am living now. Still it is full of contradictions, I love amazing food, but I know people are starving elsewhere ... The capitalism has a purpose for me. I want to use what I've got to make a difference, and my narrative needs to have a purpose.

This need for meaning and a purpose to one's activities at this stage will be central in the Baby Boomer's approach to giving back. We are reminded of Erikson's stage of late adulthood when the significant task is to perpetuate culture and transmit values of the culture ... and strength comes through care of others and production of something that contributes to the betterment of society. So when we're in this stage we often fear inactivity and meaninglessness.[6]

Volunteering and mentoring

If you haven't got any charity in your heart, you have the worst kind of heart trouble.

Bob Hope

Even if they are not like Chai, who has created a foundation as well as private equity funds and whose entire business connection is interwoven with this theme, Baby Boomers who do pro-bono, not-for-profit or volunteer work on a smaller scale are also planning to keep control and need to see results. As has been true in other areas, society and the organizations in this sector will be adapting themselves to the generation, rather than vice versa.

Results and meaningful engagement

After having given so much to their careers and played by the rules, boomers now "want meaningful engagement."[7] But the idea of stuffing envelopes and distributing juice and cookies will not be acceptable. As Kathryn G. Jackson, a former financial services executive, says: *"I said no way. I don't do spread sheets, I don't lick stamps....because my experience was based on my work for the public school foundation."* Instead, these professionals wish to apply their professional skills – like Henri's work as a pro-bono financial and HR advisor for an association of psychiatrists and a small publishing company and

Pat Russo's work on the board of her golf club. And their contribution can be priceless for these organizations, a way to change the boards so they are run more like a public company board, to be more efficient.

Controlling time will also play an ever important role when choosing to volunteer, suggesting that flexible project-oriented missions similar to Henri's work will have to be developed if even a small percentage of this human resource is going to be tapped into.

Coined "vigilante volunteers" in *Boom, Bust & Echo 2000*, many boomers come from a post-parenthood group of middle-aged professionals with significant finances, seeking fulfillment through serving the community (Foot and Stoffman 2000). Still active in the workforce, they are specific about how they commit their time and resources toward volunteering. And while many boomers fall outside the privileged socioeconomic profile of a vigilante volunteer and will have to work throughout their retirement years just to make ends meet, boomers from all different segments of society will have numerous aspirations and obligations during later life, including caring for their parents and/or grandchildren. Accordingly, boomers will look for volunteer opportunities that meet not only the needs of the community but also their own yearnings to connect in a meaningful way with friends and family and to learn new things and develop new skills.[8]

As a result in our research, we found many different options for volunteering emerging with possibilities to work overseas, to help small businesses or to work in Encore programs and much debate over how to tap into this source, because with the numbers involved, even a small percentage could make an enormous difference.

Our next interviewee Marv Berenblum has found his solution for giving back during his "third" career in an organization which taps directly into this human resource. Like Hank who spoke "*of bringing your business skills and applying them to (non-profit) organizations,*" Marv's solution, and those of the executives in his organization, is also a way of mentoring-sustaining social contact with the next generation and a developing a sense of what Levinson calls "generativity,"[9] that is, a sense that one has accomplished something worth passing on to one's successors in the profession. On a smaller scale, mentoring can include Henri's teaching activities or Chai's role of Director General whose role "*is to highlight the key issues, set it up then step aside. Like when you have grand children you can always give them back.*"

Marvin Berenblum: Three lives

Marv Berenblum worked for Continental Grain Co. as Senior Vice president of Human Resources and was on the Board of Directors. He then became Senior Vice President of Human Resources and member of the operating committee of Knight Ridder Inc. before joining Heidrick and Struggles in 1989 where he worked for 14 years. Marv joined National Executive Service Corps (NESC) in June 2003 as President and CEO. He became Chairman and CEO in June

2005. Marv's is therefore also an example of a different career path, moving out of the corporation after many years into the smaller structure of executive search and then finally to his third career in the non-profit sector.

One piece of advice from Marv for this next stage is the importance of preplanning. At the same time when he looks back on his own preplanning, he remembers being slightly rattled:

> *I think that we have the continuing and special obligation at certain stages of our lives to do a self assessment. There are many ways of doing that. One way I've always found helpful is asking yourself these questions: What are the 20 things you most enjoy doing? Of those what are the five you most enjoy doing? How many of them are job related? How many of these are things are things your parents wanted you to do? Of these things you like to do, how frequently do you do them? When you go through these questions, you learn more about yourself and you might recognize opportunities that come up. Otherwise you might not recognize things that are right in front of you because you haven't thought about what your interests are and the things that really turn you on.*
>
> *Once I went through this exercise in a group and I was sitting next to a person who had his own company. We were filling this thing out and I was looking over his shoulder and noticed that 18 of the things I most enjoy doing were actually related to my job. In his case, it was maybe three or four related to what he was doing. And I thought "wow, running your own company must be exciting," and that I would like to be running my own company. But that was not where his interests were. This was scary in a sense because this new phase of life was a real opportunity for him, but scary for me because I liked what I was doing!*

Three lives

Marv let himself be guided by this passion for work, and lived what he considers to be "three careers."

> *I pinch myself sometimes because I've always been doing something that I enjoy. Some people might imagine there was a guiding hand but I am not religious, I have just been fortunate enough to recognize opportunities which have seemed to simply fall right into place in some special way.*

Learning about other cultures

The majority of Marv's corporate life was Continental Green where he spent 20 years and was a member of the Board. But first he worked for several other companies.

> *I started out in Indiana right out of Cornell with an MA in industrial and labor relations with a job at Cummin's Engine Company as an Assistant Foreman on a manufacturing line. I remember I walked into the plant and a guy came over to me and said, "Heh, I haven't seen you before, you must be new." I said, "Yes this is*

*my first day" and he said "Wow, I've heard people on television talking the way you
do, but I've never heard anyone actually talk like that." And I thought, "I'm really
in another culture here."*

*But that was the best thing that could have happened to me. Otherwise everything
was just based on theory because I had never had an experience in the industrial
workplace. I was going into the HR field but I had never had that experience. So
I went to another part of the country, learned something about another subculture
in our country and I found out what factory life was all about. Then I worked for
the largest company in this country, Exxon. So by the time I got to Continental I had
had a fantastic grounding and I was ready to contribute.*

His transition out of industry was motivated by family and location.

*My last corporate role was Head of Human Resources at Knight Ridder. What
happened there was that my wife Susan was mugged a couple of times. We were in
Miami, so she went back to Connecticut and I really had to think about the next
step. This was in the late 80s and the country was in a deep recession. The question
was what was I going to do? I contacted a person in the Executive Search business
who had been a classmate of mine and said I'd like to get back to the Northeast, and
he said, come have lunch and one thing led to another.*

*So I began what I consider a second career in the recruiting business. In the
corporate world I had a huge staff, and in the recruiting business I was going to be
novice. I'd never done business development myself so this new mode was a challenge
and as it turned out I enjoyed the work that I did in the search business more than
I anything I had ever done before. It was fantastic. That lasted 14 years.*

Marv then reached traditional retirement age, which he called a "third
stage" allowing him to learn and refine existing skills while mentoring for
others on a volunteer basis.

*For this third stage I was flying back from Seattle and found myself sitting next to
the Chairman of the Board of National Executive Service Corps. We were talking
about what you do in the next stage of your life. It was just an informal conversation, but I went home and said "Susan, I've found something. This person has
articulated something that I think makes sense for me." I could recognize it. This
was an opportunity where I could use all the things that I had done in my life and
still continue to grow, which is in fact what has happened. A few weeks later that's
what I was doing. I never thought that in this stage of my life I would be growing,
actually learning and still refining skills and taking advantage of all of the things
I learned in corporate America and the search business, but I am.*

Giving back through mentoring

Today Marv is Chairman and CEO at NESC, a company that does business
advisory consulting and search work in the non-profit world.

We have 250 consultants, all volunteers. These are people who have completed their primary careers, former Presidents of companies, COO's, CHRO's CEO's, CFO's – a whole gamut of backgrounds and skills so we do strategic studies, board development, executive searches and coaching to provide services for non-profits to help strengthen their management. Some of these clients are large such as Lincoln Center and The Metropolitan Museum of Art. Others are small neighborhood groups such as Western Connecticut Youth Orchestra and Dancing in the Streets. Our services are affordable and they all get the same, high quality service. NESC is like a small McKinsey devoted to non-profits.

Refining skills

Marv had a long history in the non-profit world: he was President of the Board of the Boys & Girls Clubs and now serves on the Scholarship Committee, but NESC has been a real learning experience, and a chance to transfer his skills from the corporate world.

I've been involved in leading strategy development for clients, marketing and board development, things that I knew a little about from doing board work but as a consultant it's another story. And I've learned about running a non-profit organization with all of the challenges of how you find financial support.

One of the surprises comes from the organization of non-profits and the difficulty in generating the financial support they deserve. When I started out the whole 2/3 of income was coming from philanthropy and 1/3 from earned income. Today, 75% comes from earned income and 25% from philanthropy and that is actually good, because then you are able to manage your business on your own terms, as opposed to being too reliant on philanthropy which is fine when things are going well, but these days, you have all sorts of non-profits going out of business because the funds aren't there.

A lot of the elements in the corporate world are relevant, it's just in a different form. You are working with people who are motivated by mission rather than by profit. You may be dealing with people on boards who have never been on a board, or are now in staff roles. Or someone who was a CFO of a private company is now the CFO of the non-profit.

Family and passions

Besides his work at NESC, the point for Marv, "*is to stay active, mentally and physically and meaningfully.*" To do this, Marv keeps his plate full:

There are two things I've done all my life, swimming and singing so I continue doing them; I did kayaking as a kid, and I still like it, so I do it with my daughter and granddaughter. And I travel the world for a choral group. I'll be in Cuba in June, we're going to be in Turkey and Armenia and Georgia next year. Then

I do a cultural exchange program so we will be in Turkey this summer, we were in Japan last summer, in Australia the previous summer, and China the summer after.

Family is also very important:

We all live close together in the same community and my mother's family is very large. My daughter puts on a family reunion once a year maintaining the tradition of my mother's close knit family.

Despite all these other things, and although he is "*not singularly involved in NESC,*" Marv admits that "*it's a full time commitment.*" And that he is probably spending 75 percent of his time with NESC and 25 percent of his time with the other activities.

When we insist and ask Marv how much time he spends "for himself," he responds:

Let's make it clear. I'm a volunteer. I'm not paid for anything I do. Even the CEO and Chairman role. Everything. So what I'm doing is because I want to do it. It's not because someone is paying me, or they have an expectation. That's why I'm constantly rebalancing what I'm doing. I'm playing tennis, I'm swimming, and I'm doing my own exercise program, so that everything I'm doing, it has to fit. It's not like I'm a peripatetic person, and I have to fill up every space in my schedule. I have granddaughters who live about 10mn from my house, I like to spend time with them. We're doing all sorts of things. I fit it all in. But I don't feel like I'm doing anything because I have to, I'm doing everything because I want to.

And he notes other differences:

Stress

There's no stress in what I do. There may be pressure, which is different but not stress. I think if I were being paid for some of what I'm doing I might feel stress. I'm doing the best I can, and having an impact.

Control

It's a different mentality. I'm still very concerned about the quality of what we do, I'm not satisfied unless things are done to the highest level of standards. There are still some things that are applicable today that were applicable then, it's just the way I feel about myself today. It is more collegial and less hierarchical.

And motivation:

When I was in the corporate world I think it was the sense that at the end of day I hoped that there was a list of things that I had accomplished that was positive. Today it's the fact that we are helping organizations that are performing a wonderful service for people in need. I very much identify with the organizations we are helping. So I feel as if I am leveraging myself so that thousands of people are being helped. I feel like I'm giving which is great. I'm giving time, financial support, helping others. It's a wonderful time of your life that you can do that. And I have the material resources to do it.

When asked how he defines retirement he says:

It's an interesting question because we do not use the word retirement at NESC. We say that there are 250 consultants who have completed their primary careers. If you ask my wife if I am retired today, she would say absolutely not. Today as far as commitment, dedication, and the kinds of things I'm doing, compared to 25 years ago, it all looks the same.

Then he tells an anecdote using those old demons, Florida, and golf.

I'll give you another scenario now. Susan and I bought a getaway place in Boca Raton, Florida; and the first week or so when we were there I was thinking, maybe that's it. I could strip back some of the things I was doing, make life simpler, spend some time on the beach, enjoy it. We were sitting across from this fellow at a restaurant who had sold his two grocery stores and went down to Florida. He was a handsome fellow in his early 50s and I said "George, I'm thinking of spending more time here, and just give me a sense of what do you do, what's a day like." And he said "well, I like to get up early in the morning, and I go down and take a very vigorous walk on the beach, then I have breakfast, and then I go and have a swim then I have lunch and take a nap. Then I go back out I take another walk and another swim and I take a short nap and then we go to the early bird dinner, and then because I actually have a very active day, we like to get into bed early, by 7.30 at the latest." And I said "George, how about a movie now and then?" He said "Oh, I love movies but truthfully, I haven't got the time for it."

Although Marv says he imagines the next step might be to cut back on his leadership responsibilities at NESC. "*I enjoy so much everything that is involved at this stage, that as long as my health holds, truthfully, I'll keep doing the whole thing.*"

Marv's advice is in fact not to necessarily "*do something different*" at all.

I think that if you really have enjoyed your career, to the extent that you can preserve it in what you do next is a desirable thing. You don't "have to do something different." Although someone who has been used to being in a regimented life may think he doesn't want any more regimentation, without it he may be lost. And golf, for example could help this. So you don't necessarily have to completely change things. If there are things about what you are doing that are part of you, try and see if there is a way to include them. Express them. Not be ashamed or afraid of it. If you like regimentation or if you like being in a group, then find a group.

Marv also says:

> *Don't wait to jump off a cliff. Plan ahead. Don't think about taking a break; focus on taking the next step as soon as you can. That can be a terrible mistake especially for people who are very active. Your system is just not made for that kind of pause. This is where you see health coming in, people having strokes.*

Book title: *Life is a Dichotomy*

> *It's a dichotomy because there is always that part of your life where you have a sense of not fitting in and then there is the other part where you get over it and may even surpass what were your most far-reaching goals and expectations.*
>
> *I've had my share of setbacks, personal struggles and self-doubts like anyone else. I may have come across in my professional life as self-confident as if I moved easily through barriers and prejudices that came up. However, I was also fortunate to have the support of many people who helped me reach most of my long-term personal and professional goals.*

If our interviewees are any indication the intention to give back will be an integral part of this stage and will take many forms, from hands-on volunteering to full-fledged foundations, non-profit board work and consulting. Giving back is also a way for them to become and remain anchored in the community (public school boards, national parks, golf clubs) establishing connections outside the primary career which may gradually increase in importance as they readjust and interweave their personal and professional activities into this new multiple lifestyle.

7 Pursuing your passions

Chase down your passion like it's the last bus of the night.

Glade Byron Addams

Choosing to pursue one's personal passions after transitioning out is a challenge requiring a qualitative leap into another sector which may be far removed from the primary career and motivated by desired potential selves that have been placed on the back burner because of the demands of work. Carole St Mark, former President of Pitney Bowes Business Supplies and Services, shows how this passion can become a business connection, while Jean Jacques Strauss, a media executive, gave his passions a place early on.

This period may seem an ideal one to live a completely different possible self, a time to pull out those many things one has said "no" to and dust them off (See Figure 7.1). Many quite seriously pursue their passions in their patchwork – Henri plays saxophone and has organized several stage productions of musicals with his choral group while Hank hikes, skis, and fishes–but Carole St. Mark has made this a central focus and her business connection.

Carole's is the story we have chosen but there were others, a Director of Research at the Institut Pasteur, who today has chosen to return to the bench while spending the rest of her time learning to play the cello. A former dentist who at 66 is now restoring paintings and "has more work than he can handle." Carole's story is interesting for the organic way it has evolved and as an example of combining existing skill sets (business) with new skill sets (interior design, horse farm) to fulfill unexplored creativity during this stage. But it also suggests that if you choose this as your main focus, it can result in greater initial disarray after a highly successful career just because it is so "totally different" representing a qualitative and quantitative break from the past. We are reminded of Marv saying "*You don't have to do something different. Someone who has been used to a regimented life may think that he doesn't want any more regiment, but he can get lost.*" However when as in Carole's case, the desired self is strong enough, an entirely new chapter can indeed begin after the initial period of transition, bridge work, and structural reorganization. Finally, Carole's story provides insight into the specificities of being a career woman in a man's world, which we will explore further in another chapter.

Carole St Mark: The evolution of Carole

Carole St. Mark worked for General Foods, St. Regis Paper then GE. After she moved to Pitney Bowes, she went on to become Vice President of Senior Planning and Group President. One could easily imagine Carole as the person in Marv's story whose shoulder he looked over to see that *"only three or four of the 20 things he enjoyed doing most were related to his job."* Carole says: *"I feel that I wasn't naturally in my element in the corporate world. I left behind the things I really loved and enjoyed, and did what I found challenging intellectually."* Obviously, in this case, this new stage would seem a real opportunity involving not so much a lateral move into related areas, board work, foundations, or consulting but to something truly different. Carole's transition involved a major reassessment of her interests to find *"the things that really turned her on."*

After a degree in Russian and an MBA, Carole got a commission-only job at an employment agency. Then she placed herself at General Foods in their personnel department as a recruiter and remained there for eight years. From there she went to St. Regis Paper, then GE. It was here, Carole says, that she really learned about HR succession planning, personal discipline, and accountability. She says: *"They beat me into shape: it was the best education."* She was at GE for about ten years.

Succession planning

Then she began her career at Pitney Bowes, originally a company that produced postage meters.

> *In 1979 the CEO of Pitney Bowes was frustrated with the succession planning there. He was in his mid-60s and hadn't thought about who was going to succeed him. He had a guy with a PhD who developed a program on succession planning that he spent a lot of money on and it didn't work. He admired GE so I was recruited to develop the management succession planning process at Pitney Bowes. First I threw out the old system. I figured the best way to figure out who the talent was, was to interview them and I went around the world for a year assessing everyone above a certain level. Then I came up with a summary which said, here is your top talent chart, with the whole management team. After that we developed a process and met with the head of each unit, asking them about what they thought about their team. The boss thought it was marvelous. Then he appointed the President to replace him. The new CEO thought it was useless until I presented it to him. After that he loved it because it was fact based and he jumped on it and pushed it through the organization.*
>
> *From there we created a department. One of my jobs was coming up with all the candidates for senior jobs and they were looking for a vice president of senior planning. I found internal candidates and presented them to the CEO but he*

didn't like them. He said; "How about you?" I said, "I don't know anything about strategic planning," but he said "Why couldn't you do it?" I thought about it, and thought maybe I could do that – and he gave me the job which was very controversial because I inherited this very large department of all guys and they all thought they should have gotten it. They made my life a living hell. It was the toughest thing I ever did.

The CEO then sent me to Wharton. I also went to my GE friends and said teach me strategic planning and I put in the GE process of strategic planning which I ran and it worked. The CEO was inclined to like it because I could explain things to him that other people couldn't because I kept it clear and focused. He also gave me new business development. We needed some growth businesses so we started some ventures and one of them was outsourcing before outsourcing was done. We got IBM as our first customer and ran IBM's back office, then we made an acquisition and merged it into that. Then my life changed.

I went to the first class of Wharton's Advanced Management Program. It was extraordinary. I was away and the CEO had offered me the management of a third of Pitney Bowes. When I came back I got that job which was controversial too, because of my being a woman with very little operating experience. I was a group president and I was handling separate lines of business and there were more and more acquisitions. A little venture I started grew very well. It was a service business, not highly profitable but not costly, no capital investment. That went from 1988 to about 1995. By that time the company I'd started was a billion dollars in revenue, 12 0000 employees and I ran that. It was both US and global. I was traveling all the time. I averaged five plane trips a week for about a year and a half. That's why I don't go out to dinner anymore, I've done that. That's punishment.

After many more reorganizations, the CEO retired and an internal candidate became CEO. Carole says:

I got along fine with the CEO but not with the new President. There had been no separation between Chairman, CEO and COO with my former boss the CEO, he had all three. Then suddenly they created this extra layer, and had me report to the President, but it didn't work. I cut a deal, I was 53, and I decided there was no way I wanted to stay.

Remembering your passions

Carole's initial transition out was not easy, requiring a true reassessment of what she wanted her focus to be once the corporate skin had been shed.

I went through six months of "who the hell am I?" I had no personal life when I was working. I was in the office at 6 am until 8 at night. I felt a loss of identity for those six months. I got help from a therapist, someone I'd know on and off for years and learned to accept what I was and focus on what I really wanted and who I really am.

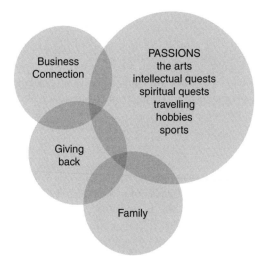

Figure 7.1 **What's next? Pursuing your passions**

She realized that throughout her career she had *"forced herself."*

> *I am very creative and I sort of forced myself into being an analytical business person, although I did create things. That's what I loved and was good at. Being in business was about being successful, getting an A, getting that bonus because I did really well and I worked my butt off. I would never do it again.*

Ultimately, Carole's choices and steps were more radical and thus perhaps more difficult than those that are still close to the mainstream of the past career (consulting, board work, private equity, foundations) leading to a dramatic sense of initial loss and requiring more profound personal reconstruction.

Developing new skill sets

Once Carole had decided she did not want a corporate job, she could move forward. It then became a question of deciding, learning a new skill set, and taking action.

> *I had always had so many interests I had never been able to do, I decided I wanted to pursue my passions; antique houses, interior design, gardening. I wanted to have a business finding and restoring antique houses and selling them. First I went to Fairfield University and took classes on interior design. Once I did the interior design course, I was taking action. It was a hard class and I had to do scale drawings and that was new, and I really loved that. During that class I was at Madison Square Garden, at the horse show, and I heard this distinctive voice and it turns out that it was a woman in my Fairfield class! And she became a riding friend, so things sort of evolved.*

Then one thing led to another:

> *Someone suggested Litchfield for the first house. I bought one and I designed it.*
> *I moved from Stamford in 2000 and I found an antique house that I bought as my*
> *own, with two barns in the back. I thought it would be a good place to retire my old*
> *horses and brought one there on the weekend. I had always had horses which I rode*
> *when I could. It kept me sane.*

And another:

> *If you ride in Litchfield, you need to have an inside ring. So I thought, why not build*
> *a big one, then have other people ride in it. That meant I needed a barn. So I built*
> *this building, then that building. It grew and grew. I decided I wanted to create*
> *a full service stable, which I have. It's very upscale and it's three times more expen-*
> *sive than elsewhere. Now I have an office person, a barn manager, and a training*
> *manager. I come in on Fridays to pay the bills and on weekends with my husband.*
> *But running a horse farm was certainly not in the plan, there was no strategic*
> *planning there!*

Today Carole's focus is completely outside the corporate career environment, but early on, she did go the consulting route. By remaining in contact with the corporate business connection as she was gradually trying out her hand at renovating houses and as the horse farm grew, she created a bridge from one world to the other and weaned herself off her corporate activities.

> *I did have a lot of calls at first, I was a good candidate. So I set up a consulting busi-*
> *ness, and I got some jobs but I didn't want to do that, so as I got closer to opportuni-*
> *ties I said "no." I'd had it, I was tired and I thought, I'll just take some time.*
>   *I was also on several Boards: Supervalu, Inc. (largest food wholesaler), Grand*
> *Metropolitan PLC in the United Kingdom (UK) (which owned Pillsbury, Hagen*
> *Daz, Green Giant, Burger King, etc), Polaroid, Royal SunAlliance Insurance,*
> *PLC in the UK, and Gerber Scientific, Inc. I traveled to the UK once a month, and*
> *around the United States (US) to meetings. Then it was okay.*

Over time as her other activities gained in importance, her participation and interest fell away and her knowledge became less topical. Carole naturally shifted her focus because she was aware that there is a shelf life to one's knowledge as a non-executive director that must constantly be renewed if one is to remain pertinent.

> *Today I'm still on the Gerber Scientific Board. But I am not an operating person any*
> *more. My current knowledge is pretty stale. When they get into talking about the latest*
> *manufacturing techniques, I'm lost and not interested. One board is enough now.*

Today Carole has truly found her balance, still structured by the horse farm but a real flexibility so that she no longer feels "pinned down." Both of her main activities have also created a family connection and are something she has done with her husband.

> *I continue to buy and sell houses. I make money on it, but not a lot. I bought a big house that we restored with my husband and I have a business called "Vintage Homes and Gardens." It's not a proper business, it's a passion. The horse business is the main activity. But it's the world's worst business, you can't make money on that.*
>
> *But I'm free to do what I want, because I have someone here and I want the phone answered. I pay bills. I try and ride three–four days a week. Get up in the morning exercise, do gardening because there are extensive gardens, then make an appointment to ride. Yesterday I went to Massachusetts to a garden center and an organic food shop. I have total freedom. I don't like to be pinned down. Eight meetings for the Gerber Board a year, that's plenty.*
>
> *Now, I try to do all the things that interest me and have fun and enjoy the moment. I spend my time doing creative things. I do a lot of photography for example. Years ago, I had my own darkroom, now I've learned it again and with digital you can make anything out of anything. I try to make the horse farm break even. At one point I thought I would sell, and my husband said, what the hell would you do then? The horse farm gives me a structure.*
>
> *I still get up at six in the morning. If I don't, I'm unhappy because I'm very disciplined. When papers come in they get organized. I still do things because I am driven, I still have a time – organization structure and I won't ever relax completely.*

Mentoring

And like so many others she has an idea for giving back which she has included in her structure:

> *I formed a not-for-profit organization – Women's Enterprise Initiative – with three other retired senior business women. It's an organization that identifies and supports women in Northwestern Connecticut who need help starting or managing their businesses. We act as mentors, and each of us now has several active clients whom we are working with. I like that. It's fun, and it's giving back.*

Carole advises people not to jump at anything,

> *Because as you get further away from the incident of leaving, things fall into place, you explore things, you start seeing things. Do all the things that you haven't done. I think you really need time to let it all happen and let it all settle in. Get over the emotion and panic. Men seem to have a harder time. Women have had other roles multiroles, had kids. Also talk to people. I networked with a lot of people.*

And she definitely considers herself retired:

> *I didn't need the power or the visibility. Pitney Bowes was the largest employer in my city, and I couldn't go to the supermarket without people knowing me so it's nice*

to be anonymous. I didn't really love the business executive role, but I was successful at it, and got lots of recognition – I was on the cover of Business Week and Fortune magazines and was a member of the Committee of 200 – an organization of women who are senior executives. We met twice a year and learned a lot from each other. I met many interesting women and I talked to many of them when I left the corporate world. But today my whole social focus has shifted, so it's totally different. Today I see a group of very interesting and accomplished women regularly, but none of them want to be in the corporate world anymore.

Book Title: *The Evolution of Carole.*

Refusing to be pinned down

Refusing to be pinned down is Carole's way of refusing to have her time controlled by the external forces of a 24/7 job, to leave her free to pursue her passions at her own rhythm, with the all important structure of paying the bills and running the horse farm to reassure that "driven" self, that will never totally relax. To reach this balance, Carole had to retrieve those activities and selves she had said no to throughout her career. Although we describe this as pursuing your passions, it could involve a seminar on urban planning that you didn't go to because of work obligations, a musical instrument that you stopped playing, a spiritual quest such as Loh Meng See's bible study group, or even a doctorate in another less "career worthy" subject. In order to "reach the top" these have often all been left virtually aside, and because of the career embeddedness of the primary career, making this the central focus when transitioning out may be more difficult psychologically, and a less obvious choice.

Even golf is a possibility

Jean Jacques Strauss, our next interviewee had a career in media advertising and his passions have influenced his choices throughout, pushing him to zigzag in and out of the professional world, and take breaks to challenge himself. The field of media communications itself made this possible, as he had a career in France during a time when radio and television were being privatized, and later on when the Internet exploded on the scene. His career is also interesting because today he very seriously pursues his passion for golf. Because it has come up so often as the negative image of the isolated, disconnected retiree, his story allows us to take a look at how one person's negative self can be "what's next" for another.

Jean Jacques Strauss. Even golf is a possibility

Following the period of protest and causes, most of the B2-generation entered the working world and played by the rules (proposing change from within), but all of them did not. After being a student in the thick of the student protests of May 1968 at Nanterre University in France, Jean Jacques' approach to career and work was about "keeping control" from the beginning.

> *Because work is made to normalize, to have you become part of the norm, and I resisted this. So in a way I couldn't have a career, but I was lucky I was able to keep control of my life. My idea of working was doing what I liked. I always respected the company, I was reliable, but I couldn't become a company man, I didn't give my heart and soul to the company. Basically that was my approach. People were not always happy about that. You are marginal, you refuse to adapt, but you're doing a good job, so they can't blame you. That was just the way I was.*

So Jean Jacques never quite "bought into" the race to the top, instead he became a specialist in all aspects of the field of media communications and was always looking for new projects.

> *I was in Media Advertising which is very bling bling with gurus and stars and that was never my thing. So I always tried to keep things in perspective. It's still just business and it's not vital. My mentors would be scientists or writers. In media you meet very creative, competent people who are very charismatic, but I always kept a certain amount of distance from that. There are people who stayed in the same company for 40 years, but that wasn't my trajectory. I was transversal and I went for innovative projects, and I had a career in a period where you could do that. So I had a pretty good time, and I never took it too seriously. It's true I was a little amazed by colleagues that took it absolutely seriously.*
>
> *Still, I got the prizes and I wrote a book* Television Sponsoring. *Because there was no television advertising in France before TV was privatized and since I had been the head of the department at TF1 (privatized TV Station), I was a good candidate to write the book.*
>
> *So I never really thought of my professional life as a "career." I call it a path, and I changed often. I studied Sociology during a period when people who had studied sociology had a "reputation" because the May '68 student protests had begun from the sociology department at Nanterre where I studied. At that time a résumé with Sociology/Nanterre on it went directly into the garbage. But that didn't matter; I still found a job because I had always worked during my studies. I was an intern at Europe 1 (Radio Station) from the time I was 17 and I gradually became an official intern. When they needed some extra help, they'd call me. So I went to the University and did that at the same time. When I got out, there was an opening at Europe 1 in the Media Sales Department and I took a job there.*

The golden years

Jean Jacques began his career at a time when you could cross the street and get another job, the "golden years" of full employment.

I found it was actually quite difficult to change from being a long-term intern to part of the team, so I didn't stay very long. It was fine, but after I while I thought, I've got to leave. I didn't go far, I just went across the street to RTL [a radio station] and at the time it was easy. At that time you could find a job and when you already had experience you could find another job. I went to the Media Sales Department at RTL for five5 years, it was a great experience, a very nice experience.

Then, someone from Radio Monte Carlo contacted me. They were installing radio transmitters in France and they were in a major phase of development. They were recruiting people to manage all this massive development.

Jean Jacques then found himself working in radio when the sector was in complete transition in France, moving from public to private status with all the resistance that this can entail.

I was interested so I accepted to leave for Monte Carlo. That was a pretty crazy experience, because I arrived in a place where the people basically had no desire to work! They were very happy where they were, they were making a lot of money. They were either Monegasque or French residents of Monte Carlo, so they didn't have to pay taxes. Life was easy, and they were not at all ready to make any effort to develop the radio, especially since you have to realize that at that time RMC was a government owned radio. That was in 1975–76 before the Radios Libres (Free Radios) and the government had a monopoly on most radios except Europe 1 and RTL which had their main offices outside (called radios péripheriques) of France.

But I arrived in this crazy situation, where every time I tried to do something, it didn't work. I was in charge of development. To do that you had to organize major PR campaigns in towns with podiums and a technical set up etc. but everyone refused to do anything. Suddenly things were breaking down! I'd regularly go see the Managing Director who really didn't care much either. This radio was a government radio – but at the same time it was a radio, it's media, it's supposed to be dynamic. It wasn't really a bad radio, there was just this incredible resistance to change. I'd regularly go to see the Managing Director to ask him why I was here, and at one point he said, "Look, you've got a great situation here, you've got a beautiful villa, buy yourself a boat, work a little less, and you'll see, thing's will work out better." I told him I was a little young to do something like that, that wasn't the reason I was there.

One senses, in Jean Jacques' story, the impatience of the young B2-generation who refused to buy into "the system" and in his case a desire to continue searching and to live his passion in the deepest sense.

At that point I'd been working for ten years, (the experience at Monte Carlo lasted about a year) and I thought either I return to Paris to get a job doing what I was doing before, or I do something totally different and take advantage of life. I thought I should go to a place where I didn't have all my different familiar support systems, my regular habits, the easy way out, and try something unknown, where I would feel a little lost.

Jean Jacques decided to place himself in the unfamiliar environment of the country and try to make his way while respecting nature and the planet. His lifestyle was his own personal challenge, living off the land, using renewable energies, and recycling.

From lumberjack…

I thought "What don't I know?" The country, rural life. I'm a city dweller, I've only lived in the city, at a certain level of comfort, in radio studios, the easy life. Let's see what I can do in a totally unfamiliar situation where I know no one. I was 30 years old and I wanted to test myself, it was a way to test myself. To see what I was capable of doing when I was not in my easy familiar environment. So I rented a house, and I had a few months of unemployment to get settled. Then the question was, how can you live in an isolated rural area near Cahors in France? It was out in the country, with farms and lots of woods.

Jean Jacques' break occurred in mid-career and was a way of pushing himself completely out of his comfort zone. A Baby Boomer's way of proving to himself what he could do. It was a radical choice at a time when radical was possible, and a model for some.

I couldn't be a farmer because I didn't have any land. And in the area there was a lot of wood and not a lot of people to cut the wood. So I thought, maybe I could live here by doing that, and I decided to try. So the first thing I did was get myself hired at a lumberjack's. I worked for a couple of months with them, with some pretty crazy people and when I decided I knew how to use the tools, I went out on my own. I went and signed up as a lumberjack. So I lived that way, by cutting wood for people. To avoid having to sell my wares from door to door I signed up in an association at the Chamber of Agriculture, where they had an engineer who would recommend me once he decided I was competent. That way I would get calls when people needed wood cut and I didn't have to go out and look for it. I did that for more than five years. So I proved to myself what I could do, and I learned how to grow a vegetable garden, to keep bees for honey. I also built a house (with help) half wood, half masonry. After six years or so, I had made the rounds. I had young kids and I thought maybe I should give them contact with another environment too.

To radio and television…

Once again because of the dynamics of media at the time and in France in particular, Jean Jacques was able to return to field he had left behind seven years before.

At that point, I was lucky, I returned to Paris in a part time situation, while I was still living near Cahors. So I started working in radio again, writing radio ads at an affiliate of RTL, and it so happened that this department also did the advertising for a station called SudRadio in Toulouse. As luck would have it, there was a position to set up the advertising network for the radio in Toulouse. I said I was interested. So the lumberjack episode lasted seven years. I stayed in Toulouse for five years. I found clients who wanted to advertise on the radio, and I also wrote basic ads. So I did a little of everything because I've done just about everything in this field.

When he changed again, it was to ride the wave of the privatization of television networks and return to Paris – which he needed to do for personal reasons.

Then I got a call from a colleague who was working in TF1 (Television station) which had been privatized. They were building a team for advertising for this network. That was in 87–88, and for lots of personal reasons I decided to return to Paris. I worked for TF1 for several years but it was a pretty difficult environment.

After that I started working in Advertising Agencies. They were interested in me because of my media experience. I advised clients on how to communicate in radio and television. Instead of working at the TV and radio stations, I was helping clients communicate in the media. So I changed sides and I worked for large advertising companies like Publicis, Regis etc. for several years. I was still in media advertising, but it was another step.

To the Internet…

Jean Jacques continued this until 2000, where he participated in an Internet adventure. His experience was emblematic of many: a novel technology (transferring video onto the Internet "*we were pioneers*"), an entry on the stock market "*a little too late*," the burst of the bubble and the slightly wistful comment "*I could have been a millionaire.*"

He continued working in Internet (the first European Internet marketing company, where Jean Jacques was in charge of Media) until a little before 60 when he began to consider transitioning out because he "*wanted to take time, have less stress, get away from management problems and living for results.*" Like Hank McKinnel, place was important. He chose a place to live where he could be close to his grandchildren and which was reminiscent of his seven years as a lumberjack.

So I thought, maybe this is the moment to leave Paris. I was a little sick of Paris, I was never really attached to it. So we settled in the Perche about an hour and a half outside of Paris near Chartres. It's the country, it's rural.

Going back to a rural environment allowed Jean Jacques to live in an integrated environment not only for age, but also to be in touch with the local inhabitants rather than bathing in the ultrasophistication of Paris. He and his wife have done the major renovations on their traditional stone house themselves, and Jean Jacques works side by side with local artisans for many of these projects. They have a large vegetable garden, cherry, plum and apple trees. They eat from their garden for half the year – canning, preserving, and freezing vegetables, fruits, and wild mushrooms, keeping potatoes, carrots, and cabbages in the cellar and buying half a cow, a lamb, and eggs from nearby farmers. This connectedness was essential to his choices.

For his business connection, Jean Jacques' idea from the beginning was to become a consultant two days a week. This choice

> was both financial and to stay in contact. To see if I could advise people, use my network. I spent a year thinking about it and seeing if it was doable. I wanted to see what type of structure I needed, and keep it simple. The first year I got calls and I had an assignment 15 days later and it never stopped. But in 2009 it was soft, so I was more active, I called people, had lunch. I want jobs without too much stress, with honest people, on my own terms. The idea of stopping full-time work was to get rid of certain negative aspects of life. So I'm not going to go back to that. I'll work within a certain context.

Even golf is a possibility

Golf is one of the patchwork of activities in a numerous interviews (Chai, Pat Russo, Marv, Kathleen Flaherty, Jean Jacques Strauss). Although for some, and especially Americans it seems to represent a "negative self" associated with retirement, it also provides a social connection, a family connection, and a physical activity that can be continued until quite late, and was often begun during the primary career. There are 61.1 million golfers worldwide; 6.9 million in Europe, 13.6 million in Asia, 1.7 million in Australasia, 1 million in South America and 500,000 in South Africa and 35% are over 50, so it is a huge community.[1] It may therefore also serve as a bridge from the primary career to the next step, without necessarily being the full focus.

And golf ...

Jean Jacques also has lots of projects: music (he plays guitar), writing a novel, and golf.

> Golf is an important element. I play every day if possible, to improve my handicap. I participate in one tournament per month. I have always played sports competitively – tennis for years, so it is a focus. I was also the President of the Golf Association for a couple of years on the course where I play in the Perche, a course where you have a good mix of people from the neighboring towns and Parisians who have moved in, like us.

He even organizes an annual "Winter Cup" in February with a group of 30 or so. "Last year it snowed! You should have seen everyone arrive in their *ski suits with fluorescent golf balls – It shakes everyone up during the darkest month of the year."*

Thus, Jean Jacques is far from the chic golf clubs of Paris and the bling-bling environment he never quite bought into. But there is also a cultural difference to his choice, because in France golf is not automatically associated with the entire "retirement" experience, thus less, perhaps, apt to be a "negative retirement self" than in the US culture. Jean Jacques does not live the age-segregated existence of the golf communities mentioned in the US and Florida, but the game is a central element in the activities of his new structure. It keeps him in touch with the local community and his family (he plays with his wife and would like to teach his grandson), and is an obvious way to keep healthy.

Jean Jacques has also recently bought several acres of woods near his home, and is using his skills as a lumberjack, to cut his own lumber for his wood stove, but also to manage this area, making sure that it is controlled. His other activities include martial arts: *"because health is very important, and after a period when my career made this impossible, with cocktail parties and business lunches, I'm very careful about keeping in shape,"* giving back through local volunteer work: *"I did the publicity and sponsoring for the 100 km walk in the Perche, and I helped a local mayor get elected,"* and teaching: *"I give a Masters seminar at the Nantes school of communication which I like a lot."*

Jean Jacques *"considers himself retired, but with an activity on the side"* and he is realistic that there is a timeline. *"I still have something to give, even if I know it is not going to last forever. You can't be half in and half out and I know I am out of the mainstream. I don't go to cocktail parties, media events etc. But suddenly time exists and you can appropriate it. It's not easy because you never had to do it. So you create structure, you can become overactive. That is part of learning during this new status."*

Book Title: *Keep Moving to Stay Live.*

8   It's all in the family

The focus upon family may increase when there is more freedom from the primary career and family may become part of the business connection, as illustrated by our interview with Eric Christin, an entrepreneur. An interview with Soek King Ko, former CEO of Motorola, shows how Baby Boomers may be making up for lost time with family during this period, and how the relationship with family may differ among cultures.

The connection with family after retirement may seem evident. Obvious things come to mind, traveling with your spouse or simply, like Patrick Gallagher or Patricia Hewitt, being more available for family crises and difficult periods for children when they come up. For this group, which has devoted so much time to career, often at the expense of time with their family, it can be a way as Loh Meng See said of "*making up for what has been missed with the children.*"

At the same time, this connection can take many forms—from structured caretaking of grandchildren (Kathleen Flaherty) to sharing passions by running marathons with family members to traveling, or like Chai Patel and Lien Siaou Sze, creating family foundations. We have observed that this family connection can and does also include caretaking of aging parents, for although the B2-generation has a long child-free period ahead of them, many have parents who are still living, and others have children who return to live home after school. The connection with family, like the pursuit of one's passions or the business connection is more or less part of one's multiple activities, and varies greatly depending on culture, profession, and gender.

As an entrepreneur, the family connection was intimately related to our next interviewee's choices to transition out.

Eric Christin: A cool glass of water or melting butter

Eric Christin, like Chai Patel is an entrepreneur. After 20 years in the corporate world he worked for Mergers & Acquisitions for a time until he found a business he was interested in. Eric began diversifying his activities more than ten years before he transitioned out, and today he is still a brainstorming session on his own, fulfilling potential desired selves on the way.

From nuclear physics to parking lots

After specializing in nuclear physics in a French Grande Ecole (Ivy League school) and working on nuclear military weapons during his two years of military service, Eric Christin was hired by IBM where he stayed for nearly 15 years. First he worked on difficult calculations on large machines, then became a technical engineer *"in a blue suit with the white shirt, the perfect IBM uniform."* By 1993–4, Eric was in marketing and financial development at IBM and he was recruited by another computer company called Amdahl.

> *I worked with Gene Amdahl for four years. I opened Amdahl France. When I started I was alone, and when I left there were 120 people. We sold many very large computers but the problem was how to finance them so little by little I found myself in contact with the banks until finally I was recruited by a bank into Mergers&Acquisitions (M&A) because financing was not as well developed back then.*
>
> *In M&A I was evaluating dossiers for the banks and for bank customers who wanted to sell their companies. One day the bank President gave me a dossier and asked me to look at it and on Monday morning, I told him that I had found a customer for the dossier—me! It was a parking lot company. The president laughed and said "have you seen the price?" I said yes, it's a high, but it's a good dossier. Then he asked me how I was going to finance the company and I told him, with the money that he was going to lend me!*
>
> *So the bank funded me and I moved out of industry and into this completely different business. It was great, there was no development needed, and I was the owner of my own group. There were no social issues really, there were only twenty people working for me because it's all electronic. It's all stone, you buy the parking lots, and it's an asset. At the same time it's a complicated job. The biggest issue is security, plus the quality of the air and the quality of the electrical circuit of the fire alarm system but I'm an engineer so I have no problem with that. If you ask me to talk about philosophy, I might have a problem, but with technology, I'm ok. It also has to do with location. How the streets are, the access, who the competitors are. Some lots work very well, others don't. Sometimes you can make a lot of money and sometimes you lose because there is a one-way street! It is more difficult than you think. Today I have several parking lots in Paris and Marseille and my business is buying old parking lots, refurbishing and selling them. I've been doing this since 1996, for more than ten years.*

Eric went in as CEO and Chairman. But then, as he says: *"at a certain age you realize that you either sell everything or you stay in, which is a difficult problem. This is something that you must think about."*

A cool glass of water or melting butter

For Eric there was no catalyst, he took his time deciding and it was a long decision.

The choice was to sell or not. If you sell, sure you get a lot of money but what do you do next? Money is like butter, it melts in the sun, while the company gives you a cool glass of water everyday. So I decided to have a cool glass of water everyday instead of a pile of melting butter, to keep my group and company and find a way for it to work without me.

This is a central problem for entrepreneurs and business owners and may delay their transition out of the work force. In fact a study in 2006 by Northwestern University's Family Business Program including a series of interviews with ten CEOs in manufacturing, commercial services, real estate, and retail showed that these B2-generation entrepreneurs are not looking forward to retiring at all, and if they do, many would like to keep their business in the family.[1] Thus, most Baby Boomer business owners were postponing retirement because they did not have a qualified successor in their family. Luckily for Eric, the solution "was simple" and allowed him to keep some control, change gradually but leave with confidence.

It was simple because my daughter was interested and has become managing director of the company. Her basic training is law and she was a lawyer for France telecom for ten years. So she came knowing about business law and then we had a trial working period. It took me one year to transition, but this was only possible because of my daughter. I had to have someone run the business, but if I had hired someone, the motivation would not have been the same. Besides, this is a cash business and you have to be careful of who you hire. It's working well, which is lucky for me, and my daughter is happy.

So today I am still in this business, it's mine and it's a family business. My children are in the company, one is on the board and the others have shares. I am still the Chairman and I make decisions about acquisitions and my daughter is full-time COO.

Eric now spends about 1–2 days a week in his primary business and he transitioned out two years ago, at 60.

Filling the open space

After that Eric says, "*there was a lot of open space.*" However, he had begun diversifying his activities more than ten years before leaving and he did not limit his participation with family to his daughter.

Art

I wanted to do something together with my wife. She is creative, she paints and she likes contemporary art. I finally found it—I created an investment fund of contemporary artists. This was possible because of tax incentives created by the French government, making investment in art deductible. So that instead of paying your full taxes you can invest in these funds. With this money we buy paintings, then hopefully the paintings increase in value.

He has called the company Art Finance. The first investors were "*a good group of friends*" but next year Eric hopes to open up participation to other groups. Eric and his wife travel to find the artists.

> *This year we went to the London Fair, the Madrid Fair, then New York, then Bale. That's our job. When we decide to buy we refer to a group of five who are used to investing and before buying we have a meeting with our experts.*

Eric explains that the paintings are not necessarily kept in storage, "*the investors can have one or two of our paintings in their house for several months, so the art work is shared.*"

Finally he and his wife have also recently opened a Contemporary Art Gallery 1161 in Paris near Notre Dame, to giving young contemporary artists a venue of expression.

Exploring a potential self, the biomedical connection

Besides the family connection, Eric has a long history of inventing and investing in the biomedical field, which when he explains it, is clearly an unexplored "potential self," and can only be called a passion.

> *My father decided I would be an engineer since I was the oldest. I wanted to be a doctor but he said no. Still, I think I would have been a good doctor.*

In his first biotech-related project Eric applied his knowledge of mathematics to develop an algorithm, and his entrepreneurial skills to develop and transfer the invention.

> *I helped create a reference book called Incompatex (a book of incompatibility between drugs). It's an engineering product. You have 8000 drugs, so you have to imagine the combinations: this is a mathematical problem. I created the algorithm then I consulted two experts, the Head Pharmacists in Grenoble and Lyon, and they filled in the blanks. This was created in 1991, and it is updated every year. I sold my rights to this, but it was my first step into medicine.*

Eric used a similar technology to help develop a European Dictionary of Drug Names which was sold to WHO and he has developed an algorithm with medical applications with scientists at the Centre National de Recherche Scientifique (CNRS).

> *It's a mathematical product applied to the EEG to transform the CT scan of your head into a mathematical formula. Once you have a mathematical algorithm of your head, you can do anything with it. I worked with someone from the CNRS and we are selling it to Kodak for their future machines. We got the rights from the CNRS so it is our property and we created a company.*

Eric has also invested in a start up with Australian doctors as a Business Angel.

> *We created a biobank of bones for doctors, a library of bones, if you will. Bone is the only material which can be used in people without rejection, and our patented technology is for cleaning and preserving (freezing) the bones. This company took 12 years to make its first euro and at the beginning I did everything. Now I am an administrator and I go to 2–3 board meetings a year. In 2010 for the second consecutive year, we made a profit, and if this continues, we might really start making good money!*

Finding a new career

Finally, Eric is has spent more than ten years as a judge, an activity which he sees evolving into a "new career."

> *I have been a judge at the Tribunal de Commerce (Business Court) in Paris for more than 10 years. In France each type of business has a professional syndicate and you can be elected as a judge. I have been elected three times. The maximum is 14 years so I will probably be reelected again for four years. We represent a large sector of activities and deal with business litigation. There are three of us who listen to the lawyers defending the businesses and we make the decision. The first year is mainly training in law—three years of university in six months, full time for three–four months. It's just law, because you're supposed to know business!*

Eric continues:

> *It's a fantastic job. You aren't paid, it's an honor. And when I'm finished, I am preparing to do International Arbitration—the process used by large companies that want a fast, confidential decision for litigation. It's negotiating, and our decision is binding. This involved a lot of training, the exam was really difficult, but I'm nearly finished. It's a new career.*

When asked if he considers himself retired, Eric says:

> *I don't know what the word means. Maybe one day when I am too tired I'll be retired ... My mother is 90 years old and she said "son, don't retire, because when you retire you become a book on a shelf and that's all. Now and then maybe someone will pick up the book, but not necessarily." She is still very active. She's treasurer of a senior group, plays bridge and tarot, and this was an important message for me.*

Family and culture

Thus for entrepreneurs, the role of family, and passing on the business is often the starting point for a transition. Once a replacement (family or not) has been found the business owner can gradually move into a less operational role, train his/her replacement while shifting the focus toward other interests and activities.

Beyond this, there seem to be cultural differences in the relationship with family and its place after the primary career. Although Hank McKinnel states, *"I clearly spend more time with my children than before,"* he also says *"The other thing I see people doing is that they retire and build the biggest house they've ever had in their life because their children will all come and visit, but they don't. They have their own lives. This expectation that all your kids are just going to be with you in this big house is a fiction."*

And yet, several of our interviewees have indeed created a living space— often a vacation house or country house that can and does accommodate "the entire family"—Kathleen Flaherty on the beach, Henri Balbaud in Corsica to name two—where their family does come regularly.

One of the keys to this difference is distance. As we remember, Hank has daughters in New York while Henri's and Kathleen's children live close by, allowing them to take care of grandchildren regularly and get together more easily with adult children. But it is also a matter of choice. Jean Jacques Strauss, for example, chose to live in an area that was close to his grandchildren.

Loh Meng See sees it this way:

> *If there is a difference between Asia and Europe or the United States (US), it is urban versus not urban. In Singapore and much of Asia we are always in the city, we don't have the country to retire to. Second, I think that for Asians the family dynamics are different. The children tend to stay close to us. In the US and Europe there are open spaces. My daughter lives 5–10 minutes by car. This is a choice too. And we tend to try to be close to the next generation. Grandparents help look after grandchildren. We do a lot more.*

We found that the importance of taking care of grandchildren was also still strong in France, where grandparents are willing to set aside Wednesday to take their grandchildren and easily spend school vacations with children and grandchildren alike. Once again, the country is smaller making access easier, and the expectation is still there on both sides.

Loh Meng See's role as consultant shows that the importance of family in Asia can go beyond the intimacy of caretaking. Besides his advising on corporate governance, he also has a role *"advising the children. The company I consult for is a family group and there is a family office. The children are young, around 30. I work as a coach for sibling harmony and the allocation of roles to avoid parental bias or pressure. Should succession be in order of child birth, or merit? Thus, I have a role advising and mentoring the children to help them along the way and maintain objectivity."*

The sandwich generation

But globalization and changing living patterns may have their way with cross-generational caretaking and close family support, and the B2-generation lifestyle and child-rearing patterns are part of this transition. Our next interviewee's story begins and ends with family, and is an eloquent illustration of the transformations that have occurred in education, around gender issues, professionally and in the family in Asia. Soek King Ko also discusses a theme which was only mentioned in our Asian interviews during this transition—a spiritual quest, which may play a role in the final choices of one's activities, and the search for meaning when preparing for what's next?

Soek King Ko: A precious journey

Soek King Ko begins by saying, *"I was born in old Asia and my family had a very traditional Chinese upbringing. There were nine siblings and all of us were told to go to a Chinese school."*

But in typical Baby Boomer fashion, she rebelled strongly and early on against gender and cultural stereotypes, family pressures and imposed religion.

At 12 Soek King decided that *"the world was English, not Chinese"* and she transferred herself to an English school.

> *It was a missionary convent school. They wanted me to be a Christian and learn the bible. But I wanted to decide for myself, so when I was 15, I found a technical institute for bright kids, mainly boys, and I got in. There were only 4 girls in that school and when I picked the primary subject I wanted to study they said "You can't study that, that's for boys." I went to the headmaster and threatened to go to the Ministry of Education if they refused to let me choose what I wanted!*

They accepted, which motivated her to graduate with a distinction because *"she was doing something that no one had ever done."* Soek King's story is a continuous series of challenges to do things that had never been done and of adapting to family responsibilities.

She did not go to the US to study, because *"I had to help my family, and support my younger brothers."* She received a scholarship to the University of Science, Malaysia majoring in Chemistry and fought once again, because she didn't wish to teach. At her first job at Intel, she broke barriers as the first woman engineer then moved on to IBM as a systems engineer. Soek King again met with resistance when she attempted to change jobs because her husband held a senior position in the same industry. *"I would write letters but as soon as they found out who my husband was they said no. For one job I didn't tell them who I was until the last interview and when they found out, they wouldn't hire me."* She was finally hired by Motorola which was working in two-way radios, where she stayed for 23 years. *"After three years, they wanted to hire a materials manager at Motorola. They hired two people who didn't work out and an American colleague said, 'why don't you try that lady?' So I eventually got the job but as usual I was not the first choice."*

Later on, Soek King was chosen to run a factory with another male colleague, proving that a local team could do as well as the expats, and ended up running a factory of 5000 it on her own "*while also managing the family business.*"

Soek King's catalyst to transition out was a combination of a personal wake-up call:

> *In 2001 I had to participate in a retrenchment program with my HR person. It was very difficult for me the first time, it was very hard. But after the second, third, fourth time, it got easy. This upset me. I thought what has happened to me, why have I become so heartless? Why is it so easy for me to tell them they can't come back to work? I was very disappointed that the compassionate side of SK seemed to be lost.*

And the gods calling:

> *In 2001 we had set up the equivalent of the Chicago 911 emergency system in a town in Southwest China. After we celebrated the end of the project, I got sick. I had a lot of symptoms of SARS, but without a fever. I was sick for months and the doctor didn't know why. So I had to stop traveling during a period when SARS was at its peak. Then several months later they figured out that I had a bacterial infection, I was still very weak so my kids and my husband said, why don't you stop working? I retired in 2003 at the age of 52.*

A spiritual quest

The early period of Soek King's transition out took the form of a spiritual quest. This was also true for two other Asian interviewees and finally became a central focus for Loh Meng See, serving as a vector for giving back, a family connection and a passion. For others it was a way to take stock and go through the important process of self-reassessment—learning "to know thyself" again, and finding the meaning that seems to be so important for this stage. Soek King says:

> *So I was 52. It took me slightly more than year to build my immune system up, and there was a lot of soul searching, because I wanted to look at the spiritual side of things. I wanted to learn the true teachings of Buddhism was. My mother was a staunch Buddhist, and I tried to understand the different types of Buddhist practices. Some are focused on liberation, others on services mankind. I went to India, to Nepal, and listened to the Dalai Llama. A spiritual person once told me the major thing we have to do, even with Christianity, is to find happiness, and for this everything you do must from your heart. And my conclusion was I don't have to be religious. It's how you live your life, how you treat each other, how you behave as a person. So that was my very simple journey.*

Soek King's humanistic conclusions are similar to Chai Patel's—that even without an active club faith, one must do "*the right thing, from the heart*" in relation to others to find happiness. Once this basic moral and philosophical foundation has been identified she can begin the process of constructing her lifestyle. For Soek King, this spiritual side should be cultivated and is closely linked to her family experience. *"We have eight siblings, my oldest brother died at 29, and I saw my mother's grief then and it affected me greatly. Two brothers passed away on the same Chinese calendar date years later and I witnessed my mother's grief again. I saw that and it affects you, it makes you a different person."*

Education

In the meantime Soek King's husband had retired, and they worked together on creating a college, a technical campus to improve the competitivity of the education provided in China, a continuing education arm of a University. Once again this was a family effort.

> *We had a family meeting and decided that it would work. We had family and friends who invested and we left to China to do this together. At first I said I wasn't going to help because I was still recovering and on my spiritual quest. But in 2005 I saw that they needed someone to do help with the business.*
>
> *Today we have two campuses, 500000 sq ft, and the other 1.2 mil sq ft. with 9000 students and a software company. The second college is a software college. That was my baby. I work out of Singapore, go there, then we work at home too. Since the company is very sound financially now, I felt like I had to let go, because I am almost 60 and continue my spiritual quest.*

Today, Soek King has slowed down, stopped traveling, and is at a crossroads, but feels that her next step will be in services, giving back to the community.

> *Maybe counseling, I am already doing a little now. But I'm getting back to basics because I don't want to be sucked in again. I am struggling because part of the goal for the education was to have a foundation. Every year we give scholarships—you can get money from equity. So it would be good to make the foundation successful, spearhead it, but then I would have no time again.*

And family

This break was also motivated by her family and children because she *"hasn't had time."*

> *A big part of the last two or three years has been being with my children. That is what I have been focused on. Because next year my son will get married and my daughter is based overseas so that it is a window of time, and if I miss it, I miss it.*

For example I have worked on improving my relationship with my daughter in the past five years, and now we are friends. My son recently said he didn't want to have a career like mine because he wants to be able to spend time with his children and I suggested he be a professor. As a professor you can have the joy of learning and reading so I think that that lifestyle is probably more enjoyable. Your success in the corporate world should be measured according to whether your children are well taken care of or are beautiful individuals. I measure success by the happiness of my kids. If they are successful in their own way then I feel I have had a successful life, because the next generation is very important...

Soek King goes further, speaking of the B2-generation's relationship with family for Asian Boomers, giving us a peek at the "family friendly" approach and policy in Singapore and speaking of how she thinks it will evolve.

We are the sandwich generation. Our generation is dedicated to our parents. My father lived with me until just before he passed and my mom too. And our generation also hopes to serve our children. But once my son gets married, I am personally of the opinion that he can leave or stay in the family home; I hope that we will continue this relationship but things are changing. In Singapore, communities are building apartments with a main apartment and a smaller apartment that are connected so that the parents can still be there. But the kids are going for a Western education and family values are no longer taught the way they were when we were young. It's not so much Western, the world is now technological. When I was young, I would go in the supermarket and the decision was easy. Today, the world lives on marketing. In that kind of world it is not the younger generation's fault, the world is just changing.

Book Title: *A Precious Journey.*

What's in the sandwich?

The world is changing, and the model for change has long been the US, where children have been systematically moving from their parents' home since the 1950s to create their own nuclear families. Soek King's story is emblematic of this change, starting from her traditional Chinese upbringing, to her role today with her children, "*who will go overseas to study, and who she does not expect to take care of her.*" The US model is in marked contrast with the Chinese, which is traditionally more collectivistic than individualistic and thus more family than work oriented. This dichotomy ran through Soek King's entire story (choosing between Chinese and English, not leaving to take care of her family, seeing her children leave to study abroad). It also shows the obligations of filial piety within the family structures and Soek King's obligations to her immediate family and elderly parents. Indeed, in a Confucian society the family is seen as the fundamental unit for women in particular and the family takes precedence over the individual members, complicating the relationship between family and career.

Soek King has had to manage both the traditional and the Western model in her life. She thus finds herself sandwiched between the two, and aware that her retirement and old age will not be the same as her parents, because her children will no longer necessarily live by family values.

A research paper titled "Life Cycle Saving and the Demographic Transition in East Asia" by Ronald Lee, Andrew Mason, and Timothy Miller shows how dramatic the metamorphosis has been in Asia since the end of World War II. They found that the proportion of Japanese elderly living with their children declined by 30 percent between 1950 and 1990. In 1973, more than 80 percent of elderly Taiwanese lived with their children while this had decreased to 60 percent of elderly men and 70 percent of elderly women in 1993. Finally in 1950, 65 percent of Japanese women thought they would rely on their children in old age but this had declined to 18 percent by 1990.[2] Nevertheless, for the moment the respect of the traditional family remains intact in Asian culture. As we saw with Soek King, she remains emotionally and physically very close to her children and for both she and Siew Hua Lim the extended family is still the general rule, with the different generations sharing holidays, weekends, and childcare, and the younger generation still paying homage to elders and their role.

9   Business as usual

It's not a question of dividing up your life between work, family and pleasure, instead you fuse them.

Elisabeth Brenner-Salz

After leaving the primary career there may be a desire to "go plural" and remain closely involved in the corporate process. The specific activity of non-executive board work – both for-profit and not-for-profit is discussed in this chapter in an interview with Jeff Yusi,[1] a CEO in telecommunications, and Elisabeth Brenner-Salz an economist and urban planner. The cultural and structural differences of different board activities are discussed and compared.

We have now focused on various elements of the multiple lifestyle that may be given a greater place after transitioning out of the primary career and become a vector for other activities: giving back, family and pursuing passions. A business connection of some sort is maintained, but many times this represents a shift away from the primary business career, the corporate world and corporate structures. In some cases completely new skills are learned and a new working/living culture is discovered. The choice of board work allows one to maintain direct contact with the corporate world and our next interviewee, Jeff Yusi has made this choice so the focus and magnet is almost entirely the business connection itself.

Jeff Yusi. Seizing opportunities

Jeff Yusi comes *"from a small town in Idaho where many people did not go to university."* Today he has 32 years of experience in technology industries in the United States (US) and Europe and his career is a dizzying example of someone who helped create, then rode the incredible wave of the telecommunications industry. Jeff spent 17 years in corporate telecommunications, where he says he went through the ranks of his first job from trainee to manager to director to VP *on a straight line path.*

Car phones for the rich and famous

Jeff says his career has been *about seeing the opportunity and seizing it, being willing to move and taking the risk.* When he left his first position to go into the car phone business, he remembers people said "*Get off it, you're nuts. Car phones are for the rich and famous.*"

Jeff admits to being

> *rather forward looking in that case. I got excited and knew it was going to be a consumer item. That was in 1983. I was a sales manager then became a VP. When I went to my first board meeting they asked me to leave the room. Then they fired my boss and put me in his place. So in 1983 at 27–8 I found myself president of this little mobile phone group.*

Jeff continued this straight line path *in high speed mode on steroids* and was COO, CEO then president and CEO of different companies between 1989–2000. In his last position Jeff helped lead the US wireless industry into a phase of explosive growth and into the wireless and internet convergence.

During this period he took his first seat on a board as a non-executive director, taking Steve Davidson's and Patrick Gallagher's advice and learning about non-executive board roles while he was still in the corporation.

Board work: learning to back off

After resigning as President and CEO, Jeff went overseas to develop the cable television business. It was then he decided to "go plural."

> *I moved overseas because I believed there would be tremendous growth in the broadband industry. I was CEO and the chairman was a mentor for me. It was a partnership – he was Chairman and I was CEO. (He said, "you're the new president, kid").*
>
> *That was when I went consciously plural.*
>
> *I understood the difference between owning a company and running a company – so this new role intrigued me. What motivated me was being a Chairman versus being an operating Director. I had learned some of the skills on my first board when I was still within the corporate structure. That taught me a lot. For example during the first few board meetings I wanted to dig into details – but you don't do that in a board room. You realize you are not managing it, other people are managing it. If you are used to being operational, you have to learn to back off. And some of it is just people skills. Sure, you make mistakes but you learn to deal with people – it's part of growing up.*

Jeff was especially interested in Chairman roles.

> *A Chairman is a bit more advisory but you are still involved. Besides governance it's about succession, both in management and the board and it is a consuming process.*

"*In 2001 I became Deputy Chairman of Noxy which was huge – we were publicly listed so we were under close scrutiny.*" Jeff completed this by becoming a Director at Renytall a company which went public and is now listed on the NASDAQ. He has been Chairman of the Board since November 1, 2004.

Asking the right questions

Then he joined Tarmel and says "*I had my plural set up.*" He had help from mentors but he also asked himself these questions:

▷ *Can I add value? If you don't have a clue about what's going on in the industry, it probably won't be a good fit.*
▷ *Is it a service company to consumers or industrials In my case I had done technologies and service, so I know how to do that and I could do it elsewhere.*
▷ *Is it a Non Executive Director or Chairmanship? In US, Europe, or Asia? It makes a difference.*
▷ *Is it public or private? You can make changes more cleanly in a private company vs a public co setting.*

As for numbers, Jeff says:

> *A mix is important. Some people can do five. As long as there is no major event you are okay, but otherwise you can be consumed by the event. So you are playing the odds as to whether the company is going to go into the event. That means two or three non-executive directors and one or two chairmanships, for example.*

A case in point was Tarmel. Jeff says: "*I was supposed to be executive Chairman for 1 year, then step back, but three months in we saw that the CEO was not going to work – so I temporarily took the CEO job too.*"

Without the CEO position, Jeff was working 50–60 percent of the time with his plural set up. But the odds were against him, and the "event" occurred, so that he is still CEO and COB at this writing, (and quite happy about it) emphasizing that a commitment to board work, and especially a Chairmanship includes the possibility of unforeseen events requiring a willingness to be flexible with time and commitments, and even find oneself in a CEO role once again.

Besides the for-profit board work Jeff "*serves on Advisory Committees for the Michigan Cancer Institute and Michigan Equity Partners. I'm a trustee at the American School. That opened my eyes to academic involvement. And I've been invited to work for my Alma Mater – my wife urged me to do that. That gives me some balance.*"

Giving up the perks

For Jeff the main difference between his corporate role and going plural "*is gaining independence. And you give up perks: jets, hotel suites, everything.*

You live in another realm. Before you were in the limelight with television interviews and all that. People wanted to listen to you. Some people love that, but when you go plural, you are your own employer. You get independence, but out of the limelight. You may be in the hinterland for a while."

Like so many, Jeff does not consider himself retired and is still trying to imagine how he will adapt his life and his relationship with his family but imagines himself 5 years down the road (and further) with "*a significant portion of my time tied to the development and well being of a business or two. I wouldn't want the intellectual emptiness that would come with not being engaged in a business.*"

But above all one senses how excited Jeff remains about the technology:

It's easy to get enamored with this business. Take Tarmel, for example. It was created because it was recognized that at sea there was no communication. It's an international effort and we provide free equipment and financial support to restore communications in disaster zones. If there is a natural disaster, we set up the communications during that. The hurricane in Haiti, for example. Bang, we were there, which is very satisfying. So you can get attached to the company, but as a Chairman you have to remain independent – which is very different.

Book Title: *Seize the Opportunity.*

For profit board work

Jeff's cluster of activities remains focused around the technologies he helped develop during his career but he has now organized himself a portfolio of corporate boards, so that, even without the CEO position, he would be working in several companies in a more strategic, independent role. Independence was Jeff's motivation, as well as remaining in close contact with the industry and technologies that he loves on a different level. Access to board work is the privileged opportunity of a number of our interviewees who are former CEO's, COO's, and CFO's. It is an ingredient in the recipe of many and the main ingredient for Jeff, who cannot imagine himself not being "*tied to the development and well being of a business or two.*" This choice provides a true bridge, allowing the person to maintain direct ties to the primary career. Jeff's interview gives an idea of how to organize this type of lifestyle, but also the salient features to be considered when seeking the proper balance, in particular the possible complexity and difficulties of managing time and commitments.

Thus board work is a viable avenue to exploit corporate experience in a new manner. It can be limited to one or two non-executive director roles, leaving ample time for completely different pursuits or like Jeff become a nearly full time, but plural activity. Besides the business connection it can be a way of giving back, living out a passion and even mentoring. But whatever the commitment to board work, it is important to understand the learning curve associated with this pursuit. There are different skill sets to be developed and an understanding not only of governance issues and one's potential role in a particular company or organization, but a certain number of basic cultural differences when working on boards outside one's country.

What's to learn?

Before one can imagine one's role or fit as a potential board member or Chairman, the basic workings of the board – profit or non-profit – and basic governance must be understood.

Patrick Gallagher says, "*I learned by observing and reading everything I could find and emerging myself in understanding the IFRS (International Financial Reporting Standards) and all of the governance issues associated with boards. I did a lot of reading about this to keep current and to learn what was expected of me.*"

Learn by doing

Besides the book knowledge, Patrick Gallagher and numerous other interviewees recommend learning by doing. This means, like Jeff did, taking advantage of the opportunity to be on a board while you are still full time and committing

---

Governance made simple

The **Board of Directors**, aka board of trustees, board of governors, board of managers, or executive board is a body of elected or appointed members who jointly oversee the activities of a company or organization.

Typical activities of a Board include

–governing the company by determining general strategic policies and goals
–choosing and evaluating the CEO
–risk management, succession planning
–budget planning and monitoring.
–reporting to shareholders

The Board is composed of both executive and non-executive (outside independent) members in either a one-tiered system (US, UK) (executive and non-executive together) or a two tiered system (Germany, Japan and others) composed of a supervisory (non-executive directors) board which oversees the management (CEO and executives) board. Boards are also often organized into committees that evaluate and report on long term or topical corporate issues (nomination, remuneration, risk management). During regular meetings the board discusses, advises and guides the CEO on subjects ranging from the annual budget to mergers and from going public to succession planning.

The Chairman of the board

The culture and tone of the Board emanates from the Chairman – he chooses the team, defines their roles and sets the stage for the way the board will operate. As Chairman it is up to him/her to create an environment where each member has the space and a forum to fully express his/her expertise and background in open communication and exchange, so that it can be used to the fullest advantage of the company.

The overall influence of the Chairman of the Board depends on whether s/he is also the CEO and on the number of Board members. Separating the executive role from governance is a means of checks and balances to reduce a risk of making decisions while wearing two hats, and ultimate conflicts of interest. In cases where the CEO and COB are one, a Vice Deputy chairman is sometimes named, especially when the CEO is to be evaluated. This separation also increases the importance of maintaining a fluid, open relationship with the CEO to avoid eroding the board's knowledge of the business of the company, as well as the authority and accountability of executive management. The time commitment can be between 1–3 days per month. More involved, more operational, Set agenda for board meeting, run board meetings, send out papers to board members, sit on more committees etc....

Non-Executive Directors

Are external to the company, thus a source of outside expertise and insight, bringing independent judgment to the company culture. Increasing the number of non-executive directors is intended to stimulate more independent behavior by the board and bring a fresh and broadened perspective into the corporate ecosystem. Today the non-executive director is brought onto the board for his/her specific background and capabilities, and is expected to prepare thoroughly to discuss what are often substantial corporate issues. The term for a Non-Executive Director is between 1–3 years which can be renewed. But many are no longer considered "independent" after approximately 7 years.

Supervisory boards

European supervisory boards are significantly rethinking how best to fulfill their responsibilities in a time of economic turbulence, changing markets and accelerating globalization. A good part of the discussion focuses on the issue of supervisory board composition and the qualities to be sought in individual directors and on the board as a whole. Historically the supervisory board's mission was to provide the oversight that comes from experienced, but more general, business judgment.

The make up of a board, the right cocktail

Where once all of the board members were from the same 'culture' (mostly CEO's and men from the same industry and country) today there is an awareness of the need for mixity and to move across industries, as well as to find the right balance of personalities to stimulate dynamic pertinent exchange while at the same time obtain group cohesion. This means that nominating committees may now look beyond the conventional CV and outside their personal networks to obtain diversity in gender and culture while also looking for candidates in adjacent industries with both operational and strategic experience to keep the broad perspective necessary to give the company a leading edge in a global market.

US, Europe, Asia Boards?

Besides the basic structure of boards themselves, and deciding upon the interest of the roles of non-executive director versus Chairman it is important to realize that corporate governance differs in the US, Europe, and Asia for basic historical, legal and philosophical reasons that can affect day to day workings of the board itself. In the US and UK corporate governance is based on a goal of maximizing the wealth of shareholders while in Japan and other countries, such as France and Germany the goal is to "ensure that firms are run in such a way that society's resources are used efficiently by taking into account a range of stakeholders such as employees, suppliers, and customers, in addition to shareholders." With this system of *codetermination* the latter companies have supervisory boards in which employees may have an equal number of seats and thus play an important role in the strategic decisions of the company.

The size of boards is roughly the same in the US and the UK and is usually around 10–15 people. In the US a majority are typically from outside the firm while in the UK a minority is external. Traditionally, the size of Japanese boards is much larger, with an overwhelming number of directors coming from outside the company, although with the pressure of globalization certain Japanese companies have reduced the size of their boards to that of US.

To remain competitive on a global scale many of the emerging Asian nations are also reforming their corporate governance systems. Indeed, in the Asian landscape approximately two-thirds of listed companies, and nearly all private companies, are family-run. Although these family-business owners have been the motors of the strong economic growth and increase in living standards in these countries there is now great international pressure for them to begin working toward full convergence with international standards and practices for accounting, auditing and non-financial disclosure.

The Anglo-American model provided by the US and UK provides one possible direction to go – recommended for example by the OECD (convergence), these other models are also a possibility.

As a result, each governing board is unique- the story of the company culture, the national culture, the personal culture of the Chairman, as well as the separate professional, national and personal cultures of each of its members. It also means that the expectations for a Chairman or non-executive director will differ from one board to another.

Moreover, the recent financial crisis has also had an enormous impact, creating a demand for greater professionalism, accountability and transparency by boards and board members and meaning that the consensus on the ideal board structure and governance itself is in the state of flux. In the US, for example, where traditionally the CEO and Chairman role was held by the same person, a certain number of companies are now separating them. The Chairman therefore plays a more active role in making policy and business decisions, requiring more time and investment.[2,3,4]

to a non-executive position before leaving. Elisabeth Brenner-Salz, our next interviewee, says you must start doing the plurality thing early. "*Don't wait until you've finished full time to be plural, because you are going to make some mistakes on your CV.*"

Know thyself. What's my added value?

By taking a hands on approach you see the players in action and get "to observe excellent chairmen and not-so-good chairmen" gaining direct experience while beginning to determine your added value. Steve Davidson says, "*You need to be very clear on what set of skills you bring to a board or a non-executive position.*" When deciding to work on boards, Steve looked closely at his strengths and experience in deals, finance, Wall Street and US/UK governance and today he has specialized in remuneration. Patrick Gallagher meanwhile, decided to work in emerging markets after realizing that his added value was in the telecommunications industry with experience in merger acquisitions, high growth and transformation.

For Elisabeth Brenner-Salz, there is an even more basic need: to figure out what you like.

> *First you have to know what you like. You have to find out. If you do it alongside a main-stream job, you can work out where your talent is, and what you can add and what you enjoy and you need to know that when you finish your mainstream. If you wait until you're there doing it, it's too late. Even if you don't have time, talk to people who do it.*

Thus, there is a need to become self aware, looking at your résumé from another angle, to decide what role you would like to play and where, and then think about the impact you could have on a particular firm or organization over the next five years.

Do your due diligence

Finally, care must be taken when making choices.

Steve says he was caught *right between the eyes* on his second assignment for a board, because "*I trusted the person who recommended me.*" This can make for a complicated exit, and may be a delicate task because you are committed and as Elisabeth Brenner-Salz says, "*it's a small world.*"

Not profit board work: another culture

If Jeff Yusi's main focus is the technologies and a business connection in for-profit, corporate board work, our next interview with Elisabeth Brenner-Salz plunges us into a world with a majority of not-for-profit boards and chairmanships in the community and the arts. Her experience and that of others shows that this choice can be a way to give back, to mentor, and is often a passion.

Elisabeth Brenner-Salz: Giving back and staying in touch

Like Soek King, Elisabeth Brenner-Saltz, an economist, urban planner and an academic, is a woman of firsts: first woman Dean of Berlin Frei

Universitat, first to chair the The Society of the Friends of the National Gallery of Berlin and to lead the Urban Heritage Conservation Program. Elisabeth Brenner-Saltz developed a strong sense of community early on. Her father died when she was seven and she was:

> *brought up by a tough career women. She always gave back to sport, she was headmistress of a boarding school. I was brought up in a household where you not only worked, you gave back to the community. And early on in my career I always gave back to the community.*

Community and culture

This sense of community and of doing work "plus," has been a focus through-out her career. After getting her degree in economics from Harvard, she initially worked as an academic economist at the Berlin Frei Universitat and at the Sorbonne organizing and directing the German-French Economics degree, the first of its kind in Europe. She then became a partner at Deloitte where she says "*they had community hours on the time sheet. There was an ethos of giving back to the community.*"

She was also multitasking long before she began a "plural" existence allowing her to pursue both intellectual and cultural passions. "*I never thought I would do only one thing. I've always done that. In school I did a mixture of science and art. I settled on economics because it sort of gave me all of that.*"

Even at the height of her career at Deloitte, Elisabeth felt:

> *I was never full time. I was theoretically full time but I was part of the Urban Development Program and Heritage Conservation in Berlin at the same time. I was an independent expert and I didn't represent Deloitte on that. I represented Berlin and negotiated with the government and Senate Department to determine the rede-velopment areas and with private investors to raise funds. It was an amazing role.*

Elisabeth was a member of the group of 17 experts guiding this program and became Deputy Leader, then Leader.

> *I was doing this while I was at Deloitte. If they needed a strategy for a particular bid with a private investor I was brought in. I played a strategic role, was a strategic advisor and had moved well beyond the role of being an economist. So it was econom-ics plus government. In fact I had two big jobs and was working 18 hours a day. I wasn't married, and it was fun. It meant meeting interesting people at a pivotal time. So my role was well beyond just being a partner at Deloitte. In fact I ended up as senior advisor in the end because it was easier to do the other things I was doing.*

Elisabeth left Deloitte when she was no longer Leader of the Urban Planning Group. "*I had just gotten married and I thought that maybe I needed a change.*"

Due diligence and an "oh-shit" moment

Her next role was a return to academia and as near as she got to an "oh-shit" moment, which, as we have seen in other cases, had to do with due diligence.

> *I was approached to head* Frei Universität Berlin, *which had to be turned around. They were in deep trouble and needed a trouble-shooter to sort it out. This was an absolute nightmare. It was in much worse shape than what they said. And I was so flattered to be the first woman Dean, I guess I hadn't done enough due diligence. I should have wondered why an academic wasn't taking it on.*
>
> *I was supposed to turn that around, and it was nasty. It affected my reputation because there was a vicious anti-woman group and I got attacked in the press. There was a lot of stuff in the paper that was inexact and some pretty nasty personal stuff. I wondered "why I have I arrived at the end of my career and suddenly have this happen?"*

At the same time Elisabeth had become the first woman to Chair the Society of the Friends of the National Gallery; and she decided to leave her role at the University.

Commercial, cultural, and community boards

After that Elisabeth consciously began to build a portfolio of activities. She went on to the main board of Lehman Brothers and started to look for Non-executive Roles and Chairmanships from that point on.

Today Elisabeth is still on the board at Lehman Brothers, but has a number of community service and cultural chairmanships on her plate allowing her to exploit her "economic plus political" experience.

> *I'm Chairman of the Ersatzschule Council (private schools council) but I represent the private schools to the government. The goal is to change the boards so they are run more like a public company board, to be more efficient. You are a change-agent, a corporate trouble-shooter.*
>
> *I am also chairing the Urban Improvement Council in Hamburg. It's a business improvement program – like they did for Times Square in New York. This is a pilot program in Germany. One of the first programs combining private initiative in economic development, so we are still working on the German model for this. This is a major shift in paradigm in Germany, so I play a role in brainstorming on strategic issues and economic development.*

For Elisabeth there are several essential issues to consider when contemplating doing a portfolio of board work, with independence gained, and structure lost.

There is a difference in having executive and non-executive roles, and if you have to ask how to become an entrepreneur you are probably not meant to. Some people jump out of the corporate structure because they are really meant to be entrepreneurs and then there are others who you might call 'one of life's employees' – if you're one of life's employees you will probably not want to try the non-exec role, you will do a career in business and then once you get to be a certain age you decide that you need a core non–executive structure – so you get a secretary and an office and maintain the corporate structure even then. These may be very senior people, they are very good non-execs but they have never gone the entrepreneurial way and perhaps they don't really think about 'Can I cope with being truly independent? Can I truly cope with hiring and paying for a secretary? Employing and paying for a driver? Having to think about how to do my own IT, and having my own Blackberry?'.

She also discusses the commitment to time. "*When you start something, you spend more time than you think you will. There's always more time up front. I am currently in theory committed to about 3 days a week. That doesn't count the reading and the occasional visit. People would say the* Ersatzschule *Council was 1 day, but I had to fire, hire and restructure, so I was doing three days a week.*"

The Urban Improvement Council in theory half day a week, but I have had to meet everybody, so this has meant a couple of days a week. I may work it down to one day a week but never to a half day. Initially it's much more, then you can structure down.

Lehman Brothers was supposed to be two days a week but in the credit crunch it was 3–4 days a week, plus the travelling. And of course with the additional calls, it's night work. I go to the concert I come home and then the board calls. At Deloitte you're used to juggling. In theory as a non-exec you are in control but in reality if you have three boards in one week, you're not really in control because of all the preparatory work. In fact it is the preparation that takes time, not the meeting itself.

With Lehman Brothers and her other activities she feels she has a balance and wishes to keep it. She is careful not to become pigeonholed as someone who does public policy and pro bono and wishes to continuing doing something more commercial work "*because I have a commercial brain. I like it because it's varied. I wouldn't want to be in a full time job. And I'm married to someone who works even more than I do. He chairs a private school, and the Philharmonic, so he's probably 25% pro bono. If you do it in your own house, you don't take time commuting and people come to you.*"

Elisabeth advises:

Start doing the plurality early. Don't wait until you've finished the full time thing to be plural. First you have to know what you like. You have to find out. It's too late to come to the end of your professional life of full time work and say now what? You must train yourself all the way through, you have to start earlier, even if it is a local school board or a local charity.

She defines retirement as

Giving up. I can't imagine not doing something. And today I get my pleasure from my work.
I get as much opera ballet, theatre as I need. I could spend a bit more time gardening and traveling. It's not a question of dividing up your life between work, family and pleasure, instead you fuse them. What you need is stamina.

Book title: *Shameless Opportunism*

Non-profit board work: what's the difference?

At the heart, the difference between profit and non-profit organizations is purpose – one to make profit and the other to serve a public service (see Table 9.1). Thus, while for profit organizations are accountable to their shareholders and seek to make money, non-profits must use all income for their particular public service. This affects the day-to-day workings of the organization and their boards: non-profit board members are usually not paid and one of the major activities of board is often fund raising. Passion and dedication to a cause often accompanies the choice to do board work in this environment, for depending upon the size of the non-profit group members can also play a direct role in the day-to-day workings of the organization.

Table 9.1 Board work: For profit – not for profit, what's the difference?

For Profit	Not for Profit
Profit making organization	Public service organization
CEO may be on board of directors	CEO usually not on board of directors
Board members may receive payment	Board members are usually unpaid
Privately owned	Publicly owned
Profit distributed to shareholders	Profit used for public served
Corporate management structure	Management of volunteer staff
Business Driven	Passion driven
Roles and time well structured	Hands on, time consuming. role sharing

Being a change agent in another culture

Besides this, the change in culture when working in non-profit organisations and boards is significant. Elisabeth says:

> *"You have to get into the way the people think, because it's different. In this context accountability and the way you value time and effectiveness must be tempered sometimes, because volunteers don't understand this. They have a different agenda."*
>
> *And you have to think about the motivation and then wonder if they are going to be able to cope with doing four or five different things in the day. Can you work in different sequences? Different people, different approaches. One lot with a problem because the scaffolding is falling down and another upset about something else.*

Thus professionals must adapt their skill set and expectations to this culture. That said, executives with experience in industry can provide essential know-how to non-profit groups seeking this type of profile, becoming what Elisabeth calls "change-agents" with the *"goal of changing the boards so they are run more like a public company board, to be more efficient."*

And since the non-profit staff, even managers, do not necessarily have a background in management, mentoring these skills may also be important.

As a result, for Elisabeth, the importance of preparation is essential:

> *Professionals who haven't done other work outside the partnership suddenly say 'I want to be on an arts board but they have never done it before.' They haven't worked their way up. People suddenly realise that they haven't done a school board or a local charity.*
>
> *You have to find out if you really like being on the working side of culture. You might say I love opera but you might not like being on a board where you have politicians, or you might prefer to be on a charity, a fund-raiser, a non-fund raiser. Find out ahead of time. What's it like being on an art's board? What's its like fund raising? You might hate it.*

Being bitten by the bug

But if you don't hate it, a main ingredient for investing in this type of board work is passion or dedication to a cause, so important to Baby Boomers at this stage. One interviewee, Kathryn G. Jackson calls it *being bitten by the bug.* Her first experience on the board of the local public high school was an intense fund raising experience. Today she is the CEO of the Second Harvest Food bank in California, and her comments reflect this passion:

> *It changed the way I thought about where I lived. Am I passionate about this issue? The more I learned the more I got bitten by the bug. To the point that if they hadn't hired me, I probably would have tried to get on the Board.*
>
> *It's the hardest, most complicated, difficult and most satisfying job I've ever had.*

When it starts to feel just like a totally corporate job with too many meetings, I say "Get me out of here" and I go to a food distribution center. I roll up my sleeves and I'm bagging carrots or handing out eggs to hungry people, and they are joyous occasions. I thought it would be grim, actually, but you're giving people food and it doesn't get much more basic than that. I mean it's kind of air, water, food. And people are so appreciative. Also it's a very different work population. Some of the people are very much like people I worked with in financial services, they've got advanced degrees or whatever, but there are a lot of truck drivers and warehouse workers and tens of thousands of volunteers. It's this fascinating community mix. You go out to our warehouse and you see these people bagging food and you might see a group of women wearing head scarves, and they are next to the local high school football team, and they're next to a girl scout group who are next to a corporate group or a group in yamakas. It's fantastic. We provide food and we build community.

10   The business of people

If I had only known, I would have been a locksmith.

Albert Einstein

"Vocational" careers (doctors, psychologists, nurses, teachers, researchers) as well as professionals in private practice (lawyers, architects, freelance professionals) may also wish to remain closely connected to their primary career after transitioning out. Their career patterns will affect this, leaving them with different choices and other motivations, illustrated by Lise Small, a psychoanalyst and Didier Marchal a research scientist and MD.

Board work is a way to remain directly connected to one's primary career while taking on a new role. This provides the stimulation of having to learn new skills and discover other company cultures – or taking a deep dive in the pool of the non-profit world to transfer your skills and give back. But there are other ways to remain closely connected to one's primary career. By consulting, like Loh Meng See and Henri or for our next interviewees, who have had vocational careers, by engaging in bridge work in the same setting by cutting down and making space for the multiple lifestyle.

These next two interviews, one with a physician and research scientist who spent his career in a large government research organization and another with a psychoanalyst working in private clinical practice and as a trainer, present careers in the business of people – treating, teaching and support. In these careers the roles of mentor and giving back have been intrinsically woven into the day-to-day activity. They give us a look at the transition out of the primary career in sectors that we have not yet encountered, in particular university careers and private and public healthcare.

Here, the criteria for success are different. More focused on intellectual and technical skills, in these "vocations" advancement is based on technological progress as well as the contribution made in one's field – in the form of publications, inventions or patents, while those in private practice face the issues of a small business and with retirement, the problem of transferring the clientele or selling before leaving. Like entrepreneurs we find a group that tends not to want to transition out or to do something different at all, but to remain within the same activity as long as possible, slowing down or doing bridge work, with different choices depending on whether they have worked in the public or private sector. These interviews also bring up two important transversal issues of health and learning when preparing for "what's next."

Lise Small: More chocolate chips

Lise Small is an American Psychotherapist who has now lived in France for over 45 years. Her career has been about connectivity – finding the connections between her native US and France, between English teaching and Transactional Analysis, and between her training in different therapies and a new school of thought. When asked about retirement she says: "*I think that having worked at something that I love and feeling that I was lucky enough to have chosen a profession that really suited me, somehow makes me feel that I will manage retirement.*" She did not follow a straight road to become a psychotherapist. She discovered it later, and overcame major obstacles to attain her goal.

> *I really began working as a professional after I divorced. I was an English teacher for adults. At the same time I came in touch with a group of people who were working to establish Transactional Analysis in France. So my first idea was that I would apply TA to teaching. But after that I thought I would teach teachers how to apply it. This was about five years down the road. Finally I decided I wanted to do more in the field and not necessarily continue the teaching of English.*

Lise had multiple challenges: finding a trainer, getting a degree and undergoing psychoanalysis. Although "*no one in their right mind thought that I would ever make it,*" for Lise "*there was never any question, once I had decided that was it, that was it.*" She therefore chose to make to make a major mid-career change to fulfill a desired self and then moved on to a new career, rather than, like Jean Jacques, taking a pause to see what he was capable of.

> *My first obstacle was finding someone who would train me in TA because I didn't have the qualifications. I had several years of college but I didn't have a degree. So I went through a hard process of being turned down (three times!). Finally I went to the Chairman of the training committee and he said come to a workshop and I'll check you out. He did and said ok, fine: but you have to have a Master's degree, have done psychoanalysis and you need to train with me!*
>
> *So I said "great!" and I did it.*
>
> *At the time I continued to teach part time, and as soon as I was able to take clients I did because there is no way you can establish a practice overnight. Meanwhile I was also doing a Master's degree with a school in the US, because the French wouldn't give me credit for my college work and in the US I got credit for college as well as for my experience as a teacher. It took me a while to get the Masters, and I also did five years of Jungian analysis. During that time I was returning to the US from time to time to train with my TA trainer. Everyone said, how in the world do you manage – But I thought there had to be a way.*

And there was. Lise qualified in TA, completed Jungian analysis, did Gestalt training and Body Work. Then she says "*I worked as a simple psychotherapist for a while, for a couple of years. But when I would attend TA conferences and exchange with others it became clear to me that I had something to say and that I wanted to say it.*"

A professional community and a new approach

In a profession where the day-to-day work is face-to-face with clients, Lise understood the importance of contact with colleagues at peer conferences and through membership in associations. These gatherings provide community, continuing education, intellectual feedback and recognition, a platform for expression in the form of presentations and posters as well as avenues of research and ideas to be carried back into therapy to help the client.

For Lise, they also bridged her French and American cultural and professional identities and eventually led her to understand "*what she had to contribute.*"

> *For several years after that I was relatively active in the French TA organization as a link between the French and European associations. I was Vice President of the association. And during that period my trainer, Richard Erskine, began to develop what he was calling Integrative Psychotherapy. So one time when I was back in the States I participated in founding the New York Association of Integrative Psychotherapy.*

With Integrative Psychotherapy, Lise was able work with an approach that allowed her to use all of her training – TA, Gestalt, Jungian and Body Work in her sessions and she found "her subject" in its theoretical foundations, a subject which she has developed and now teaches to future therapists in workshops.

> *At that time I also became very interested in a particular type of developmental psychology which is Daniel Stern's work with the sense of self. It's powerful stuff. It gave me a way of talking about the development of the sense of self without the pathology. In other words, how does this develop normally. Because the descriptions that I had been reading in the Kleinian, Freudian world – Well my babies hadn't been like that! I thought, I don't think these people ever saw a real, normal baby! And I began working on this as my subject.*
>
> *Also early on Stern was very much into relational theory and therapy. Everything is in the relationship and the child structures the self based on what goes on in the relationship. And that is what I teach. This is what I have gotten deeply into and what I do my workshops on now, and I think that is where I can make my contribution.*

Thus Lise's career has included one-on-one work with clients, training and supervising new psychotherapists, active participation in psychotherapeutic organizations and finally helping found and contribute elements to a new school of psychotherapy.

Each of these moves was self-motivating, driven by the feeling that she had something to say, the desire to further understand her clients and her place within the confines of existing schools of thought and her experience. Thus the career was always a road of intellectual and emotional discovery of the self and others, something which Lise sought out and built herself. There was no predefined ladder to climb or external institutional structure to follow and adapt to. Lise's career choice, found mid-career, was a passion and a vocation.

Ramping down and creating structure

Thus, it is not surprising that Lise's retirement has also been self-motivated. Because she is in control of her activity, she can also control the pace and structuring of her retirement process. Because it remains a passion she does not feel a particular need to do something different and there is no corporation or institution forcing her to exit. Despite the age of retirement in France of 62 one can continue to work while on a pension, which is exactly what she has done.

Like those who have founded their own businesses, Lise's investment in her practice was intense: "*I was so involved ... so totally in there ...*" so we find her *gradually cutting down* first by reducing her one-on-one work.

> *There was a time when people called back and wanted long term therapy I would take them. I no longer do that. If it's one or two sessions, that's ok but otherwise I give them a reference.*

Then by increasing her focus on the mentoring roles of teaching and supervising:

> *And at this point I'm doing more supervision and training than therapy. I still have a few patients, but I'm mostly doing supervising. Then last year I did a once a month training group, I've cut that down to 4 times a year and I go to Grenoble to do a training program for a full day.*

Lise has also realized that cutting down is not necessarily enough. Today she has decided to re-structure her activities and organize her time to leave real spaces for other things otherwise she was finding herself "*swept up.*"

She says:

> *Today I am in a real process of saying I am going to put my working days on Tuesday and Thursday and the rest of what I do will have to fit into that. This is hard because I was so involved but having two days a week working is a way of structuring it because otherwise you get swept up.*

For Lise and others with multiple and self-constructed careers this restructuring is essential. It involves introducing space for desired selves into a structure that is in already in place and must be "dismantled." And there may be resistance from others, and ambiguity oneself.

Lise says:

> *The people that I work with to do supervision and training are pushing me. They say, hang in there, stay, don't go yet. We need a couple of more years.*

And even her children are a little resistant to her decision. She says: "*We laugh about it. They say 'why do you want to stop?' 'what are you doing to do'? I think they think that means I'll be old.*"

It also means finding replacements for clients, a delicate task which Lise has "lined up in her head"

> *I thought of people that I can send them on to so that they can continue working in a similar manner. I have lined it up in my head with the people I am training right now. Some people that I have trained are better than I am and they will be fine.*

Lise's motivation to ramp down includes a desire for more freedom (*it's very hard to go off and leave people and when you have put these commitments in place, you're obliged. So I would like to have more freedom*), time, (*I have an image of being able to get up more than several days a week and not have to say. "I have to be ready to go at..." So it's time, just to wander around the house and do things at my own pace. It's the sense of balance that after I have had enough of that time for myself, I can go out and make contact.*) as well as health, an important issue which we have not yet discussed directly, but which was mentioned in several interviews. For Lise, this was a "moving force" to begin the process toward retirement.

The moving force of health

> *I used to have a spectacular memory for my patients. I didn't have to take many notes, it was as if the movie just started to turn again, and several years ago, I suddenly couldn't anymore. There are still pieces, but today I have to take notes. I compensate but it was a very traumatic experience. Because it was so much a part of me, that it made me start thinking about it, it was a moving force to have me think about cutting back.*

This issue evoked the specter of a "negative self" for Lise of "*people out there, dottering around, who have been presenting the same thing for years, and continue. I don't want to become like that. So that made me stop and think.*" This idea is also mentioned in our next interview by Didier Marchal and may be especially pertinent for professions where success is based on one's intellectual capacity and contribution, and where constant renewal of one's knowledge capital is expected: University Professors, Research Scientists, Psychoanalysts, Psychologists, Doctors etc.

In Lise's case, the image of aging is being imposed not by the external word, but by her physical self and must be integrated into her transition out. Her story shows that although the B2-generation will statistically live many years longer than the last generation, when health issues emerge, they can be a major motivation for transitioning out, slowing down and the approach to retirement itself.

For Mike Critelli, for CEO of Pitney Bowes, for example there was a "wake-up call." He says about his final period as CEO: "*It affected my health. I went in for a routine physical and I had a semi-false alarm. They said: There are no symptoms but you have to do a cardiovascular NMRI. You have blockage in multiple arteries we need to go in for an operation on Tuesday. The test wasn't done right, so it was less serious than they thought. I asked a cardiovascular specialist – how could this happen? He said: 'Did you experience a lot of stress in the last year or two? Because this can happen to someone who has a large amount of stress.'*"

An ounce of prevention

For Hank McKinnel and Marv Berenblum, the issue of health cannot wait until you close the door behind you, but like the rest of one's plan should be put into motion while still working in the primary career. But the B2-generation has already begun this. As they moved through their 30s and 40s the fitness culture emerged, because like everything else, they had decided to be in control of their bodies. Today, corporations often have onsite workout rooms or offer subscriptions to gym clubs and yearly check ups. While for medicine this has meant the right to know by having access to medical records as well as a more active participation in "health" – diet, sports, and preventive medicine. Today these healthcare consumers, who monitor their own blood pressure and glucose levels and surf the Internet before going to the doctor, expect to be treated as intelligent partners when it comes to their bodies.

But the opposite is also true. Obesity, diabetes and heart disease which are scourges in the United States, United Kingdom, and Europe that are a direct result of diet, exercise and lifestyle, so the way the boomers will live out these extra years can go either way. For Hank McKinnel, prevention is a key.

Health is very important. You are going to live another thirty or forty years. I feel that one of the solutions to cost control for health is prevention. So I've encouraged a number of people to go to the Mayo Clinic for an annual complete two-day executive health review, for example. This catches the problems early, and you know your own risk factors. Good health is relative as you get older. I am assured that I won't die of cardiovascular disease or cancer because I'm kind of past that, even though I was in the bottom tenth percentile. I was active and I had good genes, I guess. But they put me on Lipidor as a preventive measure. That is what a preventive program does.

Other people who don't exercise, are overweight and smoke would focus on something else. You need to be as proactive about your health as you have been about everything else. Obvious risk factors like inactivity, obesity, diabetes, have to be dealt with. It can make a big difference over a twenty-year period. It is really one of the building blocks to move into the next chapters.

But despite prevention and "doing everything right," which Lise has, one's health is an external factor which may come into play when deciding and organizing the transition out. The issue of age is no longer theoretical but physical. Today Lise is dealing with a difficult problem in her hip and says:

The physical thing is hard, because I've had physical things; but this feels like it might be more defeating and permanent than in the past, and the worst thing is the doctors keep referring to my age!

So that part, I really have to deal with, and once I know exactly what it is, I can begin to deal with it. I've done everything that I should have and it maybe it didn't work. Retirement I am in control of, and that I am not. So it may mean that there are areas where I am not going to have the freedom. Maybe I won't get to India or the Hermitage.

Thus it becomes a question of dosing one's activities, readjusting expectations, and as Mike Critelli advises "*only taking on as much as you can.*"

A multiple structure

With the time and freedom Lise expects to have a full plate, a multiple structure for family, her passions, the business connection and giving back. Her experience as a psychoanalyst gives her an especially keen understanding of the importance of community and relationship in these next stages, and of renewing connections. Her main advice is "*be sure that you are not going to stay isolated. Make sure that you are going to be part of some kind of a group that suits you before you leave.*"

When she reassessed her own priorities she says: "*I realized that the only thing that is important to me is being in contact with people and staying in contact, professional or otherwise.*"

This became the heart of Lise's approach, motivating her to rediscover old friends and deepen contact with others, creating bridges to her bi-cultural, professional and personal selves. This includes

Family both in France and in the US:

I will have more time for the chocolate chips. Because I have only one grandson left in town, and he and I bake chocolate chip cookies and pumpkin pies. I bake. I adore it, I adore cooking, and I want to give more family dinners

and dinners with friends where I'm not just fitting it in. Take the time and do it the way that I like to have it done.

I have been very careful to keep a space for my family. Because what happens is their space gets smaller. My granddaughter is a teenager, who you don't see much of, but we still have a good contact. I had to be available when they were available while my time was taken, so that made it difficult. With my son, it's better we make appointments to meet and that works.

I will also reconnect with my family in the States. I have always gone back, but for short periods. This year I went back and saw my brother and sister and their spouses and I stayed for a long enough time to be able to see people and sit down and really know what was going on. I have son in Chicago, so I need to keep going back and forth there too.

Women friends:

At the AAWE (Association of American Wives of Europeans) group I have some very very close friends. I figure if I have trouble they will be there for me. So what I have been trying to do the last couple of years is keep that connection. Because that group is almost family. And they allowed me to drop off completely when I was so busy, and when I got back in touch they were all very happy. We were thinking of setting up a retirement group together because knowing each other's history makes an enormous difference.

And professional contacts:

There are people I will be very careful to stay connected to. I saw one woman in the profession who was 65 and she cut herself off from everyone. Then she got depressed. Finally she came back and made contact, but it didn't work. Even though she filled her time up with good activities, I wouldn't want to do what she did. It was much too abrupt. And she lost contact with a lot of people she could have stayed in contact with. And I think the people felt offended, so that made it harder.

So there are people that I will definitely remain in contact with, or try to see more often. I have a couple of people I will hold onto for the intellectual stimulation. Because talking to them is stimulating whatever the subject. The person who trained me, for example, is now a long term friend, and another one is a TA person that I got to know over the last 10 years. These are people that would always invite me in if I were in their neck of the woods.

Lise also hopes to be able to make her professional contribution in writing:

Also if I actually have the time to be able to sit in front of the blank page for a whole day, I might get the things that I am teaching written up. I've written a few articles, but I want to write one really good article that shows how applying this approach is not evident, it's not one-two-three. It's something that the therapist has to have, and keep in the back of his/her mind and pull up. It's hard to describe and that's my problem. I can teach it, but I still haven't gotten it down so that it works in written form.

Finally she will make space for her personal passions:

> *If I can get my health under control. I will continue to travel, because I really love traveling. I haven't been to Russia, I haven't been to India. I go with a traveling partner. We've been to the desert in Niger, we went to Jordan. We had to go with a group to Cuba. I want more space for this because for the moment I'm traveling within the school vacations and I want to have more freedom.*
>
> *And I will join a movie group that I have watched jealously for five years. They go to the movies and then they go out and talk about it. Then I will go to all the art exhibits all over Paris.*

Although Lise's career has been about giving back, she has nevertheless looked into volunteering. Like other professionals she is seeking to transfer her skills, wishes to remain flexible and is not willing to stuff envelopes. Her professional network may be able to help her with this,

> *I had an idea of offering my services to the Maison Verte, the Françoise Dolto (French child psychoanalyst) Foundation. I have the qualifications and I said I would come in as a volunteer, but it never went anywhere at all. I realize I need to contact someone who runs one of those, or go through someone I know to find a way in. Because I want to do work at a level that allows me to give back what I have. I think in France, volunteer work is still not what it could be. There's a center down the road, an outpatient hospital for children. But most of the time you have to sign up, and I am not ready to be completely committed. So I have information on volunteer work in France, and I will keep looking into it.*

Today Lise considers herself semi retired and defines retirement as

> *the moment when I no longer have any connection with anyone in the field. And I am no longer attending conferences, which I will probably continue to do for the contact and maintain the connection. But I don't want to lose it completely and I suspect that I could imagine doing it as long as possible and I am motivated and engaged.*

She remains forward-looking:

> *With the Integrative Psychoanalysis we are still in the evaluating process, for example. Two years ago at the meeting in Bled, Slovenia two of the people who had trained with me went through the evaluation and were accepted. This year I have a group that are doing the same thing. And one that is actually going to become a trainer. So there is still much to be done.*

Book Title: *Taking Steps One by One.*

> *Each of the people I worked with I worked with one by one. I didn't work with patients I worked with individuals. It's also a philosophy, it means that when something looks too big you deal with it in steps, one by one.*

Lise's final choice involves questions and solutions that can apply to other independent professions: lawyers, doctor's in private practice and freelance web designers, architects, or translators for example. Like small business owners, there is total implication in the primary business because this has been self-created and owned. The decisions involve how and when to slow down, readjust one's working patterns, and transfer the business or clientele to others.

Didier Marchal our next interviewee, is also in the business of people. However, as a doctor in a large public research institute his career advancement and retirement choices have been structured by the organization and his motivation to is to continue learning.

Didier Marchal: My life as a research scientist

Didier Marchal is an MD, specialist in hepatology and Director of Research at INSERM, (*Institut Nationale pour la Recherche Medicale*). He spent his career at Hôpital Beaujon, a public hospital in the Paris area, treating patients, doing research and teaching.

Didier did not enter his career with the idea of it being a vocation because he says

> *"I didn't know what I was getting into. When I first started my studies no one in my family had ever studied medicine. I chose hepatology after studying nephrology and pulmonary medicine because I realized that this was what I was interested in. I wanted to be a surgeon at first, but I discovered that didn't really interest me, and I worked as a GP in the country as a replacement, but that didn't do it for me either."*

Thanks to his contact with people he met during his different residencies *"who were doing fascinating and stimulating work"* and his mentor Dr. Jean Pierre Benhamou, Didier entered and continued his career at INSERM, a public research institution created in 1964 to do basic, therapeutic, diagnostic and public health research with more than 6000 researchers. A career which became a stepping stone for Chai's entrepreneurial work, but in which Didier found his place, because *it excited him to understand.*

Like Jean Jacques and other early Boomers, Didier spent his career during a golden age of research, in a new institute where there was a lot happening and there was funding.

Didier says *"when I started working in liver disease, they didn't know anything at all. There were no treatments. During my career they identified and can now treat Hepatitis B and C, control liver cancer better and diagnose and treat severe liver disease. The progress during my career has been enormous."*

He decided to work on the hemodynamics of liver disease to understand the vascular complications associated with this disease.

> *What excited me about research was trying to understand different causes and applying physics, because physics was a subject that I was very interested in. When*

you study hemodynamics, blood flow, pressure, resistance etc it's all about physics. It was a pathophysiological approach to liver disease.

Didier made his contribution to this progress in 1984.

I discovered that there were vascular anomalies in people with liver disease, which were unknown at the time, because everyone thought this was normal. Then I discovered a treatment to prevent these complications.

He also helped refine a biopsy technique to obtain biopsies in severely ill patients, making research, diagnosis and treatment possible.

As a result Didier has more than 400 publications and became one of the international leaders in his field, heading the French, European and International Associations for the Study of the Liver at different points and lecturing all over the world at International meetings and hospitals in the US, Europe and Asia. Didier's commitment went beyond the confines of France and his lab and he used his different roles as a platform to promote research in his field: *"I worked very hard at promoting European research during my time at the EASL and as Editor of the Journal of Hepatology so that there would be high level scientific research in our field in Europe, because for me this was a part of building the European Union."*

At the end of his career Didier was Director of his own lab at INSERM.

The lab works on the hemodynamics of the liver. We do basic research and clinical research so we see patients and perform clinical studies to identify the causes of liver disease and try to find solutions. Research fellows come from all over the world to study with me for a year or two, it's very cosmopolitan. You might have a Japanese fellow and someone from Poland and Canada at the same time. They do post-doctorate work on one of our basic research projects, publish a research paper, and work alongside French interns on clinical projects in the hospital.

Like Lise, Didier did not look to transition out of his career instead,

I asked to stay an extra year because you are supposed to retire at 65, and legally I was able to do that. I didn't want to stop early because I had too much going on. I had studies I wanted to finish before I left and I had things to finish in the laboratory. This gave me the time to reduce my activity in the lab and to find people to replace me. I found two replacements, one person to head the basic research lab, and the other the clinical lab. This was very important to me.

Thus, both Didier and Lise have not sought to transition out early or do something different but have managed, on the contrary, to continue working beyond the traditional retirement age, and continue to work closely within their fields.

And they are not alone. Indeed in one study in doctors 60 or older, 56 percent won't quit until at least 70.[1] If they are in private practice this can be possible, like Lise, by ramping down or selling one's practice. Even those who do leave intend to stay active in medicine, through volunteering abroad with Doctors without Borders for example, and writing or lecturing on medical subjects. For professors in other subjects in the university setting, emeritus status exists, entitling them to access to university facilities and sometimes an office.

Today Didier is going to be 66, has recently transitioned out and

> *has organized it so that he can have a scientific or medical activity now and for several years. I'll be continuing my clinical activity part time for at least two years – seeing patients, organizing study protocols, working with younger doctors for clinical studies to help them to do medical research. I will be helping them with their study protocols, analyzing their results and to write and publish their articles.*
>
> *I've been Editor in chief for the Hepatology section of the European Journal of Hepatogastroenterology for the past two years and I'm going to continue that. This takes about a half a day per week and it allows me to keep up with what other centers are doing.*
>
> *Also, I may be invited to hospitals in other countries to teach transjugular biopsies to other doctors. I've done more than 10,000 of them, probably more than anyone else in the world. That experience doesn't disappear.*

Didier is clear about what he will miss and why he wants to continue:

> *The way a laboratory works is that you have a Director and full time researchers and technicians, then masters and doctoral students who come to study with you. So you are constantly learning things, not only because of what you do, but from the input of these different scientists. There are discussions at least once a week in the lab meeting about the progress people are making, the difficulties they're having, new results. You develop new ideas and new directions thanks to these exchanges. It's the same when you attend scientific meetings. You come in contact with everything that's out there, all of the new research. Because that's what I'm most interested in, to continue learning.*

Continued learning

As we have seen for several other interviewees, the transition out may require learning new skills: knowledge of board work and practices, a seminar on investing in start-ups or interior design for Carole and for Eric Christin's training as an International Arbitrator. Didier's career has been based on the pursuit of knowledge and learning, and this is what he will miss most and is seeking to maintain by continuing his bridge work. His continued work as an editor and with younger scientists mean that he will be able to (and must) continue to attend staff meetings at his hospital and the most important medical meetings in his field, because this is the only way to keep up to date.

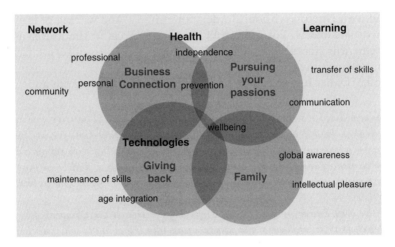

Figure 10.1   **What's next? Transversal activities**

Like Lise, Didier's wish is to remain within the professional community where he spent his career and continue his activities. But unlike those in private practice, researchers such as Didier or those in the University are not in complete control of the situation. While Lise was able to retire and maintain her clientele and activities, there is a retirement age in France and other countries for learning, research and healthcare institutions (as well as companies) which Didier was able to extend, but this has its limits. In the US in universities and elsewhere, fixed retirement has been discontinued. Despite the possibility of emeritus status, Didier and others who remain within the same structure and merely reduce their activities must confront the negative possible self of the "dottering professor" mentioned by Lise, and the pressures in the University setting of younger colleagues wishing to get ahead may become an issue. Moreover, although the study on bridgework showed that it was a highly advantageous way of downshifting gradually from high gear to the next, there were disadvantages including a feeling of loss of status and being out of the loop.[2] Nevertheless this solution also allows these professionals to get back to the heart of their profession – teaching, consulting or research work, to continue the all-important intellectual pursuit of learning, and also when the situation permits, to play the satisfying role of mentor.

Didier is keenly aware of this shelf life. He says:

In France you are not allowed to be a Laboratory Director after a certain age. And without that you become isolated, so you have to think about that, and prepare for stopping your clinical and research activity. You have to because gradually you will no longer really know what's going on. You won't be on the leading edge, so you have to stop. You become a spectator rather than an actor in the research world. I know that will happen but not exactly when.

The necessity of "keeping up to date" can involve many professions: dentists, lawyers psychologists or software engineers, and may be important if they intend to remain in their field while cutting down (see Figure 10.1). For others such as those in teaching, it may be necessary to keep a certificate, or for some like Kathleen Flaherty, it fulfills a life long ambition to obtain a first, second or third degree. Those who wish to pursue their passions or write a book must aquire the basic training this entails. Moreover, for anyone transitioning out there is a continuous learning process to remain up to date with advancing communication and information technologies. Continued learning remains an important means of placing oneself in age integrated situations, of coming in contact with others in the community, of intellectual stimulation and of breaking the ceiling of age.

Besides his work, Didier will dedicate more time to family who live close by and to his passions.

I'd like to spend more time with my grandchildren. I'll take them on Wednesdays sometimes, and for vacations. Then I'll try and see my mother more. She's 92 and lives close by so I will take the time and see her more.

I'll continue jogging and I'm going to learn golf which requires a lot of concentration. I played years ago with my father, but had to give it up because of time. First I want to take lessons to get back the basics, otherwise it's no fun. We also have two gardens which I created with my wife, and I will continue doing that and I hunt on weekends from October–January.

Didier also would like to attend conferences in History "*to try and understand how we have reached the point we have and why we approach things the way we do. Because for this you have to understand the past.*"

Finally Didier has an idea for giving back that he would like to develop which highlights the change in the doctor-patient relationship because of the expectations of aging Baby Boomers: their desire to remain in control even in the face of illness and to be treated as a whole person even in this setting.

As doctors we see people suffer and die on a daily basis. We have an intimate knowledge of illness. This gives us a special understanding of human suffering and I thought I might be able to do something with this. Work in palliative care as a volunteer for example, or in other wards with doctors.

Because of our special understanding of disease, we also have a special relationship and understanding of the patient which we could use to give support to the family. The difficulty of explaining to people that their spouse/father/child is very ill and is going to die is enormous. Doctor-patient relationships are very complicated and doctors don't really get training for that. You learn by doing, and it might be interesting to transmit this. Younger doctors need help with this because they don't learn it in medical school and it is something that is lacking. I think that patients are very unhappy in the hospital, because even if they're well taken care of from a medical point of view the medical contact is not 'human' enough. This is very complex because as university hospital doctors our goal is to take care of the patients. We are highly specialized and there is not enough contact with the patients, and they suffer from this. Perhaps I could be a bridge in this, but it's just an idea.

Didier advises:

You really have to prepare yourself, and do it progressively. You can't do it all at once, especially if you have been totally invested intellectually in what you do. I've been doing this for 35 years plus ten years of studies, so it's much more than half of my life and you can't just stop at all once, unless it wasn't important to you, or you weren't really invested, which is not my case. It should be progressive if possible.

Book Title: *Chercher pour comprendre* [Searching to Understand].

11 The boys and the girls, east and west

Health, continued learning and the network are transversal issues which affect and shape one's transition out. The vertical issues of gender and culture may also affect the career experience and the process out, but how? Women have entered the workforce massively since World War II and they will now be transitioning out. Will this process be different between men and women, between the United States, Europe and Asians? Interviews are presented of two women, Kathryn G. Jackson and Siew Hua Lim.

Kathryn G. Jackson's story is an appropriate starting point to take a look at several elements that seem to mark the difference between men and women in retirement. Like many other women in our book, she took initiatives throughout her career to craft some flexibility into her working structure, often to adapt to growing children, and which also in the end affected her transition out. Other women felt that they had to give everything to their career and may not have children at all. Thus in the first part of this chapter we will look at differences which appear in the career patterns of women in East Asian and Western cultures, then see how these might affect the transition out of the primary career for men and women.

Kathryn G. Jackson: Planes, trains and automobiles

After 23 years in asset based financial services for transportation, Kathy sometimes jokes and says she *financed planes, trains and automobiles*. She was with several different companies, in particular GATX Capital where she worked twice, saying *I seemed to have a seven year itch problem with committing to a single employer.* In between her stints with GATX, she worked for D'Accord Financial Services, a speciality advisor to railroads and airlines. When she returned to GATX after D'Accord, it was as Executive Vice President and on their board. She remained for eight years. She worked with the company to adapt her schedule to be more present for her family and in the last period with GATX had negotiated a four-day work week, with Wednesdays off.

> *What happened to GATX and caused me finally to leave was the financial after-math of 9/11. The company had a very diversified approach to business, which works out well unless all of your markets tank at one time. After 9/11, aircraft was a very bad place to be invested. Computer assets had had a boom around the Y2K issue, then financing demand slid dramatically and the bubble burst on venture lending in Silicon Valley. The economy was basically soft. GATX reached the point where they couldn't fund themselves reliably which made it tough to be effective as a financial services company.*

Kathy struggled to know what to do, and finally convinced the company to let her take a six month sabbatical motivated by the company's situation and her family.

> *My son was probably about 12 at the time and my daughter was 9 and it felt like it might make sense to be at home, since I was not doing much good at work. GATX did not have a sabbatical policy, but I said "Heh guys, I am not being very effective here and can't really help with what's going on. However I have a few things at home I would like to focus on." They were very gracious about it.*

She fully expected to return to GATX, but after declining a job as CEO in one company she went to Bank of America, and in a situation that allowed her to be even more fully present for her family.

> *We ended up crafting a job at BofA which was extraordinary. I was Managing Director and I worked from 7.30 am–2.30 am. Part of the reason I had decided I didn't want a CEO position was that I wanted to spend more time with my kids. They were entering what seemed like interesting territory age-wise and I felt lucky that no one had gone off the beam at that point.*

Resisting the final temptation

Despite this she only stayed for a year and a half because of the "culture" and deep down, because she was ready to resist the final tempting.

> *At BofA there had been so many acquisitions, so may skin sheddings, that it was a 'survivor culture'. At my former employers, the team was collaborative and the envi-ronment was supportive. But at the Bank, when I would suggest helping someone with a contact, the person would say Why??? So I found the environment very unsatisfying.*
>
> *The last straw came when BofA decided to acquire Fleet Bank Boston which resulted in two very large leasing companies coming together. The CEO at Fleet Bank took the lead in the merger and he made three quick choices. He hired his own general counsel, his own head of risk management and his own CFO, all men from the East Coast.*

For the next hire, they offered me (the first woman, the first line manager, and the first person from the West Coast) a senior position and after some real soul searching, I said no. That was the final temptation. I was done, I was ready to leave. That was about 2004.

Kathy had been preparing for this without preparing. Looking back she remembers a hiking trip she took with a group of women friends and a moment of epiphany:

I went on the first of what became annual hikes when I was six months into BofA and it was just beginning to dawn on me that maybe this position was not a match for me. We hiked around Mont Blanc. Somewhere in the course of walking around that mountain I realized, 'I'm going to move'. I didn't know when or how but I knew this was my last stop in financial services. I knew I was near the end of this road. And it was blindingly clear at the top of that mountain. By the time of the next year's trip I had left BofA. And it was important to me to arrive back to the second trip with my friends having made that change, because it had truly been an epiphany for me.

Although Kathy left BofA with no idea of what she was going to do, as others have mentioned, she doesn't really think you can plan.

When you are working full time, you are so busy you have no bandwidth. You think the missing ingredient is time and space but when you have the time and space its not like a light bulb clicks on. There's some critical chemistry that comes with the passage of time and baking and thinking and talking to people.

Interestingly, like Soek King she closed the door tightly behind her, to prevent from getting "sucked back in."

The one thing I might do differently is to stay connected. I really closed the door and padlocked it behind my financial services career, even though there were many people I really appreciated from that phase of my life. I think that I was secretly worried that I would get sucked back in, like I had gotten lured back in to BofA. I thought I was vulnerable to that and the only way I could make sure that didn't happen was to say, I'm out of here, good-by, syonara, close the door and lock it.

Initially Kathy planned on doing some for-profit board work. When this didn't work out, although she was a little disappointed professionally she found that she was very happy personally.

I loved having the time to be with my kids and getting to know them again. I got to reconnect with a lot of friends. Then I got involved on the fund raising board at the public high school, the Foundation for the Future, where I served as Board President for two years. That was a fabulous experience. My son was 15 and my daughter was 12 and both of my kids had gone to public school. The public high school in this area is extraordinarily diverse ethnically, socioeconomically, and scholastically. There is a huge population of English as a Second Language students, then AP honors-tracked kids. There are very wealthy kids and dreadfully poor kids. The school is 42% White 42% Hispanic and includes various other ethnic groups.

Doing the board work with the foundation for ten–20 hours a week I got to test out how certain lessons I'd learned in the for-profit sector worked or didn't work in the non-profit sector. I didn't think I was building a bridge to anything else and I really felt like I was retired. I had severed all ties with the financial services industry when I left, but my colleagues didn't believe it. They figured I'd last 3–6 months without working. But they didn't get it. That didn't mean that I would never ever do something again, but I was sure it wouldn't be in asset based financing.

Being in the moment

It was fun. I was very engaged and pretty happy until the fall of 2008, when my son went off to college and the financial crash occurred. We were fund raising for the Foundation at that time, so we were very busy and my daughter was a sophomore in high schoolBut by February 2009 we were breathing again at the Foundation. The bulk of the funding was done, we had confidence we were going to survive, and I woke up one morning and thought: I think I'm bored.

I was in the 2nd year as President of the Board. I felt like I could do the job with my eyes closed, it wasn't new and exciting, both of my kids were fairly settled, and I thought: Oh my God, what do I do now? Up until then I was really in the moment, but at that point I had a crisis of confidence. I thought: I don't know what I want to do, I don't know if anyone would even hire me, I've been out of work for more than four years and I'm kind of old.

Kathy says she went through several months of being very unsure and unhappy. In this situation and as we shall see throughout her transitions, she turned to "a group of women friends" an approach which was a grounding for many of her decisions.

The next chapter group

About three or four years ago I started getting together with five women in a group that we originally called "the next chapter group." We later renamed it 3C the "Caucus for Creative Change," so I am a founding member of 3C! There are six of us now, and we get together once a month. We are all in our fifties. We've all had successful careers, all have kids pretty much grown, and are all feeling somewhat unsettled in some element of our life, personally or professionally. We just get together, sit around the table, have a couple of bottles of wine and a meal and share.

I went to one meeting around that time and said: I don't think I know how to do this, I think I may have to go back to work. I remember they all just looked at me and said how can you possibly be as undone as you seem to be? Then one of the women mentioned a career coach she had seen speak at a forum. She said he was a little bit different, kind of provocative and she dug out his name.

I sent him an email. He will only meet with people for three times maximum – he's an intervention guy. He said ok, so I figured that meant I might be salvageable, and I went.

Through this experience Kathy learned more based on what didn't feel right then what did, and by resisting someone else's agenda until she could finally write her own.

Don't even go there

One of the very first things he said to me was "Oh my God, you would be an incredible Executive Director or CEO of a non-profit." I said "No way, don't even go there. I don't do spread sheets, I don't lick stamps..." because my experience was based on the Foundation where the ED had to do a lot of the administrative tasks.

I also figured nobody would ever hire me anyway because I came out of financial services. At that point having financial services on your resumé was like having a toxic waste dump on your résumé. I did think about whether I wanted to go back to financial services for a minute, but it only took a minute. If I didn't like it back then, I figured I'd find it a lot uglier now.

So we did major brainstorming and a lot of it didn't feel right to me. In fact, the coach had an agenda that "by the time you were fifty you'd better not be working for someone else." He felt that "the future is in crafting your own gig, that way you can't get fired and you can't get downsized."

We are reminded of Pat Russo when Kathy says: "*But I'm not an entrepreneur, I'm a good intrapreneur. I am good at starting businesses within a structure.*" As a result the sessions were unsettling but revealing.

So I would leave the session thinking I had to find a business to start. But then I found myself waking up in the middle of the night – not in the way the coach hoped I would, full of enthusiasm – I was waking up full of anxiety, like when you have those dreams that you show up at school in your underwear and you didn't know there was a test ... I thought, this is horrible! This is obviously a sign that this is not what I am supposed to do.

Kathy listened to the signs, and finally took a second look at the idea of a non-profit role, but at a level that would not include licking stamps and would in fact allow her to transfer her skills.

In the end the coach really helped me with two things. He validated "you do not project old," so get over that. That was very helpful. The second thing was the idea of non-profit work. I said "Do you think anyone would really hire me for that?" He was also helpful there. He said many wouldn't, and the only ones that would are those that are actually run like a business and that need someone who can bring your type of expertise to the table. So that was a helpful observation.

Testing it out and getting hooked

I decided to test it out. A friend told me that Second Harvest Food Bank was looking for a CEO. And in fact they were kind of looking for someone like me. They'd had an interim CEO who was fantastic, for a year but he wasn't interest in the long term role. The Board was very cautious. They had ultimately concluded that they needed someone with a strong business background who was also a strong communicator and leader. They'd decided that the business background was important because you can learn about food banking but not the rest. So I worked my way up through the interviews. And the more I learned about the organization and frankly the more I learned about hunger in our two counties (essentially Silicon Valley), the more I got hooked.

The amount of hunger in one of the wealthiest areas in the world is astounding. We estimate that one in four people in these two counties is at risk for hunger. That doesn't mean that they are actually starving. The state of California estimates how much it costs for a family of four with two working parents to make ends meet in every county of the state. In our county it costs 86 000 USD to make ends meet, so one in four local families is getting by on half or less of that amount. If you are living on half of that you are at risk of hunger, it's that simple.

Kathy *got the nod* for the CEO job, taking a *real deep dive into the pool* after four years of not working and many other years of flexibility.

This was a CEO of an organization of about 110 employees, a 70 million dollar revenue business and majorly full time. My daughter was just starting her junior year in high school. She was frustrated and disappointed when I essentially disappeared into the Food Bank because she was used to having me around, and liked it. But you don't time these things. It probably happened a year or so earlier than would have been ideal. It was perfect from an intellectual and personal point of view, but from a life position and family point of view it was not. But these opportunities don't come around every five minutes. So you have to jump when it feels right. I kind of felt like Jack Horner sticking his thumb in the pie and pulling out a plum! It just felt right.

Today, Kathy is CEO of Second Harvest Food Bank for Santa Clara and San Mateo Counties, *"more than full time,"* participates in a Mother-Daughter book club and meets with the 3C group. She has also explored the world of microfinancing in her area with a women's group called WAM (women around microfinancing). When she has more time she says she might work on their board as an *extracurricular activity, because it's fun.*

Woman in the workplace from East to West

The affect of the women's movement on working patterns is evident. Freed from the obligations of childbearing with the technological advances of accessible birth control, these second wave feminists have broken ground for the next generations X and Y. Kathy has had a full and varied career and was able to negotiate a flexible schedule to improve the work-life balance at each step. This was not true of all of the women interviewed, but working women have become the norm during this period in Western countries and has increased rapidly in the highly developed economies of East Asia (70 percent of East Asian women are in paid work, nearly half the work force in Japan is made up of women).[1] Nevertheless, the presence of women at the managerial level remains rare in most Asian countries (often 10 percent or less, with Japan at 1.4%) compared to 42.5 percent of women in the US.[2]

The juggling game

Because of this the Asian women we interviewed are truly exceptional – a first generation of professionals having to juggle with the culture clash between traditional collectivistic, male dominant, family oriented values and the more individualistic Western values of the work place. As we saw in the chapter on family, the cultural concept of filial piety entails obligations, especially for women, which are very different from those in Western countries, and this relationship with family is intimately linked to the change in women's roles and her approach to work. Although we saw that this is evolving, a study on the relationship between work and family in managerial women in China, Hong Kong, and Singapore in 2005 showed that the dominant family type among the participants was still one in which parents lived with their children or children co-habited with their parents, described by one participant in the study as the "family dynasty system."[3]

While Anglo-American cultures tend to separate the domains of work and home, Asian women in global cities seem to perceive the domains of work and family/life as fluid and interdependent so they may find themselves completely responsible for both domains.

This collectivistic vs individualistic foundation also affects the motivation and purpose for working, and the ability to invest in the career itself. For example, it is acceptable for family time to be sacrificed for work in Chinese culture for this is seen to be beneficial to the family or a short-term cost incurred to gain long-term benefits.[4] Thus the daughters/professional women in these Asian countries may be expected go to work to earn money, while their mothers and mothers-in-law, sometimes working with domestic help, take over the childcare and daily household chores. Loh Meng See mentions this: "*my wife helps look after the grandchildren because my daughter works. Both grandmothers look after the grandchildren. Now I share that – we have two grandsons, so I am there as a role model.*" However at the same time, as in Japan, this remains ambiguous because there may also be an expectation for women to return to the home once they have children – creating an obvious dilemma if they wish to invest seriously in their careers.

Our next interviewee Siew Hua Lim, adapted her career choices to her family obligations. One senses the movement of a pendulum in her career: the pull and push of satisfying her ambitions to reach peaks in her career and her desire and obligations to be present for children and family. The weight of these two extremes is more evident in this story with a pattern of having to make difficult decisions, entailing several moves out of the work force rather than the flexibility which Kathy was able to find. Siew Hua says each step was only possible because she *let go* and today her children are taken care of and she is able to pursue other undeveloped potential selves because: "*This time I feel I have the freedom.*"

Siew Hua Lim. Letting go

Siew Hua name means Autumn Splendor. Siew Hua feels "*that there are seasons in life, and the retirement season is autumn, more mellow, with lots of colors and a chance to take more risks and do different things. It is also a time for harvesting.*"

Siew Hua studied engineering "*because we were streamed into the sciences and I didn't want to teach*" and because it was a "*challenge for a woman.*" She then worked for the Singapore government for several years to pay back her scholarship. Five years later however, she looked around at what others ahead of her were doing in this field and she *decided to move out of engineering.* She was able to go and do an MBA at UCLA, realized that she really liked the financial sector and began working in investment banking.

We are reminded of Chai Patel's description of merchant banking when Siew Hua speaks of her first position in this sector. She says "*it was called merchant banking then in Asia, while in the US it was called investment banking. There was a difference between the two but we all became investment bankers because of the influence of the US system. Many of our clients said they preferred merchant bankers. They felt there was a relationship with them when we were merchant bankers. The style was quite different. Investment banking was about products and transactions.*"

Surprising decisions

Siew Hua's choice-making came very early in her career, where she made a challenging and for some surprising decision. Surprising perhaps because she chose to be outside of the support net of family and alone with a very young child to advance in her career. Her husband's support was central to this.

During this early period I was given a chance to go to London. This was a big decision because I had a ten-month old child. They said "we would like to send you to the head office, it would be great for your career, but we know you have a child so it's up to you."

So I thought about it. My husband has always been very supportive of my career, without that I don't think I could have gone as far as I have. I decided and said if I could bring my nanny along under my work permit, then I would go. The bank arranged for that. My husband flew to see us often but it was a struggle. A lot of people were surprised I did that. The job was challenging enough without a nanny and a 1-year old child! But I enjoyed my time, and did well.

The change from merchant to investment banking changed the job itself. Thus in her mid-40s, Siew Hua made another very difficult decision and left investment banking because of intensive traveling and her children.

In investment banking, the way we did work was different. We needed big deals so it was always outside of Singapore. I was traveling constantly. I decided that my children were growing up and I wanted to spend time with them. I couldn't see any way to reduce traveling and stay in investment banking.

Her employer tried to convince her to stay, saying they would adapt and she would not have to travel, but Siew Hua knew that *"the client would never accept this. And I didn't want to end up in the back office."*

Her plan was to take a year off *"but two months into my time off an investment banking client called me and offered me a job. I refused, but he persuaded me to work on one project as an advisor. My husband was surprised – I was supposed to take a year off and two months later I was working again!"*

The collaboration with this company lasted until 2009 where Siew Hua Lim held various positions of increasing responsibility, allowing her to pursue new avenues each time and with her boss finding solutions along the way. She took another break before her final transition out.

First Siew Hua Lim changed sides and became the in-house investment banker for this large Asian conglomerate. She set up their corporate office in steered the company through the Asian financial crisis and worked on internal strategy and policy.

After I had been on the job for five years when everything was back to normal and the group was expanding to China, I told my boss that I thought that I had finished what I had set out to do. I wanted to take another break because of my children. Because they both wanted to go overseas and they both wanted to go to boarding school. I wanted to spend some time with them before they both left. That was what motivated me. That time I really took a year off.

Once her son had left for boarding school, Siew Hua thought – *"I can travel now, I don't have to be home every night."* She planned go to Shanghai on her own, but her boss again made her a proposal.

I thought I would like to live in Shanghai and planned to do a three-month business Mandarin course there first, but my former boss heard about it and called me and said "what are you doing that for?" and he made me a proposal. He had just acquired a business in Brazil and begun a greenfield business in China. He wanted to place the headquarters in Shanghai, China. He said "you can go and head this business group for me and set up the headquarters. You will learn business Mandarin very quickly."

Siew Hua went to Shanghai for three years, completely building a business this time, getting to travel to Brazil and truly learn about the culture, until, she once again returned to Singapore for her children.

After three years in China, my son had to come back to Singapore for two years of National Service and I wanted to be home for him. So I returned to Singapore and managed from there. I had built a team. I took on a position as Non-Executive Deputy Chairman, then Chairman.

Making a clean break

Siew Hua finally left for good in December 2009 saying: "*I decided to give myself a chance and make a clean break. I thought if I didn't step away I'd be drawn back in. I agreed to have them call me for a few meetings, but that was it.*"

We remember Soek King and Kathy's comment: "*I really sort of closed the door, padlocked it behind my financial services career .... I think that I was secretly worried that I would get sucked back in, that I was vulnerable to that.*"

The solution in these cases was a "clean break" closing the door and building a wall to avoid being sucked back in. Although this solves the immediate problem, it carries the risk of becoming isolated – losing the initial window of opportunity and making possible re-entry more difficult. As Kathy says "*I will say that that was part of what led to my feeling of groundlessness when I started to think of what I wanted to do. I hadn't talked to some people in four years. I had made no effort to maintain those relationships.*"

This emphasizes the importance of being aware of this window and unless the change is being made into something totally different like Carole who also made a clean break, judiciously managing one's network. Kathy's advice is: "*So today I don't have thousands of contacts but I have a baseline groundwork in that regard. I would try to maintain that. That is what I would change, just having maintained a little more of that network.*"

For Siew Hua this period is truly seen as a chance to explore new territory – She, like Soek King centered herself in the early days by exploring meditation and religion, a way of taking stock similar to Marv's self assessment, then pursued her new directions.

Finding freedom

This is a time I feel I have the freedom. My children have grown up, the nest is empty. I want to do something before my energy runs out. This is the time I've been waiting for. First I wanted to take some time off and think carefully. I had always wanted to spend some time meditating. I like reading and pondering. So I began to read books on that and today I go on Christian mediation retreats when I can.

I wanted to do something entrepreneurial, something from scratch and began looking into Angel Investing to bring more entrepreneurship into Singapore. I started investing in start-ups and mentoring entrepreneurs.

I'm also involved in social entrepreneurship which helps developing countries and communities in Vietnam and Thailand, for example come up with sustainable and self funding businesses.

Siew Hua is also a reader of Carl Jung and she says:

The second half of my life must be different from the first half because this is how you enrich yourself. We have attained success, now we must do something significant and establish a legacy.

If I had not let go of my comfort zone (e.g., a stable but unstimulating engineering career), I would not have been able to embrace the new opportunities of investment banking. If I had clung onto my previous career peak, I would not have taken the risk of scaling new peaks. My daughter who is a serious dancer says she controls her body during practice but once it is trained she must trust it enough to let go when performing on stage. A line from the Black Swan movie trailer resonated the same truth: 'Perfection is not just about control, it's also letting go. Surprise yourself. Surprise others.' I believe the ultimate in life is attained not by accumulating more but by letting go of excess baggage.

Book Title: *Letting Go.*

The signs of change

In our interviews, some signs of change were evident. Both Asian and Western women mentioned the support of their spouse during the career, which especially in Asia, represents a major shift from a male dominated social structure in which the traditional role of women is subordinate and family-centered. Spouse support remains absolutely essential in these countries, in which a high level career remains exceptional for women and in which child-care structures are limited.

Kathy, Carole, Lise, and others in the US mention the support of women friends in more or less organized groups. In fact, Kathy's advice and Lise's is all about connectivity with friends and former colleagues and these relationships represent a veritable grounding for both during their transition. Kathy says:

These groups of women friends have been incredibly helpful and supportive. The hiking group is a very diverse group of vibrant intelligent women. They'll poke a fork in you. It's a reality check. I feel really glad to have a couple of these groups to keep me grounded.

Our Asian interviewees mention helping women and serving as mentors showing an awareness of their importance as role models in this still uncharted territory. Siaou Sze, former Manageing Director at Hewlitt Packard says *"In Shanghai I'm helping younger female executives so that they can plan. I tell them to find non-profit board work. There's a Women Director's chapter so that they can start thinking about getting involved in non-profit organizations."* They do not specifically speak of groups of women friends, which may also exist, but the strong, extended family connection may also serve this role.

And our Asian interviewees seem well aware of their transitional situation. Soek King says *"I have taken care of my parents, and I will take care of my children, but I do not expect them to take care of me,"* implying a profound shift in what is expected for retirement by these women.

Early vs late boomers and men

Besides these underlying cultural differences, we found that the approach of the women at these high levels may also vary according to whether they are early or late boomers and perhaps by field. Kathleen Flaherty who worked

---

Women and board work

This chapter would be incomplete without mentioning differences in access to board work. Although both men and women we interviewed have successfully taken on board work, women are statistically at a disadvantage.

Women hold about:

–15% of Fortune 500 board seats
–12% of board seats in the top 300 European companies,
–9% of board seats in Australia,
–1.8% of board seats in Asia.

Called the 'bamboo ceiling' in Japan, because it "bends but does not break," many forces are working to bring about change in this domain:[5]

Numerous studies have been performed confirming the existence of this phenomenon and its consequences and the financial crisis has served to push the problem of diversity to the top of the agenda and into the media.
There is a general awareness that replacing the buddy system for finding board members and improving diversity (gender and ethnic) on a board will bring different skills, expertise and points of view to the table and result in solutions that are better adapted to a global economy.

Diversity has also entered the political arena. In 2003 Norway became the forerunner requiring representation of women on boards of at least 40%. This has now been achieved. Spain, Netherlands and France have since passed similar laws.

in technology states, "*I was someone who gave up everything for my career, because there was really no other choice if you wanted to succeed.*" Patricia Hewitt, an early Baby Boomer (1948), confirms this:

> *Where I was partly wrong is that women, especially highly educated women have found it more difficult than expected to change their pattern of work within organisations. High performing women do 24/7 and bring in vast amounts of child care and occasionally have a husband who participates. They adapt to the system.*

At the same time we find Kathy a later boomer (1955) seeking and obtaining flexibility to adapt to growing children, negotiating sabbaticals and time off, and Siew Hua completely changing fields for this reason. Elisabeth Brenner-Salz observed this in her career:

> *I did a lot of work on women economists and lawyers and observed that women would get to the point where they could be partner, prove they could do it and they would opt out, either to have children or to do something else. They just needed the achievement and recognition, but they didn't need the rest of it. I always say it was the luxury of choice because most of them had partners who were working and it was acceptable for them to opt out but not for their partners in those days. What I found was that the women drop out in eight–ten years in droves and I suspect that the corporate world is catching up.*

None of the women we interviewed dropped out, they played by the rules or operated change from within. And this was not limited to women. Another of our male interviewees also took the initiative to transition out, at 42, eventually finding his way back to another "full time" position. Patricia Hewitt mentions this also: "*But then what you also see are younger men saying I don't want to do that. You see the pattern of 20–5 years full up and then change.*" Nevertheless, there is still a feeling expressed by several interviewees that flexibility, sabbaticals and moves in and out of the work force have become *more acceptable* for women while *most men would not do that or have the luxury to do that*.

This pattern of moving in and out of the work force is an interesting case in point for the changing road to retirement (Kathy with her return to Second Harvest as CEO, as well as Kathleen Flaherty and Patrick Gallagher who took one more CEO position before finally transitioning to a multiple structure) or just of the late career path itself. This process of career and retirement confirms Margaret White Riley's theory that "individuals (will) intersperse over their long lives, periods of education or work with periods of leisure or time with family"[6] and later finally ease out with bridge work. This becomes possible because the career is seen as a series of changes, from company to company with continuing education, training and child raising having their importance along the way rather than an attachment to one organization or even sector, until one gradually ramps down to begin building a bridge to retirement in the later career.

But whatever the choices or the culture, the price of high intensity work on family and children in particular was mentioned by numerous interviewees.

Soek King *"My daughter says: 'Mom, Grandma was great but when we were small, you were never around.' I realized they felt empty."*

Loh Meng See *"it was so bad that if one night I found myself at home, my kids would say 'how come you are home?'"*

Kathleen Flaherty *"my daughter watched how hard I worked and rejected the life style!"*

And this has been an important driving force for moving in and out of the work force in mid and late career, and resulted in a strong desire for many to "grandparent" in a direct and participating way once the multiple lifestyle has been restructured.

Thus, we find that a certain number of women, some men and later Baby Boomers have "repaved" the career path itself. The push and pull of this pendulum has helped make further flexibility possible in certain fields. The family has had a direct and regular affect on the rhythm of the career, requiring creativity in the approach to negotiating one's work structure and the ability to take risks, reducing the fear associated with change.

What's special about the men?

When asked if she felt if there was a difference between retirement for men and women Kathy Jackson states:

For men I think that it's more solitary. I don't think that most men have that kind of support from friends. I think that they have tended to look to their spouses for support. And I also think that maybe women have already broken so many molds, one more is not a problem. By working full time in a high-octane financial services environment, I broke a mold. Pulling back and working as an Executive Vice President four days a week was another one. You could imagine people thinking: 'What's that? Are you really committed, can you really make that work?' Also by creating a sabbatical program in a company that did not have one, then to just stop working for four years. Most men would not do that or have the luxury to do that. My husband and I have been quite fortunate. We have been married for 25 years and most of the time we have both been working. But there was a period where he was working on a start up and was only paid in equity. Then I was not working and not being paid for four years. Then ironically when I started at the Food Bank, a project he had been working on for ten years was discontinued. So we have gone back and forth. I think he is now thinking "what's my next chapter?" That's ok, it's all about contribution, which is not about money.

While Soek King states:

> *I think that women are luckier, because throughout our life, we have to make sure the home front is working. We have our social circle. I retired suddenly but – for me only 30% was dedicated to the career in my head. So you do simple things and you organize. I went through my pictures, chose some for my son and my daughter. Women have an easier time, I think they get "enlightened" faster. We struggled with men in the career and got through it, struggled with our husbands and got through it. Men just have one job, their career.*

The feeling expressed by these two women is that men would have more difficulty namely because they had not had to juggle family and career and because they had not developed social networks outside the work place. Also the risk taking involved in breaking the molds would make this new step less intimidating for women, but more for men. These women identified a multitude of "identities" which they felt would provide a bridge during this transition. Called "friend identity" in one study[7] – the fact of being in social/friend relationships outside the work environment before transitioning out – has indeed been shown to be an important positive aid during this transition.

While some studies seem to indicate that the patterns or expectations for retirement are not different between men and women but have more to do with regional and cultural differences,[8] certain recent studies seem to confirm our interviewee's intuitions.

In particular the New Retirement Mindscape IISM study showed that women tend to have a more positive outlook towards retirement, while men are more likely to feel financially ready for it.

Pre-retired women feel more "enthusiastic" about retirement than men (74% vs 65%) and are more "excited with anticipation" about the day they retire (53% vs 38%). Meanwhile, fewer retired men, "enjoy retirement a great deal" in 2010 (56%) than did in 2005.[9]

This study states that one possible cause is that men have been hit harder by the recession. At the same time an Australian study, published in the Journal of Psychology and Aging suggests that retirement may be "lonely and isolating" for men unless they develop the social and leisure networks before they leave, and concludes: "There is a strong emphasis in society to plan and save money for retirement but the bigger questions are: 'What am I saving for?' and, 'What do I really want to do when I retire?'"[10]

So although the retirement patterns may be similar, there may also be differences stemming from the approach to career itself, and involving the social and leisure network which is developed outside the career. These differences emphasize several specific avenues of reflection when planning the transition out:

▷ women planning board work should be especially vigilant to gain board experience and develop contacts before leaving. They should take advantage of the opportunity to be on boards during their primary career (see inset)

▷ depending on their choices, women might seek special support during the transition out to limit the fear of being "sucked back in" rather than "closing the door behind them" to the network of contacts in their primary career,

▷ the role of mentoring other women managers could be especially important for Asian women executives when they transition out.

▷ Men should pay special attention to investing in and planning leisure and social activities outside of the primary career before leaving.

12 Seeing the connections

I try to trace the connection between the characters and that way a story or plot emerges.

Anita Desai[1]

In order for the flexible, multiple lifestyle to work, it is important to "see the connections." One no longer pursues a linear path: a lateral approach is a taken so that the business connection, giving back, family, and personal passions become combined with the help of the network and learning, and time and health are integrated. Mike Critelli, former CEO of Pitney Bowes illustrates this, placing special emphasis on the "virtual identity."

We have now gone through the various themes that may be the focus when transitioning out toward a multiple lifestyle: the source of one's business connection, family, community, personal activities and giving back, and we have explored the transversal elements of the network, health, learning and time, and some possible cultural and gender differences. However, these choices are not simply isolated activities on a list. This process is not static but dynamic and to bring it to life, it needs to be integrated, becoming part of a cohesive and evolving way of life. Thus, at some point it will be important to take a look at the connections among the different choices, and ask how they are going to work together. The connections are endless and very personal but important. Jean Jacques' golf activity is a passion, a way to keep healthy, creates a connection with a community (he organizes a yearly competition, was president and is now member of the club) and with family (he plays with his wife and is teaching his grandchild). Chai's foundation is a way of giving back, creates a connection with family (his wife works with him), and is a business connection. The element of time must be integrated and will influence the importance of activities initially and as choices are made. The network is used to create this dynamic and will also evolve as new connections are discovered with individuals and new contacts are made. These connections are what make the multiple lifestyle work, and what make it fulfilling compared to the primary career which, although intensely satisfying tended to be all consuming and exclusive. Through these connections the original seeds of new directions and choices take root and integrate one into several, often new communities. The goal being to create a more balanced sustainable structure with continuity as one moves toward retirement. A bridge of professional, personal, and community connections that is solid enough to transition into the future and flexible enough to evolve over time.

Michael Critelli carefully prepared this and is a good introduction to our road map. In his process, he first identifies his areas of interest, through the use of networking, coaching and personal discovery. He then seeks the connections among them, using trial and error to find what works and then finding a way to learn to deepen his understanding and reach his goals. Today has created a lifestyle that is decidedly forward-looking, in a continuous exchange with the world out there through healthcare advocacy, gender issues, film and music. But his story also emphasizes one of the major means of connecting today which will become inevitable if one is to remain in full contact with the evolving world: the place of new technologies, social networks, blogs, and media in this multiple lifestyle.

Mike Critelli: Under the radar

Mike Critelli was CEO for Pitney Bowes. He stopped full time corporate work at the end of 2008, moving out in stages and began preparing three years before the final transition. He reminds us once again how untraveled this path is, saying *"this area is really unexplored,* and that *I really had to go out and seek it himself."*

> *In 2008 I found out about this firm, New Directions and they did psychological tests, they interviewed me and they interviewed people who knew me. Then they provided a counseling service that helped me figure out how to think about life after being a CEO.*

He also prepared by having discussions with people who had made the same transition in his network of contacts.

> *I spent a lot of time networking with people and getting their advice. I looked at different alternatives. I made a certain number of mistakes and false starts and there were a certain number of things that surprised me. Some of that is a function of what's happened in the world out there.*

In this early stage Mike learned two important things about himself that would orient him: he was impatient with routine and creative and entrepreneurial.

> *It was a lot of trial and error, starting with some hypotheses of how I would spend my time, then testing things out. I tested things out based on what the New Directions process taught me about myself. Two things that came through loud and clear: one explained why I chose to leave a public company in general and that was I was off the charts with being impatient with compliance and process and routine. They said 'you have the lowest scores we have ever seen for a CEO in terms of patience with processes.' And the other one was that for a CEO I scored unusually high on enjoying entrepreneurship and creativity.*

This allowed him to work in relation to his "negative selves" and exclude certain options.

So that pointed me away from a public company, and also from public boards. It also helped me realize that I didn't want to be on non-profit boards because more and more non-profit boards are taking on the coloration of for profit boards. I am on one non-profit board, the National Urban League, where I play a fiduciary role, but I may not continue. I knew I was in the wrong place when I was on a non-profit board where they spent 45 minutes discussing liablility and insurance....In the meantime I've worked with a number of start ups and that has been a lot of fun. This is a new direction but when I look back at my last CEO role I realize there were clues because I really enjoyed acquiring businesses and working with the founders of those businesses. So the work with New Directions confirmed and reinforced what I already was.

By reflecting upon his use of discretionary time throughout his adult life, Mike was able to establish his areas of interest.

They told me to think about what I had devoted my discretionary time to throughout my adult life and find the things I enjoyed doing with my discretionary time. This tended to be in four areas, health care, sustainable development including trains and transportation, eliminating gender inequalities and for fun I was involved in film and TV and music.

Once Mike had established these areas he explored them by networking and seeking to establish connections between the elements.

So I started looking around and in one of my many networking sessions, I talked with a person who was mentor for me, Andrew White. He asked me the open ended question, what do you want to do with your time? When I explained it, he placed me in contact with Dr Tony Iton. I saw him and I walked him through the same conversation. I said I think there is a connection between these different issues, but I don't know what. He said there is and he told me about his work with the Bay Area Inequities Initiative. He showed me a study called "life and death by unnatural causes." He said "there are social determinants to health which have nothing to do with the healthcare system and they account for about 80% of what happens in health."

Healthcare advocacy and law and order

That gave shape to what I wanted to do organized around the general theme of social determinants of health. I still had the question of what was the interrelationship among the four groups, especially film and TV. But at a Rand Health meeting I met the producer of Law and Order, the TV show. He is a physician by training and interested in healthcare advocacy! I said why did you become an executive producer of a TV show? He said that over the years he had found that telling a story for people changes the behaviors and outlooks. So that I think to be a successful advocate, one of the chief things is being able to tell stories in films and televisions. That brought that element together.

To flesh things out further and extend his access to necessary resources, Mike embarked on a Harvard Fellowship, not so much to learn one particular subject but to further understand the connections. His general goal was to maximize health promotion potential through employer-based health programs but his approach to learning was more global: "*to obtain the resources to explore all of these avenues… and learn about other places where these resources exist.*"

Mike also has his eye on the bigger picture, and realized the importance of the government in his activities, especially in relation to healthcare.

> *So everything I do is around that. The third component is that I had to try to understand how to make government work because government was going to be a key issue to make all this work.*

Finally, another key variable in Mike's equation was his family:

> *The children have been a very important part of all this and probably the thing that has kept us young and sane and happy. That's probably been more dominant in my life than a lot of other people. I am willing to sacrifice quite a lot so that there is a connectedness. It's not so much coming together as a family, as the one on one relationships with each of them.*

Mike says his goal was to work "*under the radar as a stealth change agent, with a blend of highly-public activity, and behind-the-scenes facilitation.*" Today he is managing this and the list of his activities shows the creative solutions he has found the make the final connections.

Mike has a cluster of activities related to his interest in public health promotion. In particular, he is CEO of Dossia, an employer-based health system sponsored by several companies. Dossia gives you your own personal life-long portable health record online, promotes preventive health by making health tools available in their resource center, and is interactive, incorporating feedback from the users on its forum. Introduced with a You Tube video, it is decidedly a system for the future, and a technological response to the B2-generation's demand to remain in control of their health, to understand, and to participate in the process.

Mike is also a board observer for Navigenics, a company involved in securing medical engagement through genetic testing and counseling, was appointed to the Institute of Medicine's Roundtable for Value and Science-Based Care and co-chaired a Prevention Advisory Committee for Connecticut's Sustinet Health Board. Finally he is on the Rand Health Board.

Mike found a way to combine his interest in film, in promoting social issues and to work with this son with a film project called *From the Rough* about Coach Dorothy Starks, a black woman golf coach, which should come out in the fall of 2011.

Finally, Mike has created a blog called "Open Mike" and has a page on Facebook.

Creating a virtual identity

Rather than having a single structured role as a CEO, Mike's desire was to fashion a life that is *defined by the end goal rather than the activities*. But he also realized that the fact that he was seeking as a person (rather than a title) makes it a little harder.

As a result he had to seek innovative ways to connect through social networks, blogs and film and television, for example. He also realized the difficulty of this.

> *One thing I've learned is that I need to have not only a title but a platform. For Dossia, for example, I speak on behalf of 5 million people. The most natural way to do that is to become an Executive Director, but in that case I might have to register as a lobbyist.*

By being on Facebook and having a blog Mike has created a transversal platform to communicate and give himself a voice in a technologically connected world. These choices move beyond the static identity of the individual title and plug him into the future. Through his work with film he has made an important connection with his family, satisfied his desire to tell stories and continue making a contribution to social issues, in this case racial and gender issues. Through the blog, he now has a virtual, global forum, no longer limited to the confines of four walls of the boardroom, cutting across socioeconomic and national frontiers. Through Dossia, employees are taking an active role in prevention. The connections are not only about what you do, but how you do it, and may involve "connecting the dots" differently and outside of the box.

The importance of being virtual

One's relationship with technology and the internet in general are in fact a key bridge and an important step in remaining age-integrated, and to avoid becoming isolated. Because the world has indeed become flat, and revolutions, political campaigns and personal photographs are all played out and exchanged by a new media. This is an important challenge when moving out which has been mentioned by many when reorganizing their business connection, but in fact, it goes much further. When one's children work and live on the other side of the country or the world, new ways of communicating are essential and exist: Skype, iPhone and Facebook are now the ways to remain in contact. The phenomenon of Facebook, Linkedin and You Tube must be integrated and experienced because they have changed networking both in business (Kathy said, "*when I first left, Linkedin didn't exist*") and socially, as well as family relations by reducing distances, politics, travel, and the control of individual access to information. Mike has understood this. But it is a lateral learning challenge for all.

Today Mike *"is pretty much full time and doesn't believe in pure retirement. He says I don't see myself ever completely retiring. I see myself adjusting my activities to the level of energy I have."*

And his advice is to

take stock of what you've enjoyed in the job or outside of the job and try to make that as close to a hundred percent of your time as possible and only take on as much as you can handle. That is going to be very different for different people. I am a natural multitasker. Some people are more linear, one at a time. You have to know yourself and what you can handle. This is not just intellectual it's also psychological. I did not like deadlines. I do not like having accountability for things I have insufficient control. I do not like environments where it's a game rather than a search for truth, which is why I am not well adapted to the political arena.

So you have to look at yourself and say. What are the qualities that will make things work? That is a very difficult task. But you have to, if you are going to be sane and healthy. That's the thing. To emphasize health you have to say what's good for my physical and emotional health?

Book Title: *The Road Less Traveled.*

13 The broadest range of futures

We have no right to assume that any physical laws exist, or if they have existed up until now, that they will continue to exist in a similar manner in the future.

Max Planck

I changed financial advisors, because my advisor said, I've been doing it this way for thirty years, this is the way it works, certain things don't change…and one of the things I've learned is to be suspicious of someone who says that. Peter Drucker said "The speed of change is always overestimated in the short run but the magnitude of change is always underestimated in the long run". I think the hardest lesson to internalize is that you have more time to adjust to change than you think, but also that the world's going to be very very different.

Mike Critelli

After careers during a period with limited unemployment and within a context of unprecedented economic growth, during the writing of this book the economic crisis of 2008 hit the B2-generation—mid- or late-career extremely hard. We thought that it was essential to discuss this event and its eventual repercussions on the process toward "what's next?" as well as to discuss the differences among the Baby Boomers themselves, and explore the idea of the "multiple lifestyle" as alternative road to retirement within this context.

Reality check

As we have said, all of our interviewees are professionals and many of them are from the top earning brackets of this generation. In Asia, the women managers we spoke with are truly exceptional statistically. Does this mean that this alternative "road" is limited to only the wealthiest, to the exceptions, and how will the recent economic crisis affect the Baby Boomer's process toward retirement?

Our informal interviews were particularly interested in the process these boomers took on their road out of the primary career, what motivated them to move out, the paradigm of work in this process, the difficulties encountered and the final choice which we found to be a flexible and multiple lifestyle which included a business connection or several, for pay or on a volunteer basis, but which also sought to integrate other "undeveloped" potential selves through giving back, family and fulfilling one's passions. They were able to develop connections among the different activities and interests, creating new personal and professional networks which could bridge the transition and carry them into later stages of life.

These members of the B2-generation were one step ahead of others, and their process is therefore pertinent, but the choices that they have available to them and their financial possibilities are specific to their group. Studies have indeed shown differences in Baby Boomer expectations for retirement according to socioeconomic status, with low socioeconomic status participants planning less, because they have been unable to,[1] and less optimistic about retiring due to financial insecurity. This group was disproportionately female in one Australian study and makes up about one third of the Baby Boomers in the Harvard-Metlife study. In Asia, our interviewees were limited to countries of East Asia, whose economies have exploded in one generation, thus excluding the poorest groups, for whom finding work is the priority and retirement is not an option.

However, this leaves two thirds of US Baby Boomers, for example, with at least moderate retirement savings who were optimistic about retirement before the financial crisis of 2008 and one can imagine similar numbers in Europe and East Asia. Even before the crisis many of these also expected to work after the official age of retirement suggesting that they would also move through this process seeking a business connection which may include giving back, family and pursuing one's passions" and a multiple lifestyle, with a flexible structure and freedom of choice. The choices available and the financial possibilities will be to scale.

The Metlife study also showed that giving back may take different forms according to socioeconomic level—with lower socioeconomic groups engaging in more intergenerational and informal volunteering—in the neighborhood or for family compared to formal volunteering,[2] and in the case of our interviewees, creating foundations, non-profit board work or in the case of Soek King, a university in China. Obviously the "bridge work" will depend upon one's skills and work background, and one's personal passions remain a very—personal—thing.

When the bubble bursts

Within this context, the effect of the economic crisis in 2008 burst the bubble of even our optimistic Baby Boomers and this event will also affect all Baby Boomers according to socioeconomic level and culture.

Marv Berenbaum says: "*You have the 77 million (US) Baby Boomers ready to move out and you have the great recession. So it's going to be at least a few years and maybe even then some, before we come back to any sort of normalcy in the job market. You see kids today graduating from some of the best schools and 75% of them are still looking for a job a year after graduating. It's a very desperate situation. We haven't seen this since 87–92 which was very bad. This is much worse.*"

Mike Critelli goes further, suggesting that the result will be a profound shift in the "rules," obliging him to look outside his comfort zone, remain aware, flexible, and change.

I think that there is going to be a radically different environment once we come out of this economic downturn.

I think that we're going through a time where the rules of how someone will succeed will radically change. And we don't quite know how it's going to work out in the end. So one of the questions I wrestle with everyday is how do I need to function because the world as we know it is going to be reset.

It's become very apparent to me that the 1982 downturn and 2007 are very different and we are not going to get back to the way it was before. We are going to have a much more technology-enabled world. There are going to be new models on how people construct their careers, how they put together their lives and how they have interpersonal relationships. And I'm not sure we know what the end state is going to look like so I am struggling to prepare myself for the broadest range of futures.

For Mike, this change in situation means that the golden age is truly over, and that "security" has become a thing of the past, affecting his attitude toward work and his finances.

I now operate on an assumption that I should never assume that I'm financially secure. One of the things that the first three months showed me when my stocks were melting away was that I have to have skills to be able to jump back into the workplace if I need them. The notion that I'm secure now, and I can now can move on and do other things and won't have to earn any more money is inaccurate. It's a different paradigm.

Mike now imagines that he may have to "jump back into the workplace" at some point, and brings up the importance of "having the necessary skills" for this, emphasizes once again the importance of continuing education. We find that this group, who might have imagined themselves secure with nearly complete (financial) freedom of choice, now envision a new paradigm. For example money may now become part of the equation for some who today provide services to non-profit organizations on a volunteer basis.

Marv says:

For the Baby Boomers it's going to be difficult. There is a lot of wealth out there so you are going to have people that will be able to sustain themselves, support themselves. There was a study before the great recession (of 2008) that asked if you had the opportunity to work after you retired what would be your response? 50% said they would like to work. Of the 50% who would like to work, 33% of those would like to do it without being compensated. That's a lot of people. I think there are even more people now that would like to work, because they are retiring without the funds they thought they would have. So compensation becomes much more of a factor than it was. But there are still people that would like to continue to work and that don't need to.

Financial planning

This is a group of Baby Boomers who is more apt to have planned financially for this stage in life. Nevertheless this crisis has meant that even this planning has had its limits. More careful planning is necessary, but even then "there are no perfect answers." Mike says:

> *People are waiting longer because their portfolios have melted down. I think they will work longer, and there will be a certain risk aversion. But I have also believed all my life that if you try to run away from taking risks and seek too much security, you find yourself in the face of bigger risks. I think you have to take prudent risks and operate as if bad things can happen at any time to be secure as you can be.*
>
> *The other thing I've learned is that I am going to have to manage my financial portfolio much more actively than I thought. I am going to have to make decisions that there are no perfect answers to.*

For Soek King and others perhaps in this early group of Asian Baby Boomers, the family, once again may have taken priority over planning.

> *People like me forgot about things because we were so busy—financial planning and lots of things. Now with my children I say learn about investment, take it seriously, and gain this knowledge while you are working on your career. That way you can probably retire faster and be better prepared, and have a better understanding of how to prepare. I was so overloaded, money was important but I didn't even take the money to the bank, I gave it to my family.*

For those who hope to live on a pension, this new post-crisis paradigm of "not assuming that one is financially secure" has become a question of timing and financial need. The problem of sustainable pensions in the financial downturn is global. In response to this, numerous countries have raised the official retirement age: France, Spain, Singapore, Japan, UK and the US to name a few, meaning, that the "intention to continue work" before and after collecting one's pension may now be transformed into the "need to work" (see Table 13.1).

Indeed, 25 percent of those surveyed in the United States had postponed retirement in 2009.[3] But even this is not the panacea. The problem of ageism must also be confronted, and was mentioned, in particular by several of our interviewees in France (only 20% of French work after the age of 60). Didier was able to extend his "sell by date", while others are not, and even then there is a catch-22: a need to give space to younger professionals in countries with high unemployment, and an unwillingness to hire after the age of 55. Countries such as Singapore, Japan and France have made this a political issue, providing incentives for companies that employ after a certain age, flexibility and training in the work place, and continuing health coverage for those who continue to work after the official age of retirement. Thus,

Table 13.1 Retirement then and now

Official retirement age (men)	Previously	Extended to
France	60	62
UK	65	67
US	65	67
Spain	65	67
South Korea	58	60
Japan	63	65
Singapore	62	65

society is once again adapting to the Baby Boomers as they pass through their "next stage" in the workplace and redefine the process of retiring.

Retirement in your own image

Thus the question of financial need now means that more than ever work will be an ingredient during this new stage. But is this so bad?

Our interviewees are nearly all "work intensives," they desire and will continue working, but they are not alone. As we have seen middle class Baby Boomers had already expressed their "intention to work after official retirement" before the downturn, and bridge work clearly provides connectivity, intellectual stimulation, and structure, with the latter being a motivation to continue working for all socioeconomic levels. Finally a recent report has shown that like volunteer work those who remain in the workforce have improved cognitive abilities.[4]

For Kathy Jackson and others, this change in the work paradigm is in fact a "*very good thing*" a necessary effect of increased longevity and a way of "*hedging the bets.*" Remaining in contact with the workplace means continued investment in society, being "*in the know*" and engaged for those extra years. Kathy says:

> *I absolutely think (the economic crisis) is going to affect things. Maybe it will affect those who planned to retire in a "traditional way" where when you retired you did not work at all. They are actually going to find themselves required and/or inclined to do some kind of work. It might be part time work. It might not be hugely remunerative, but it hedges the bets a bit which means you don't have to draw quite as much out of your retirement assets. And I actually think that may be a very good thing. That there is a reinvention of retirement, partly because that's the way the Boomers think. They want to change everything and put it in their own image, which may be*

good or bad, but also there may be the necessity to do that from an economic point of view. Because I can't imagine not doing anything. Although I was pretty happy for four years at the same time I was working ten–20 hours a week and I had my kids at home.

So I think that a lot of people will change the way they retire. And maybe it doesn't really matter if it is a quasi-economic necessity or an intellectual who-you-are necessity.

But the common denominator of this generation is the increase in life expectancy, a first for humanity—marking a new life stage to be lived and evaluated. One of the most painful and severe consequences of ageing and gradual dependence is the isolation it brings. The traditional definitions of retirement are all rejected by our interviewees, confirming that they are not ready to be put out to pasture and become passive observers. It also shows their desire and intention to remain active participants in the community and the world well after the official age of retirement. Work is one facet of this, but as we have seen, it is work on other terms, with flexibility and a connection to other aspects of the self and life. For this to be successful, Baby Boomers will have to be as proactive as they have been during their careers- by first reappraising their interests and skills, by careful preplanning, and by seeking creative solutions to fulfill desired selves.

14   Road map

Alice came to a fork in the road. "Which road do I take?" she asked.
"Where do you want to go?" responded the Cheshire cat.
"I don't know," Alice answered.
"Then," said the cat, "it doesn't matter."
Lewis Carroll (1865). *Alice in Wonderland*, Macmillan and Co

This road map is based on the process, advice, and experiences of the professionals we interviewed and provides a general framework to approach this transition. It is meant as a practical guide for those who like our interviewees, are seeking in the late career to "do something different," refuse the ceiling of age, enjoy working but are looking to finally achieve a work-life balance that includes their passions, family and/or giving back and build a bridge to the next uncharted stage of 20–30 years. We have included websites with basic information to get you started at the end of the book.

Planning ahead.

Preplanning, whether you know what you want to do or you don't have any idea is important, making the transition easier, the oh-shit moments less traumatic and a way to adapt when "the phone stops ringing."

Although many interviewees felt that planning was not possible because of time, some managed. In these cases, specific time was often set aside on their agenda for this purpose. Mike Critelli, like Patricia Hewitt went to a life coach. The purpose of this step and exercise, is "knowing thyself," discovering like Mike, what you are adapted to, what you like to do and expect from this stage, projecting yourself a few years into the future and imaging what you want it to look like. For those who are imagining a radical change, this is truly an essential step. For others, who would like to do board work or consulting in the same field, it provides a head start, allows you to see the whole picture, is a way to know what's out there and to begin shifting your network and focus in this new direction.

At some point, whether before or after you leave, this process is necessary: determining your list of the hereafter, or asking the questions suggested by Marv to determine your likes and dislikes. If it is not possible before leaving, in the early days after leaving it is important to begin thinking about your future and creating a road map. Whenever you begin, you should begin at the beginning.

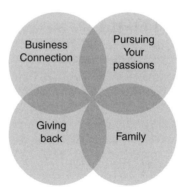

Figure 14.1   **What's next? The blueprint**

Before you leave

Start giving yourself time

Ideally 1–2 years before you decide to stop full time take advantage of your positional power and take time for yourself at least once per week; mark it off on your agenda.

▷ talk to "mentors," others who have made this step already,
▷ speak to an advisor or coach specialized in transitions to create a process and ultimately begin creating a plan or do a full self-assessment for guidance
▷ brainstorm with friends and family
▷ go on a retreat, religious or otherwise, to give yourself "time to think"
▷ begin reading books (like this one) on the subject to get the wheels turning.

Begin determining what your activity circles are going to look like

As you have seen, we found that the choices and activities in our interviews could be grouped into four circles: business connections, personal passions, family, giving back and community. You can create your own activity circles, if these don't fit, but allow this step to be a real free association at first, before restricting yourself (see figure 14.1).

Know thyself

Begin by doing an audit of what you are good at and love doing associated with work. What you want to continue doing and to stop doing. Are you an intrapreneur or an entrepreneur? Do you need to have structure organized by someone else? Do you prefer short term or long-term projects? Do you like working for deadlines? Working in groups? Working alone? Are you a communicator? Synthetic? Good at writing? Convincing people? Do you wish to create something completely new? Do an exercise similar to Marv's listing the things you love doing but also the things you do not like to become aware of your negative potential selves, being very general. Think laterally and freely. You are not committed to anything, just getting ideas.

Business connections

Keeping the first exercise in mind, define the type of business connection you think you might be interested in. For profit- non-profit a/o community board work, consulting, salaried work, beginning a foundation, private equity, start-up, project oriented work, in relation to the amount of structure you would like to have and need, the field of interest, your financial needs and the skills you wish to use.

Define your passions

List all those things you have said no to, that you would have left on the back burner. List your interest in sports, your hobbies, your unfulfilled spiritual and intellectual quests, breeding dogs, traveling, building model boats, ballroom dancing, theatre, opera, acting, gardening. Be creative, don't hold back. Include subjects you are passionate about: healthcare, history, government, the "ologies," which may become new directions for giving back, business connections, or with your family.

Family

Define what obligations you may have for ageing parents, children, grandchildren. Imagine activities that you would like to develop to include your family, your spouse, your children, your grandchildren, from a foundation to a yearly family gathering or a regular vacation trip. Are there activities which you would especially like to share with your spouse? Is there a project you have with him/her? Or with your children/grandchildren? What specific choices might be necessary to make your family connection work (location, time to integrate your family into your life, a business project to begin).

Giving back

Go back over the areas you are passionate about which could become a focus for giving back: diabetes, obesity, poverty, children, hunger, the great outdoors, environmental causes, opera, a specific sport, Chinese literature?

Define if and how you would like to give back. What level? *As a hands-on volunteer*, in hospitals, food banks, help lines, religious organizations, sports associations, clubs? *In the community*: being on the board, fund raising or participating in your golf club, your local public school, national parks, local foundations? *The world*: participating in non-profit governmental organizations? Are you interested in politics – local or national? Non-profit board work? Charitable giving? *Mentoring*: What skills are you interested in transferring? What population would you like to reach? Other professionals? Students? Children? Small businesses? Boards?

Begin talking to others around you about areas that you might be interested in if you are not sure. Read up on the subject. Go on the Internet and surf around to see what's out there.

Know thyself

Be general and put it all on the table then begin filling up the different circles. Be honest with yourself and don't scratch anything out. You are not committing to anything to start so play around with this. Take time to work on it and start investigating the various options. Then take time to think about those on the list you would like to pursue.

Create the plan

Most of us have developed business plans, strategic plans, and goals all of our lives. It's now time to apply those skills to your new endeavor, creating your own personal business plan and map of the future as no one else can make this happen. As you get closer to leaving be more specific.

Gradually decide what you want to have in each of your activity circles, your core "areas of interest," which we have defined as business connection, family, passions, and giving back-community. This will give you some perspective on an approach so that you can begin fleshing things out, begin to make use of your network, pursue learning possibilities or make contact in certain areas before leaving. In the early process this does not have to be exact but allows you to begin visualizing how your life might evolve.

Get to know your network

Here again, opinions varied as to the importance of networking. Yet even those who did not officially "network," did it unofficially. When you are working 24/7 this network seems to be intrinsic and automatic. It is important to become conscious of it as something that is available to you and that can be put to use to develop your new lifestyle. Your network may and definitely will change after you leave depending on your choices, but this network of human relations will lead to others. It's all about connectivity.

Business network

▷ Start becoming aware of your network while you are still working, first by taking stock and organizing it so that it is easily usable and can evolve. The earlier this is done, the better. Sit at the computer and list the names of everyone that you can think of that you have worked with, for, along side, as a customer or competitor. Don't worry if you don't know where they are, be open-minded and lateral in your thinking. This will be used to expand your network.

▷ Begin making lunch dates first with easily accessible individuals with whom you would like to discuss your ideas, further your project and obtain other contacts. Build upon your existing network with an eye on the future. Also contact people who have already left and who you admire, using them as guide and mentor for your own journey. Let people know what your plans are. Start getting the word out and projecting your future.

Social/personal network

Identify those friends who you have been out of contact with for years because your job made this impossible, but would like to reconnect with. Make contact. Imagine social activities which might interest you to re-establish this type of relationship and which you are interested in golf, hiking, chorus, dancing, bridge etc. Find out what's available in your area or through these new social contacts.

A living network

Increase your visibility in situations that are not directly/uniquely work oriented: you are invited to numerous conferences to speak on a panel or as a keynote and often say no. Say yes to increase your visibility in the business community...you never know where the network will take you.

Take action early

Once you have established an early plan that identifies your general approach, take action on specific activities before leaving to make the transition easier. The websites at the end of the book are a good start for this.

The Business Connection

Board work

If you plan on doing board work after your transition, the advice from our interviewees is unanimous: take advantage of your position in industry and sit on boards before leaving. So start looking while still in full time employment. Most companies will allow operating executives to sit on one board. Take the initiative to volunteer to sit on a joint venture as a representative for the company or if possible chair the board. Both will give you experience as a board member and will make it easier to transition.

To do this, you need to understand what you have to offer to a board. Work with an advisor/coach who can help you write your bio to position your self correctly. Take a look at your Resumé/CV and write a two page bio your salient expertise is: operating experience, financial expertise, governance expertise, industry knowledge, global experience, etc. You also need to begin considering how you intend to sell yourself for this activity. Meet with search firms and also connect with board chairmen who you know to make them aware that you are open to a non-executive position. Also contact private equity or venture capitalist partners in your field, they are often looking to create new boards.

Investigate the local Institute Directors (United Kingdom (UK)) or Conference Board (United States) to see if you can obtain formal training to learn about the responsibilities for a Non-Executive Director.

If you are interested in non-profit board work, once again, begin by doing some community or charity work prior to leaving, through the company if this exists. Try it out to see if you like it, determine the size of the non-profit organization you are interested in, the role you wish to play, take a try at fund raising. Gather information on the structure, time and dynamics of non-profit board work from others who have done it.

Consulting

Begin talking about your future activities with others around you, like Loh Meng See. Investigate the possibilities within your existing structure (as a lawyer, doctor, psychologist or other vocation) to continue on a part time basis. By beginning to speak with those around you before you leave, you are planting the seeds, a first step in establishing potential collaborations.

Determine what being a "consultant" means in your country as far as status. Do you need to create a legal entity, if so try to do this before you leave. Determine the size of your consultancy. If you must raise capital, begin discussions. Do you want to work alone, or on a project basis? Do you wish to be part of a group of consultants such as Marv's or be on your own? To work on a project-by-project basis, to travel or not etc. Depending on your choice, research the possibilities on internet, with those in your network, by reading.

Start up, private equity. small business

If you are interested in investing in or beginning a start up attend entrepreneurial seminars before leaving to increase your knowledge capital, to become aware of existing projects depending on your field of interest (biotech, information technologies, renewable energies etc.) attend conventions on the subject.

Identify the small business status in your company, the possible fiscal aids for this type of project etc. Draft your business plan.

If you are interested in becoming an operating partner in private equity, identify the venture capitalists in your sector. Expand your network in this direction and begin making contact.

Pursuing your passions

If you have identified passions and interests which you would like to deepen your participation in, do some research and see if the company you work for contributes to a cause that is synergistic (if you breed dogs, perhaps your company has a relationship with the Humane Society). See if you can become involved while you are still in your primary career so that you can continue after you leave. If there is interest in music, theatre or opera many companies are associated with some of these in the local community.

If you wish to turn this into a business connection, begin fact finding to determine exactly what this shift would entail. Identify and contact others who have done the same thing. This may require specific training, which you may be able to begin before leaving in a continuing education program. Identify what this means and where you can obtain it. Increase your visibility in this area – by contacting associations, foundations, or organizations that are involved in this activity and which you might like to be associated with.

If you were an artist, sang in a choir or were a musician before you started full time employment, start thinking about taking lessons again or joining a local community effort before you leave.

Giving back

Mentoring

Investigate the possibility of giving seminars, classes, at universities or colleges, local or community programs while you are still working, or providing strategic help to small business owners. Talk about this with colleagues and identify anyone in your network who might be able to help you with this. Meet with them. Discuss your idea, get advice and others to contact.

Community Work

Gather information about organizations where you might consider doing community work, then make initial contact. See what kinds of roles are available, and if any of them correspond to what you had in mind. Begin talking about this idea with colleagues, people in your network and social acquaintances to establish a contact; fund raising for your club, your children's schools, the local church, the boys club. Begin increasing your visibility, let it be known that you are interested.

Charitable giving, foundations

Identify the charitable causes you are passionate about and the foundations or organizations which exist for this cause. If you are thinking of charitable giving, consider a "giving pool" with a group of friends. Most companies have a specific department focused on charitable giving which can be contacted to help you take the first steps and obtain addresses.

Family

If you have identified projects with family, get the ball rolling before leaving, by discussing and formalizing the project with the family first. Draft the plan and allow the family team to begin initial steps.

Health

If health has not been on your list of priorities up to now, consider working with a personal trainer, like Henri, to get things going. If you have no particular sports that you play, join a club, a hiking group...or even learn to play golf....Set aside a minimum of time for this as you approach your departure date. Before leaving, take advantage of the opportunity to get a thorough check up through your employer. Do this regularly after you leave.

Learning

Depending on your choices your need to "learn" may be necessary or just a passion. Eric is participating in intensive training to become an Arbitrator. Kathleen was interested in the "ologies" and has taken a minimedical course outside her scientific PhD. As a doctor you may need to do continuing education if you wish to keep consulting in a specialized field, or begin work abroad.

If you wish to do something totally different like Carole, this may require taking certain courses (interior design, seminars on creating a start-up etc.) to begin the process. If you have decided to write a book, classes may also be an important first step. Someone interested in investing in or beginning a start up should also attend seminars. All of these may be possible before leaving through the continuing education program of your primary job.

As D-Day approaches

Finalize your plan

See the connections

Once you have identified your areas of interest and filled your activity circles, begin looking at and for the connections among them—if you want to mentor and travel with family, is there an organization with consulting projects overseas that would make this possible? How can you make this work? Are you like Mike searching for a connection between a passion and a business connection? Develop this, as he did through networking until it becomes clearer.

Fill in the gaps

Based on these connections begin to look at your personal and professional network to determine who you will be contacting, and how. See where the gaps are in the project and the network and work on developing further contacts and any learning that may be necessary.

A new paradigm

Seek age integrated activities and structure, exchanging with the younger generation to avoid isolation, by mentoring, learning situations, volunteer opportunities. Beware of hearing yourself say: this is the way it has always been done. Allow yourself and try to think laterally now and then. Push yourself outside your comfort zone.

Where?

Determine where you want to be based and if location is a priority for you to be able to optimize this new structure- Do you want to be close to your children? To your sports activities? To be near enough to an airport to travel easily? Determine where home base will be.

When and how?

Also begin imagining how much time you want to spend on each and what kind of time. Do you want Fridays off? Long weekends? Summers free? Determine your mobility: Are you still willing to travel? How and how far? How much financial return do you expect?

The first six months out

A room of one's own

Establish your home base and create a space for yourself in your house. Some already have an office, some do not. Find a place that you can spend time in on our own. It may become an art studio, a place to study or to read board papers. But make it yours, do it yourself and think about what you need.

Get wired

Get your house wired. You are accustomed to having the technology work because you have tech support at the office. If you do not have a state of the art wireless set up and computer system get it installed so that you can begin with a solid foundation. It is here you will begin to build the lists, expand your network and create the database for your activities.

Make sure you are fully capable of exploiting this technology, by attending classes, investing in a tech support contract, regularly going to your Apple Store help desk.

If you have not already, begin further exploring the possibilities of internet, iPods and iPhones: from simply managing your travel plans, using Linked In, to creating a blog, using Skype or placing yourself on Facebook. Children and grandchildren can be great help getting started.

The final plan

Complete your plan if it is not already done. Your plan should now be detailed with projected deadlines and weekly/monthly goals. Based on these goals you will fill your agenda with meetings, lunches and coffee with people you have identified. Allow yourself to move out of your "safety zone" in the early days with these contacts, to explore possibilities, to try things out.

Continue expanding your network

Take the list you have created earlier, the gaps you have identified, the connections you would like to establish among your activity circles and work on it. Google the names, start asking around (six degree's of separation) make phone calls, send emails. You can find most people today if you look or ask. Begin having one or more days a week with appointments (coffee, lunch meetings, golf dates) with the people you have decided to reconnect with. When you have these meetings be sure you are clear about the message you want to give depending on your goal, that is, you are looking for a board, want to create a start up, begin community work, pursue a passion etc.

Making it happen

- Be disciplined about your approach in this early period. Plan and meet regularly with those you have targeted. Fill your agenda. Make the phone calls yourself, see the recruiters.
- Finalize your CV if necessary. If you plan to do board work target the companies you are interested in, and obtain contact through your network. Plan your interview with a coach.
- Sign up for any necessary classes, seminars, brush up courses, degree programs.
- Make social connections through the activities you have identified, establish regular contact with the personal friends you have decided to meet with.
- Be disciplined about your sports regimen, even by just walking a half hour a day.

Health

Establish a regular routine for physical activity, sports, but at least walk a half hour per day, or continue with a personal trainer.

When it comes to deciding

You don't need to fill the diary on day one, take the time to choose the right things. If after six–nine months you only have two board assignments the world will not fall apart.

Patrick Gallagher

Making choices

Before making commitments do your due diligence, being careful about the quality of the company, the project, the offer. Carefully consider the time factor and the level of commitment. Take your time, you have a window of opportunity. Don't rush into things, your plate need not be too full, or too empty.

Keeping your eyes open

Keep an eye on the balance of not having too much or too little, so that you do not get "sucked in" or "overwhelmed" leaving no time for yourself, your family or your passions once again. Keep an eye on the connections among your activities, so that you do not get pigeonholed too quickly into one area.

"Oh-shit" moments

If you have an "oh-shit" moment identify the problem and find the solution. If you make a bad choice, see it through and learn from your mistakes. Do not be afraid to ask for advice, it is amazing how many people want to help. You have helped numerous people in the course of your career and this will be returned but you must take the initiative. Don't be afraid to make the phone calls rather than wait for the phone to ring.

The road continues

> *Question yourself every day ... am I doing the right thing? Life is full of choices and if you need to change the path then change it, not necessarily a U turn but at this time of life you have an opportunity to veer to the right or left.*
>
> Patrick Gallagher

It takes about two–three years to get your initial plan together and it will be worth it. Most of our interviewees are happier than they have been in a long time. It is essential to remember that the plan is always evolving, networking is not just about getting started, but a lifelong process. Boards have terms in certain countries (three years in the UK for example) and can only be renewed a certain number of times, bridge work in universities or hospitals may also be limited so the road will continue. What you will have gained during this initial period are the tools to take you through the others: an understanding of your desired future selves, the capacity to be flexible about your choices, to think laterally about your options, to keep your network alive and ultimately to change when change becomes necessary.

The road map

1–2 yrs before leaving	Put time (even a little) aside in your agenda to begin working on What's next?
	Identify and list your professional, personal and community areas of interest through brainstorming, going on a retreat, speaking with mentors, family, others in the same situation, or a coach. Start reading up on the subject.
	Create your main "activity circles" and fill them up.
	Take a look at your network: professional, personal, and community. Begin imagining how these might evolve into the next step. Begin organizing this for future use. Keep this in mind when meeting with others and bring up your plans.
	Recontact people in the personal and professional network that you have identified, to make contact, develop your plans.
	If you have identified specific activities you would like to pursue gain experience before leaving: ▷ Obtain board-work experience through your corporate position ▷ Begin community, charity, fund raising work to see if it suits you ▷ Take up a passion that you will increase when leaving (bridge, sports) ▷ Give one or two classes in your area of expertise ▷ If you have a specific learning project, see if it can be begun through your corporate/professional training program
6 months before	Health: take advantage of your position to obtain a thorough check-up. Begin working with a coach, join a club or begin a regular physical activity, even just walking to get back in shape, and so that it becomes a routine.
	Draft a basic action plan, including your "activity circles" and what they contain and basic connections among them. The major actions that need to be completed to reach your goals: CV, interviews, learning, network needs etc.
	Key words: Know theyself

cont'd

continued

The first 6 months out	Finalize a structured plan, with detailed and daily actions to be followed. Establish and see the connections among different activities and in relation to time, to make it workable, mixing business with pleasure, family with health, learning with passions … Determine where you want to be located
	Set up your personal space. Get wired. Establish your working model, and learn through courses or otherwise, the technological possibilities for agenda planning, travel plans, shopping, LinkedIn, face-to-face phone contact etc…
	Finalize your CV and if necessary work with a coach to prepare for interviews.
	Take administrative steps to create your company, consulting firm, start-up etc.
	Expand on your network Based on your plan, begin looking for the connections with your existing network. Make contact with new sources in the community to develop business, personal or giving back activities. Recontact personal friends that you have decided to reconnect with. Plan and begin making business contacts for your new structure.
1–2 years	Begin living your plan
	Be disciplined, and take initiatives yourself, send emails, make phone calls, set up appointments: no one will do this for you.
	Take the necessary steps to pursue any learning activities you may need to move forward for the transfer of skills, to keep up to date, or for technologies in general.
	Meet regularly for coffees, lunches or dinners with business, personal and community contacts, explaining your plan or getting new ideas. These meetings are not only for your business connections, but also to establish a place in the community, to reconnect with friends and to continue developing your ideas.
	Health: continue a regular physical activity with or without a coach, make connections with community or family through sports activities.
	Before making decisions: Do your due diligence before making any commitments and be realistic about the time involved.
	Don't be afraid to say "no." Don't be afraid to say "yes."
	Key words: structure, discipline, due diligence, seeing the connections

15 Conclusion

The road taken by the professionals we interviewed was not seen as retirement, but as a step toward regaining control of life and work in the late career and a way to begin constructing a new flexible lifestyle that would provide a bridge into the final career and retirement. This was a multiple lifestyle seeking to integrate work-family-giving back-and personal passions into a smorgasbord, a patchwork, or a plural life. Some sort of work or business connection was always part of this process, and some are nearly full time, but with flexibility and more control than they had in their primary careers. This process sometimes included a final return to a full-time position, to fill in the gaps or to be completely ready for a multiple lifestyle, a sign that the image of the career itself has changed. There were differences in the choices made depending on the type of career: business owners were seeking to turn over their businesses to family before cutting down, those in vocations tended to want to remain in their primary career activity longer and slow down, giving themselves space for their other activities, while those in corporate career did board work and consulting. Pursuing one's passions and turning this into a business connection is possible in any field. The relationship with family was affected by career choice and culture: entrepreneurs remained connected with family after transitioning out through foundations or by turning their business over to a family member, in Asia the extended family and its responsibilities are still a unifying force in their choices. The importance of choosing was also essential. Many of the Boomers in industry were in their 50s when they took these steps, far enough ahead of "official retirement" to exploit their professional networks and change directions with time to plan. There was a search for and desire to integrate meaning into this new, multiple lifestyle. Rather than the greediest generation we found that they were keenly aware of their debt to society and toward future generations and have chosen to give back in the form of non-profit board work, foundations, volunteer work, creating universities, or volunteer consulting. These interviews showed that the extra 20–30 years available to the B2-generation will be dedicated to a flexible fusion of work, family, giving back, and pursuing one's passions. Our road map is a practical guide to the process these early Boomers have followed, from knowing thyself and seeking core values and activities to taking the steps in the first days out, and as the road continues. We hope that this will make it easier for other members of the B2-generation who wish to keep control of this period, give it meaning and remain active and engaged, making retirement in the form of a life of vacations obsolete and a thing of the past.

Our Interviewees

The following people have been interviewed for the book:

Name		Present activities	Full-time role
Siaou-Sze Lien	SING	BC – Coaching Mobbey Group Pacific Consultant HUHTAMAKI OYJ Independent Board Member; Luvata Oy Director Board Member: Confucious Institute Giving back/Mentoring-women to become Board Directors. Family-Foundation Chinese Literature Passions: dancing	Hewlett Packard Managing Director
Henri Balbaud	FR	BC – Consultant HR, Giving Back/Community – SOS Suicide, financial advisor for associations/Mentoring – Master's professor Passions – biking, running, choral Family – active grandparenting. Family home	Director HR and Communications Indosuez, Credit Agricole Group
Marvin Berenblum	USA	BC/Mentoring – Ch CEO NESC, Sports/family-personal training, kayaking Giving Back/Community-Boys Club Passions/Family – choral group, traveling. Active grandparenting	Managing Partner: NY, Wall Street, Greenwich, CT. Heidrick and Struggles
Eric Christin	FR	BC/Family – President Parc-Etoile-Foch. BC/Passion – Biotech, Business Angel; inventor biotech applications Family/Passions – Art Investment fund, Art Gallery, Giving back – Judge BC – Learning – Internat'l Arbitrator.	IBM. Ahmdal. Investment Banking. Founder, CEO C° Parc-Etoile-Foch
Steven Davidson	UK	BC – Board Work – Ch Memcom Group, Digital Marketing Group, Datatec; EBT Mobile China; NED Tele Columubs Gmbh, Inmarsat Group, Enteraction LTD	MD Bear Sterns/ CEO Telewest/MD Deutsche Bank
Kathleen R Flaherty	USA	BC – Board Work. NED Yell Group, Inmarsat. Passions/Family – gardening, traveling, cooking, dogs Learning – mini-medical course JHopkins Family – active grandparenting. Family home	CMO ATT/President COO Winstar/MCI VP Product

cont'd

continued

Name		Present activities	Full-time role
Patrick Gallagher	UK	BC – Board Work NED Ciena, Harmonic; Sollers. Ch Ubiquisys; Passion: tennis, music, hiking, Family – greater investment in family	Golden Telecom NED; Flagg Telecom CEO Chairman; BT Europe President
Patricia Hewitt	UK	BC – Board Work NED Groupe Eurotunnel; BT; Chairwoman UK India Business council Passions – traveling, yoga, gardening. Family: Greater investment in family/aging parents	UK Department of Health Secretary of State; UK Cabinet Office Cabinet Member UK Department for Trade and Industry Secretary of State
Chai Patel	UK	BC/Giving back/Family. Foundation: Bright Futures Fdn BC/Mentoring-Court Cavendish Group Chairman; Bridges Community Ventures Advisory Board Member Passion: golf Family: investment in aging parents, family	Priory Healthcare Group CEO; Westminster Healthcare CEO; CareFirst CEO
Patricia Russo	USA	BC – Board work-NED KKR, HP, GM, Merck, Alcoa BC/Giving Back-NP Board Work Ch of Partnership of Drug Free America, BC – Community – Ch Board Golf Club Passions/family-traveling, golf	Alcatel Lucent DEO; Lucent Chairman CEO; Eastman Kodak President COO; Avaya Chairman; ATT Group President
Loh Meng See	SING	BC – Consultant: HR Consultancy BC/Giving Back; Nanyang Business School Advisory Board. Passion/Giving Back/Family Bible Study Group. Financial manager church. Traveling Family – Active grandparenting	Singapore Airlines SVP HR; parliament of Singapore Elected Member; Keppel Corp Group HR
Carole St. Mark	USA	BC/Passion/Family – Far Meadow Farm Founder (Horse Farm). Restoring antique houses. Gardening BC – Board Work. NED Gerber Scientific; Growth Management LLC President; Learning: interior design classes Other passions – photography Giving Back/Mentoring-Women's Enterprise Initiative Community: Women's groups	Pitney Bowes Division President CEO

cont'd

continued

Name		Present activities	Full-time role
Dr Hank McKinnell	USA	BC – Board Work. Moody's BC – Giving Back: World: Ch Academic Global Health Foundation. Community: Science Foundation for Children. Titon Nat'l Park Passions/Family. skiing, hiking, fishing	Chairman and CEO Pfizer Various senior roles Pfizer
Didier Marchal	FR	BC – Consultant-Hepatology BC – Editor Biomedical Journal Mentoring – Clinical studies with young MD's Passions/family: Golf, jogging, gardening, hunting, Learning: history seminars Family – active grandparenting	MD Hepatologist Director of Research (Hepatology) INSERM.
Mike J. Critelli	USA	BC – Giving back – Dossia President/CEO; Navigenics NED; Capitol Advisor CVC; Eaton NED; Rand Advisory Board Member Learning: Harvard fellowship Family/Passions – filmaking	Pitney Bowes Chairman CEO
Jean Jacques Strauss	FR	BC – Consulting Media/Advertising, Mentoring: Master class prof Family/passions – Golf (amateur competitions) gardening, lumberjack Giving back/Community: Media and PR local political election campaign, local assns.	Europe I, TF1, Radio-Monte Carlo. Lumberjack
Lise Small	US-FR	BC – psychotherapy consultations Mentoring – training psychotherapists Family: more intensive investment in family US-FR Passions: traveling, cooking, film Community – Women's groups	Psychotherapist
Elisabeth Brenner-Salz	DE	BC/Giving Back – NP Board Work: Passions: opera, ballet, gardening	Deloitte. Economist. Urban Planning
Kathryn G. Jackson	US	BC – Giving Back/Community CEO Second Harvest Food Bank Family/Passion – book club. Community-3C club. Woman's group Passions-hiking	GATX D'Accord Bank of America

cont'd

continued

Name		Present activities	Full-time role
Siew Hua Lim	SI	BC – Entrepreneur/start-ups Giving back – Mentoring young entrepreneurs Global: assisting companies in developing countries Passions/learning – Jung, religious retreats Family – active family support	Morgan Grenfeld
Soek King Ko	SI	BC – Learning-Giving Back – created branch University China Community Coaching Passions – religious quest Family – Active role in family	Motorola

Key
BC: Business connection.
NED: Non-Executive Director.
Ch: Chairman.

Helpful websites

General

www.bbhq.com Baby Boomer Headquarters. Useful US Baby Boomer information.

About the interviewees

www.nesc.org National Executive Services Corporation.
Professional volunteer consultants for non-profit organizations (Marv Berenblum).
www.mikecritelli.com. Open Mike. Mike Critelli's blog.

Volunteering, mentoring

www.worldvolunteerweb.org Volunteering worldwide. News and resources.
www.doctorswithoutborders.org/www.msf.fr Doctors without Borders/ Medecin Sans Frontières.
www.fsvc.com financial services volunteer corp.
www.score.org service corps for retired executives who would like to provide their support and know-how to small businesses.
www.cdcdevelopmentsolutions.org international volunteering.
www.reserveinc.com ReServe helps nonprofits, schools, and public agencies fill skills-based, part-time positions with experienced, age 55+ professionals.

Foundations, donor advised funds etc.

http://grantspace.org information on foundations, donor advised funds etc.

Encore career sites

www.encore.org Encore careers a worldwide organization.
www.jobsover50.com
www.jobs4.0.com
www.yourencore.com for "retired" scientists, technical specialists, and engineers.

Board work

Search under Institute of Directors for your country.

www.iod.com Institute of Directors (UK).
www.icd.ca Institute of Corporate Directors (Canada).
www.sid.org.sg Singapore Institute of Directors.
www.conference-board.com Conference Board (USA).
www.hkiod.com Hong Kong Institute of Directors.
www.jacd.jp Japan Institute of corporate directors.
www.companydirectors.com.au. Institute of Directors (Australia).
www.ifrs.org International Financial Reporting Standards Foundation.

Private Equity databases/directories

www.privateequityfirms.com
www.preqin.com
www.pseps.com

Small businesses

www.sba.gov Small business administration (United States).
www.yoursmallbusiness.co.uk Information on creating a small business in the United Kingdom.
www.j4b.co.uk funding information for United Kingdom and Ireland.
www.business.gov.sg Entrepreneurs guide to planning, starting and running a business (Singapore) pdf.
www.servicecanada.gc.ca starting a small business in Canada www.business.gov.au starting a small business in Australia.

Notes

1 The disappearing point on the horizon

1. See www.bbhq.com/bomrstat.htm, Baby Boomer Headquarters, accessed July 20, 2011.
2. Christopher Woods (2002). "Asia's Billion Boomers." CLSA Asia-Pacific Markets. Report.
3. John Berthelsen (2003). "Asia's Consumer Revolution Gets Serious." *Asian Time Online*, March 15, 2003. www.atimes.com.://www.atimes.com/atimes/Asian_Economy/EC15Dk01.html.
4. Tamara Erickson (2008). *Retire, Retirement. Career Strategies for the Boomer Generation* (Harvard Business Press: Boston, MA).
5. Ibid.
6. Ken Dychtwald (1999). *Age Power. How the 21st Century Will be Ruled by the New Old.* (Penguin Putnam Inc: New York, NY).
7. AARP Study (2004). "Baby Boomers Envision Retirement II."
8. Daniel Feldman and Seongsu Kim (2000). "Bridge Employment during Retirement: A Field Study of Individual and Organizational Experiences with Post-Retirement Employment." *Human Resource Planning*, March, 23(1): 14–25.
9. Tamara Erickson (2008) *Retire, Retirement.*
10. Geoffrey Colvin (2006). "Does Your CEO Have What it Takes?" *Fortune Investors.* February 6.

2 Reigniting passion

1. Hermina Ibarra (2003). *Working Identity. Unconventional Strategies for Reinventing your Career.* (Harvard Business School Press: Boston, MA).
2. Daniel Levinson (1978). *The Season's of a Man's Life.* (Random House: New York, NY).
3. Gail Sheehy (1995). *New Passages. Mapping Your Life Across Time.* (Random House: New York, NY).
4. Robert Morrison, Tamara Erickson, and Ken Dychtwald (2006). "Managing Middlescence." *Harvard Business Review*, March 1, 84(3): 78–86, 149.

3 Preparing for an encore and plurality

1. Forbes list of the 100 most powerful women of 2006, http://www.forbes. com/2007/08/28/biz-07women_all_slide_10.html, accessed August 20, 2011.
2. Hazel Markus and Paula Nurius (1986). "Possible Selves." *American Psychologist.* September, 41(9): 954–69.
3. Tamara Erickson (2008). *Retire Retirement. Career Strategies for the Boomer Generation* (Harvard Business Press: Boston, MA).
4. Hermina Ibarra (2003). *Working Identity. Unconventional Strategies for Reinventing your Career* (Harvard Business School Press: Boston, MA).
5. Alan Leighton at www.going-plural.com, accessed July 20, 2011.
6. Matilda White Riley (1998). "The Hidden Age Revolution: Emergent Integration of All Ages." Syracuse University Maxwell School of Citizenship and Public Affairs/Center for Policy Research Policy Brief. Distinguised Lecturer in Aging Series.
7. Ibid.

4 Multiple questions, multiple choices

1. Brendan O'Neil (2006). "Baby Boom ... and Bust." BBC News, August 17. http://news.bbc.co.uk/2/hi/uk_news/magazine/4798825.stm, accessed July 6, 2011.
2. Joe Queenan (2002). *Balsamic Dreams: A Short but Self-Important History of the Baby Boomers* (Picador: New York, NY).

5 The business connection

1. Daniel Feldman and Seongsu Kim (2000). "Bridge Employment During Retirement: A Field Study of Individual and Organizational Experiences with Post-Retirement Employment." *Human Resource Planning Journal.* March, 23(1): 14–25.
2. Ibid.
3. Daniel Feldman (2007). "Careers: Mobility, Embeddedness and Success." *Journal of Management,* June, 33(3): 350–77.
4. Joseph Quinn (2002, 2003). "Reinventing Aging Baby Boomers and Civic Engagement." Harvard School of Public Health–MetLife Foundation Initiative on Retirement and Civic Engagement Center for Health Communication Harvard School of Public Health MetLife Foundation, 2004.
5. Jeffrey Sonnenfeld (1988). *The Hero's Farewell. What Happens When CEOs Retire* (Oxford University Press: New York, NY).
6. Hermina Ibarra (2003). *Working Identity. Unconventional Strategies for Reinventing your Career* (Harvard Business School Press: Boston, MA).
7. Kenneth S. Shultz and Gary A. Adams (2007). *Aging and Work in the 21st Century* (Lawrence Erlbaum Associates: Mahwah, NJ).

8. Michael Useem (1986). *The Inner Circle: Large Corporations and the Rise of Business Political Activity in the US and UK* (Oxford University Press: New York, NY).

6 Giving back. Foundations, volunteering, and mentoring

1. James Gambone and Erica Whittlinger (2004). "The 75% Factor: Uncovering Hidden Boomer Values." Refirement® Inc in *Reinventing Aging. Baby Boomers and Civic Engagement.* Harvard School of Public Health–MetLife Foundation Initiative on Retirement and Civic Engagement. Center for Health Communication, Harvard School of Public Health, MetLife Foundation.
2. "Australians Keen to Volunteer," at www.worldvolunteerweb.org/news-views/news/doc/australian-retirees-keen-to.html, May 15, 2006, accessed July 21, 2011.
3. Harvard School of Public Health–MetLife Foundation Initiative on Retirement and Civic Engagement (2004). *Reinventing Aging. Baby Boomers and Civic Engagement.* Center for Health Communication, Harvard School of Public Health, MetLife Foundation.
4. Dana Lacey (2010). "Baby Boomers are Changing Perceptions about Charity." *Financial Post.* January 26.
5. Ibid.
6. Arlene F. Harder (2002). "Erikson's Developmental Stages." At http://www.learningplaceonline.com/stages/organize/Erikson.htm, revised 2009, accessed August 17, 2011.
7. Monash Baby Boomer Study (2009). KPMG.
8. David K. Foot with Daniel Stoffman (2004). *Boom, Bust & Echo 2000.* Stoddart Press in *Reinventing Aging. Baby Boomers and Civic Engagement.* Harvard School of Public Health–MetLife Foundation Initiative on Retirement and Civic Engagement. Center for Health Communication, Harvard School of Public Health, MetLife Foundation.
9. Daniel Levinson (1978). *The Seasons of a Man's Life* (Random House: New York, NY).

7 Pursuing your passions

1. Wikipedia, "Golf" at http://en.wikipedia.org/wiki/Golf, accessed August 16, 2011.

8 It's all in the family

1. "Baby Boomer CEOs shunning retirement." Laura Palotie at www.inc.com, November 14, 2008, accessed July 28, 2011.

2. Ronald Lee, Andrew Mason, and Timothy Miller (1999). "Life Cycle Saving and the Demographic Transition in East Asia," in C. Y. Cyrus Chu and Ronald Lee (eds) *Economic Change in East Asia*. A special supplement to *Population and Development Review* (26), 194–222.

9 Business as usual

1. This interviewees in this chapter asked to remain anonymous. The names and companies have been changed for this reason.
2. White Paper on Corporate Governance in Asia, *First issued June 10, 2003 Second, revised printing July 15, 2003 OECD*.
3. Lilian Miles (2010). Transplanting the Anglo-American Corporate Governance Model into Asian Countries: Prospects and Practicality. A Context Statement submitted to Middlesex University in partial fulfilment of the requirements for the degree of Doctor of Philosophy by Public Works.
4. Franklin Allen and Mengxin Zhao (2007). "The Corporate Governance Model of Japan: Shareholders are not Rulers." Abstract at www.finance. wharton.upenn.edu/~allenf/download/Vita/Japan-Corporate-Governance.pdf, accessed July 20, 2011.

10 The business of people

1. Kathleen McKee (2005). "Financial Survey. Retirement Plans are Lagging." *Medical Economics*. August 19, http://medicaleconomics. modernmedicine.com/memag/article/articleDetail.jsp?id=174467, accessed August 15, 2011.
2. Daniel Feldman and Seongsu Kim (2000). "Bridge Employment During Retirement: A Field Study of Individual and Organizational Experiences with Post-Retirement Employment." *Human Resource Planning Journal*, March, 23(1): 14–25.

11 The boys and the girls, east and west

1. "Executive Women in East Asia: Still Few and Far Between, But growing in Number." September 4, 2009. www.theglasshammer.com, accessed July 15, 2011.
2. Ibid.
3. Thein and Austin (2007). "Working Life, Working Family: The Case of Professional Women in Asia," in Therese Jefferson, Linley Lord, Nadia Nelson and Alison Preston (eds), *Proceedings of Inaugural International Women and Leadership Conference* (Curtin University of Technology: Bentley, Western Australia), 310–21,
4. Yang, Chen, Choi and Zou (2000). "Sources of Work-Family Conflict. A Sino-US Comparison of the Effects of Work and Family Demands." *Academy of Management Journal*. 43, February 1, 113–23.

5. "Women on Board: Breaking the "Bamboo Ceiling" CNN Kyung Lah, April 10, 2010. www.edition.cnn.com/2010/BUSINESS/04/22/japan.woman.on.the.board/, accessed July 18, 2011.
6. Matilda White Riley (1998). "The Hidden Age Revolution: Emergent Integration of All Ages." Syracuse University Maxwell School of Citizenship and Public Affairs/Center for Policy Research Policy Brief. Distinguished Lecturer in Aging Series.
7. Donald C. Reitzes and Elizabeth J. Mutrane (2004). "The Transition to Retirement. Stages and Factors that Influence Retirement Adjustment." *International Journal of Aging and Human Development*, 59(1): 63–84.
8. "The Future of Retirement. The New Old Age. A Gender Perspective." HSBC-Oxford Institute of Ageing. 2007.
9. New retirement mindscape IISM 2010 The *New Retirement Mindscape II^{SM}* and *New Retirement Mindscape®* studies were commissioned by Ameriprise Financial, Inc. and conducted by telephone by Harris Interactive. The 2005 study was conducted in conjunction with Age Wave and Ken Dychtwald, PhD.
10. June Petkoska & J. K. Earl (2009). "Understanding the Influence of Demographic and Psychological Variables on Retirement Planning." *Psychology and Ageing*, 24(1): 245–51.

12   Seeing the connections

1. www.indianetzone.com/4/anita_desai.htm, accessed July 11, 2011.

13   The broadest range of futures

1. "Averting a Bust for the Boomers. Remarks on the McKinsey Global Institute Study, The Economic Impact of Aging US Baby Boomers," Phillip Longman Capitol Building, Washington, DC June 5, 2008.
2. Harvard School of Public Health–MetLife Foundation Initiative on Retirement and Civic Engagement (2004)."Reinventing Aging. Baby Boomers and Civic Engagement.". Center for Health Communication, Harvard School of Public Health, MetLife Foundation.
3. "An End to the 'Golden Years': Increasing Longevity Changes the Work-Leisure Equation." December 6, 2010 at http://knowledge.wharton.upenn.edu/article.cfm?articleid=2643, accessed July 20, 2011.
4. Ibid.

Additional sources

Gary A. Adams and Terry A. Behr (2003). *Retirement. Reasons, Processes and Results* (Springer Publications: New York, NY)

About the Authors

DONA ROCHE-TARRY is Managing Partner of the European Board Practice for CTPartners. She has over 10 years of experience in talent advisory services and has successfully completed assignments for Non Executive Directors, Chairmen, CEOs, C-suite and Managing Directors across Europe and the United States. Dona has assisted large public multinationals and high-growth emerging companies to strategically structure their boards and leadership teams. She is a certified executive coach and advises senior executives across industry sectors. Prior to CTPartners, Dona was with Heidrick and Struggles as Managing Partner in New York and London, Barclays Plc. as Director of Human Resources in the Commercial Bank reporting to the CEO, and in her earlier career was General Manager at British Telecom. She has a Bachelor of Science from University of Edinboro, Pennsylvania and was a Trustee of The Work Foundation.

DALE ROCHE-LEBREC is a Freelance Writer, Editor, and Translator. She spent 15 years working for France Innovation Scientifique et Transfert, the technology transfer affiliate of the CNRS, the largest French scientific research institute, where she negotiated patent licenses, performed industrial partner searches, and was Director of Operations. Prior to this Dale was Managing Editor for the *Journal of Hepatology* and was an editor and translator for various other scientific journals, websites, and books. She transitioned out of her full-time career in 2007 and today is pursuing the plural lifestyle described in *What's Next?* Dale has a Bachelor of Arts from University of Connecticut, a Master's Degree from University of Paris VII in Linguistics, and a Diplôme d'études Approfondies from the University of Paris VII in Literature.

Index

Page numbers followed by *b* indicate boxes.

194 INDEX